Constantine
Revisited

Constantine
Revisited

*Leithart, Yoder, and
the Constantinian Debate*

edited by
JOHN D. ROTH

PICKWICK *Publications* · Eugene, Oregon

CONSTANTINE REVISITED
Leithart, Yoder, and the Constantinian Debate

Copyright © 2013 John D. Roth. All rights reserved. Except for brief quotations in critical publications or reviews, no part of this book may be reproduced in any manner without prior written permission from the publisher. Write: Permissions, Wipf and Stock Publishers, 199 W. 8th Ave., Suite 3, Eugene, OR 97401.

Pickwick Publications
An Imprint of Wipf and Stock Publishers
199 W. 8th Ave., Suite 3
Eugene, OR 97401

www.wipfandstock.com

ISBN 13: 978-1-61097-819-4

Cataloguing-in-Publication data:

Constantine Revisited : Leithart, Yoder, and the Constantinian debate / edited by John D. Roth.

xvi + 200 pp. ; 23 cm. Includes bibliographical references.

ISBN 13: 978-1-61097-819-4

1. Leithart, Peter J. Defending Constantine. 2. Constantine I, Emperor of Rome, –337—Influence. I. Roth, John D. II. Title.

BR180 .C66 2013

Manufactured in the U.S.A.

Contents

List of Contributors vii

Foreword—Stanley Hauerwas ix

Preface—John D. Roth xi

Acknowledgments xv

1. A Yoderian Rejoinder to Peter J. Leithart's *Defending Constantine—John C. Nugent* 1

2. "Converted" but Not Baptized: Peter Leithart's Constantine Project—*Alan Kreider* 25

3. Against Christianity and For Constantine: One Heresy or Two?—*Mark Thiessen Nation* 68

4. What Constantine Has to Teach Us —*William T. Cavanaugh* 83

5. Yoderian Constantinianism?—*D. Stephen Long* 100

6. *Defending Constantine* Taken Seriously —*Jonathan Tran* 124

7. The Emperor's New Clothes—*Branson Parler* 133

8. History and Figural Reading: Another Response to Leithart—*Timothy J. Furry* 144

9. Leithart's *Defending Constantine*: A Review —*Charles M. Collier* 155

Contents

    10   Is There a Christian Ethic for Emperors?
            —*Craig Hovey*   160

    11   Constantine and Myths of the Fall of the Church:
            An Anabaptist View—*J. Alexander Sider*   172

    12   Afterword—*Peter J. Leithart*   184

           Bibliography   189

Contributors

WILLIAM T. CAVANAUGH, Professor of Theology at DePaul University, Chicago, Illinois.

CHARLES M. COLLIER, Editor at Wipf and Stock Publishers, Eugene, Oregon.

TIMOTHY J. FURRY, Religion and Philosophy teacher at Cranbrook Kingswood Upper School, Bloomfield Township, Michigan.

STANLEY HAUERWAS, Gilbert T. Rowe Professor of Theological Ethics at Duke Divinity School, Durham, North Carolina.

CRAIG HOVEY, Assistant Professor of Religion at Ashland University, Ashland, Ohio.

ALAN KREIDER, Professor of Church History and Mission at Anabaptist Mennonite Biblical Seminary, Elkhart, Indiana.

PETER J. LEITHART, Senior Fellow of Theology and Literature at New Saint Andrews College, Moscow, Idaho.

D. STEPHEN LONG, Professor of Systematic Theology at Marquette University, Milwaukee, Wisconsin.

MARK THIESSEN NATION, Professor of Theology at Eastern Mennonite Seminary, Harrisonburg, Virginia.

JOHN C. NUGENT, Professor of Old Testament at Great Lakes College in Lansing, Michigan.

BRANSON PARLOR, Associate Professor of Theological Studies at Kuyper College, Grand Rapids, Michigan

JOHN D. ROTH, Professor of History at Goshen College, Goshen, Indiana.

Contributors

J. ALEXANDER SIDER, Assistant Professor of Religion at Bluffton University, Bluffton, Ohio.

JONATHAN TRAN, Assistant Professor of Theological Ethics in the Department of Religion at Baylor University, Waco, Texas.

Foreword

IN HIS ESSAY FOR this book Bill Cavanaugh observes that "Peter Leithart has written a book that needed to be written." I am sure Cavanaugh is right that Leithart has done a great service by challenging the presumption held by many of us that something went terribly wrong when Caesar became a member of the church. But if Leithart's *Defending Constantine* was a book that needed to be written, it is equally true that this book of essays responding to Leithart needed to be written. The high quality of these critical engagements with Leithart is a testimony to the significance of the issues Leithart's book raises.

One of those issues is, of course, whether Leithart gets right Yoder's understanding of what was at stake when Constantine became a Christian. A "Foreword" is not the place to "take sides" on that question. I think it is surely a sign, however, of Leithart's good will that he has acknowledged not only in his response to these essays but elsewhere that he has learned from those who have directed his attention to aspects of Yoder's position that would qualify some of the criticism of Yoder in his book. Nugent, I think, rightly observes that the shift that Yoder calls "Constantinian" is first and foremost what happens to the church when worldly power is used to accomplish what God has given his people to do without such power.

However I suspect Yoder would have little interest in defending his position as an end in itself. I think he would find more interesting a question Leithart's account forces those of us influenced by Yoder to address. That is, what is it about Christianity that tempts Christians to assume a Constantinian stance? To suggest that Christians simply could not resist worldly power does not do justice to the complex reasons inherent in the Gospel itself that would lead Christians to rejoice that worldly powers were now ready to confess that Jesus is Lord.

One of the lessons I think these essays exemplify is that the Constantinian/anti-Constantinian alternative can be quite misleading. If not misleading, at least the alternative can hide from us questions that need to be addressed if we are properly to understand as well as live out what it means for the church to be an alternative to the violence of the world. In particular, Leithart has quite rightly called attention to the importance of sacrifice as crucial if we are to understand the challenge the church presented to Roman politics and life. Several of these essays explore that suggestion, but I suspect we are just beginning to appreciate how important sacrifice is not only for questions surrounding Constantinianism but for our own day.

Leithart's book raises serious questions about the "historical Constantine." Several of the essays in this book respond to his attempt to give us the "real" Constantine. It would be a mistake, a very deep mistake, however, if the questions raised by Leithart were thought to be primarily questions of getting the history right. For as Leithart observes in his "Afterword," like Yoder he believes that history and theology are two dimensions of the same inquiry. That I take to be the central question the essays in this book engage and why by doing so this book becomes so important.

I have long thought Yoder's claim in *The Christian Witness to the State* that we live in two times to be crucial if we are to understand how and why Christians are tempted by the various Constantinian alternatives. It is not easy to live in the tension between the two ages. How that tension is to be displayed in terms of the writing of history is by no means clear. The witness of Scripture is obviously a crucial resource for that endeavor, but we need to see how that resource looks when spelled out. For example, it would be salutary for Anabaptists to think hard about Augustine's *City of God* as an exemplification of how history might be narrated from an eschatological perspective. That Leithart makes such questions unavoidable is but an indication of the importance of his work. As these essays make clear, those of us influenced by Yoder are in his debt.

I cannot resist one closing observation. How strange it is that a defense of Constantine is mounted from New Saint Andrews College in Moscow, Idaho. Goshen College in Goshen, Indiana, is closer to Washington DC than is Moscow, Idaho—a geographical fact to which I direct attention only because it makes clear that Leithart and his respondents are not soon to be tempted to take over the world. I suspect they would have trouble "ruling" in Moscow, Idaho, or Goshen, Indiana. God is great.

Stanley Hauerwas

Preface

JOHN D. ROTH

SOMETIME AROUND 1570, HANS Schnell, a Swiss Brethren lay minister, published a pamphlet in which he summarized a view of church history widely shared within the Anabaptist circles of his day. The Roman emperor Constantine, he wrote:

> was baptized by the pope Sylvester, the Antichrist, the son of perdition, whose coming took place through the work of that same loathsome devil. Therefore he received the name Christian falsely. For the Christian church was at that time transformed into the antichristian church. . . . When Constantine assumed and accepted the name Christian . . . then the apostasy came, from which apostasy may God protect us eternally. Amen.[1]

Schnell's deep conviction that Constantine's alleged conversion to Christianity in AD 312 marked the fall of the Christian church echoed a view expressed repeatedly by earlier Anabaptist writers. In his *Exposure of the Babylonian Whore*, for example, Pilgram Marpeck denounced Constantine's conversion as setting in place a fateful fusion between ecclesial and temporal power marked by the introduction of infant baptism, the substitution of Mass for the Lord's Supper, and, most troubling of all, a new readiness on the part of the church to resort to coercion and lethal violence in matters of faith.[2] And even though *The Hutterite Chronicle* acknowledged that Constantine converted "with the good intention of doing

---

1. A translation of Schnell's treatise can be found in Gross, "H. Schnell: Second Generation Anabaptist," 358–77; quote from 375.

2. Marpeck, *Exposé of the Babylonian Whore and Antichrist*. Online: http://www.anabaptistnetwork.com/node/250.

Preface

God a service," it went on to describe the consequences as a "pestilence of deceit" that "abolished the cross and forged it into a sword."[3]

Although individual Anabaptists differed about the exact date of the church's apostasy—Menno Simons, for example, regarded it as happening even before Constantine, whereas others dated it to the late fourth-century reign of Theodosius, or even to the official sanctioning of infant baptism by the ninth-century pope, Nicholas I—Free Church theologians and historians since the Reformation have generally regarded Constantine as a symbolic marker of a fundamental shift in the history of Christian faith and practice. Constantine's conversion set in motion a process that would create the "Holy" Roman Empire, enlist the civil authority of the state in the church's prosecution of heresy, entrench infant baptism as an orthodox practice (to be defended with the threat of capital punishment), and transform the very character of Christian catechesis and missions.

Although debates over church-state relations continue to rage, few contemporary Catholic or mainline Protestant scholars today would openly advocate a return to the theocratic vision of Christendom often associated with Constantine's conversion. Thus, it bears notice—perhaps especially so in the United States, where claims of divine favor on a Christian nation have long served to sanction military interventions and to defend an imperial mandate—when a prominent contemporary theologian writes a book titled *Defending Constantine* that intends to challenge head-on the assumption that Constantine's conversion was somehow problematic in the development of Christian history.

On the surface, Peter J. Leithart's *Defending Constantine: The Twilight of an Empire and the Dawn of Christendom* is simply a work of historical revisionism—a critical reassessment of the historiography of the Roman emperor Constantine. Beyond that, as Leithart himself acknowledges, the book also has a more "practical" aim: "Far from representing a fall for the church," he writes, "Constantine provides in many respects a model for Christian political practice."[4]

But the primary target of Leithart's avowedly polemic work is clearly neither historical nor narrowly pragmatic. Instead, the book is intended as a sustained critique of the pacifist theology and ethics of the Anabaptist-Mennonite tradition, and especially the writings of the well-known Mennonite theologian John Howard Yoder, along with Stanley Hauerwas "and their increasing tribe" of Anabaptist-oriented students. According to

3. *Chronicle of the Hutterian Brethren*, 1:31.
4. Leithart, *Defending Constantine*, 11.

Preface

Leithart, because Yoder "gets the fourth century wrong in many particulars" it "distorts his entire reading of church history, which is a hinge of his theological project."[5] By exposing the presumed errors of Yoder's understanding of Constantine, Leithart seeks to undermine the entire edifice of his theological legacy.

Ordinarily, one might think that the proper place to debate the merits of a book would be in the Book Review section of academic journals. But because Leithart's intentions in *Defending Constantine* are so explicitly polemical, his arguments so sweeping, and the critical reception of the book so positive in mainstream evangelical circles, it seems appropriate to respond to his claims more broadly.

This collection of essays is devoted to an extended conversation about the history of the Christian church in the fourth and fifth centuries, with particular attention to the role of the emperor Constantine. Although the primary point of departure for the essays is Leithart's *Defending Constantine*, the themes addressed here are wide-ranging, touching on history, theology, biblical interpretation, and, of course, social ethics.

I am deeply grateful to all of the scholars who stepped forward to engage the conversation, each bringing a distinctive insight to the conversation. And I am especially grateful to Peter J. Leithart, Senior Fellow at New Saint Andrews College (Moscow, Idaho), for his willingness to engage the conversation in a patient and gracious manner. Nothing in this volume is likely to resolve the debate in a definitive way. But the exchange that unfolds here does push the conversation forward. And in sharp contrast to the disputations with the Anabaptists organized by state churches in the sixteenth century, it models the manner in which deep disagreements among Christians can be debated today in a spirit of Christian charity, without fear of torture, imprisonment, or death by fire, drowning, or the executioner's sword.

One final comment: the recent movie *Of Gods and Men* (*Des hommes et des dieux*) recounts the moving story of seven Trappist monks living in a monastery in Algeria, who found themselves caught in the crossfire of violence between radical Islamist groups and nationalist partisans in the early 1990s. In the face of threats, and then a bloody massacre, most Europeans fled the region. For the monks who had long worked among the villagers—bearing witness to Christ's love by sharing fully in their lives—finding an appropriate response to the political crisis became a central question. Should they too leave? Should they openly declare their

5. Ibid.

Preface

allegiance with the nationalists? Or should they simply continue in their long-established disciplines of prayer, offering compassionate aid to all who asked, and seeking to promote understanding and reconciliation wherever possible?

Here we return to the ancient question, focused anew in *Defending Constantine*, as to whether the Christian community is obliged to provide a political narrative for those in power—a narrative that will justify the righteousness of one side of a conflict and that, presumably, will "redeem" the inevitable violence that follows by blessing it with the sanctity of God's name. As Christian history has shown, responses to this question are never simple, especially in the face of innocent suffering. In the end, the monks of Notre-Dame de l'Atlas refused to either flee or to submit to the logic of redemptive violence. Instead, they opted simply to continue living among the villagers, pursuing their practices of prayer and compassion. That decision sealed their earthly fate. But the sacrifice of their lives forces Christian viewers to assess anew their own convictions regarding the resurrection and the nature of true Christian witness.

For Christians committed to the Gospel of peace, *Of Gods and Men* is both inspiring and unsettling. It reminds us that Christian pacifism is never passive; nor does it come with any claims regarding short-term "effectiveness." And for Anabaptist-Mennonite viewers in particular, the movie is a powerful and humbling reminder that the same tradition that produced Constantinianism, Christendom, and so much violence directed against their forebearers, has also carried within itself a faithful witness to an alternative understanding of the Gospel. For the gift of that witness within the Catholic Church, those in the Free Church tradition have good reason to be deeply and eternally grateful.

John D. Roth

Acknowledgments

The essays by John Nugent, Alan Krieder, Craig Hovey and J. Alexander Sider first appeared in a *The Mennonite Quarterly Review* 85 (Oct. 2011) and are reprinted here by permission of the editor.

The essay by Timothy J. Furry is revision of a review that first appeared in *Journal of Lutheran Ethics* 11 (Sept. 2011) [http://www.elca.org/What-We-Believe/Social-Issues/Journal-of-Lutheran-Ethics/Issues/September-2011/Review-of-Peter-Leitharts-Defending-Constantine.aspx], and is reprinted here by permission of the editor.

Portions of Branson Parler's essay were first published as "The Emperor's New Clothes: A Review of *Defending Constantine*," *The Other Journal* 19 (2011) [http://theotherjournal.com/2011/09/06/the-emperors-new-clothes-a-review-of-defending-constantine/] and appear here with permission from *The Other Journal*. Additionally, portions also appeared as chapter 6 of Branson Parler, *Things Hold Together: John Howard Yoder's Trinitarian Theology of Culture* (Harrisonburg, Va.: Herald Press, 2012), available at www.mennomedia.org.

The essay by Charles M. Collier was first published in *Pro Ecclesia* 22.2 (2013) 225–29 and is reprinted here with permission.

1

A Yoderian Rejoinder to Peter J. Leithart's *Defending Constantine*

JOHN C. NUGENT

CONSTANTINE ON TRIAL

THOSE CRITICS LOOKING FOR another excuse to dismiss John Howard Yoder and the Free Church tradition are sure to find it in Peter J. Leithart's *Defending Constantine: The Twilight of an Empire and the Dawn of Christendom*. Though Leithart takes Yoder quite seriously, readers who are less familiar with Yoder's work may be left with the unfortunate impression that he was a sloppy thinker, blinded by the pacifism of a naïve tradition, and ignorant of the complexities of history. I am sure this is not Leithart's intention. Leithart intends to start a "fight" (10) and his admittedly polemical tone sometimes borders on patronizing not only his primary foe, but also the Anabaptist heritage and all theological traditions that interpret the church-empire merger as an unfortunate development in the self-understanding of God's people. This should not deter readers from persisting with this rather long work. Some of its most stimulating suggestions come near the end.

Leithart's well-crafted and articulate case deserves substantive rejoinders both to his historical portrait of Constantine and his theological critique of Yoder and the position he represents. Alan Kreider's essay in this collection focuses on the former; this essay focuses on the latter. Though no one can speak for Yoder, least of all a non-Mennonite like myself, I will nonetheless enter the fray by presenting Leithart's basic case and evaluating his polemic against Yoder (and, by extension, all who share similar convictions about faith, history, and social ethics).[1] Though Leithart challenges the work of multiple historians and theologians, I focus only on Yoder because that is where I can most constructively enter the conversation, and because Leithart claims that the main polemical target of his book "is a theological one" (10) and that most of his theological argument "is directed at Yoder" (11).[2]

Leithart's task is ambitious: to write a life of Constantine, to rebut popular caricatures, to demonstrate that Yoder's work on Constantine is wrong both historically and theologically, and to make a case for Constantine as a viable model for Christian political practice (10–11). This task is complicated by the nature of the extant sources. Leithart's preferred source is Eusebius, a contemporary of Constantine who adoringly portrays him as God's providential instrument in ushering in the millennium. Leithart grants that Eusebius' work is replete with exaggerations, contains accounts of questionable historicity, and intentionally omits incriminating material (228). Nonetheless, it remains the earliest and most comprehensive account available, so Leithart makes extensive use of it. He makes less use of the account of Zosimus, a late-fifth-century pagan who portrayed Constantine as a violent ruler who was politically motivated in the worst sense of that term. Beyond this, Leithart had access to an oration of Constantine, published legal decrees, coinage, letters, and miscellaneous excerpts

---

1. For a while it appeared as if the Free Church tradition was headed for some long overdue academic respectability. With the widely celebrated decline of Christendom in the West and unsolicited support from scholars as reputable as Karl Barth (*Church Dogmatics* IV) and Jürgen Moltmann (*The Church in the Power of the Spirit*), it seemed like Free Church thinkers might have finally earned a seat at the ecumenical table (though neither of these scholars joined the Free Church tradition, both exhibited free-church sensibilities in their ecclesiological writings). Yet due to philosophers like Alasdair MacIntyre and theologians like Stanley Hauerwas, the late twentieth and early twenty-first centuries have witnessed a long overdue resurgence in appreciation for tradition. Whereas this development has reaped much healthy fruit, it has also sewn the conviction that the only traditions *not* worth appreciating are those with a reputation for not appreciating tradition. What critics of the Free Church tradition fail to recognize is that, like everyone else, the most thoughtful Free Church thinkers (the ones who should be engaged in serious scholarly work) have long since repented of and renounced a dismissive stance toward the Christian tradition and the ancient creeds of the church (e.g., Anabaptist scholars John Yoder and Alan Kreider, and Campbellite scholars Paul Blowers and Fred Norris).

2. Indeed, Leithart engages Yoder by name on approximately ninety pages (a little over one-fourth of the book).

preserved among Eusebius' writings. This is hardly an ideal situation for a historian or a theologian.

The title of Leithart's book (which was not his idea) gives a sense of his strategy for dealing with this difficult historical material. Consistent with his aims, Leithart plays the part of a defense attorney in a court setting. The last several decades of historians and theologians—for example, Jacob Burkhardt, James Carroll, Stanley Hauerwas, and, of course, Yoder—play the role of prosecuting attorneys who have been overly critical of Constantine and unfairly suspicious of favorable testimonies in the primary sources. To Leithart, it seems as if they have sought only to find fault. As defense attorney, Leithart tasks himself with demonstrating Constantine's innocence, or at least furnishing fourth-century details that make his client's actions more defensible. Making extensive use of Eusebius, he brings forward as many positive testimonies as possible. Evidence that does not support his case is either ignored, chalked up to exaggeration (126), or re-interpreted with the help of more sympathetic secondary sources (227–230). This kind of reading, swinging the pendulum from one extreme to another, is sure to encourage constructive historical work insofar as careful historians are spurred on to revisit the primary sources, apart from their interest in either the prosecution of or the defense of Constantine.

Leithart's biography of Constantine may be summarized as follows:

1. Constantine sincerely believed that he had converted to Christianity and subsequently became a "missional emperor" who ended the unjust and horrendous persecution of Christians, united the church by healing divisions, and spread God's truth throughout the world (chap. 4).

2. Constantine practiced religious toleration, and all actions that critics cite as evidence that he pressured people to convert—including his prohibition of sacrifices, renovation of pagan temples into basilicas, repressive antipagan legislation, threats to punish Jewish converts, and persecution of heretics—are best interpreted as efforts to create a favorable environment in which all citizens were encouraged to embrace Christian faith (chaps. 5–6).

3. Constantine's successors—especially Theodosius—escalated violence against pagans and relegated the church to a department of the state; yet they should not be interpreted as a continuation of the religious-political trajectory established by Constantine so much as a departure from it (chap. 6).

4. Constantine convened, attended, and contributed to the doctrinal formulas of the Council of Nicaea with no intentions of meddling inappropriately, bolstering imperial unity, or promoting a self-serving political agenda; rather, he recognized the bishops' collective authority in matters pertaining to faith and sought to unite the church for the sake of witness (chaps. 7 and 8).

5. Constantine used legislation to reform or "baptize" (to use Leithart's term) the Roman Empire according to Christian standards by extending clergy exemptions, outlawing gladiatorial contests, protecting the weak, reinforcing traditional Roman social distinctions, and exhorting pagans to abandon false religions and sacrifices in order to worship the true God (chap. 9).

6. Constantine extended justice to all persons by establishing laws that protected the poor, appointing Christians to ruling positions, and expanding the authority of bishops to include local judicial responsibility (chap. 10).

7. Constantine claimed to have banished and removed every form of evil throughout his reign in order that the human race might observe the holy laws of God, but his exaggerated rhetoric did not match the reality. More realistically, he infant-baptized the empire, effectively beginning a process rather than fully realizing it (chap. 11).

8. Finally, Constantine's final campaign, against Persia, was not a glory-hungry crusade seeking to avenge and subdue his enemies. Instead, a letter he had written to the Persian king advising him to worship the Christian God properly and to treat his people well, along with Constantine's decision to invite bishops to join him as prayerful companions in service to the God from whom all victory proceeds, indicates that a new kind of baptized imperial warfare was emerging (chap. 11).

I leave it to competent historians to evaluate Leithart's historical construction, as Alan Kreider does in this collection. For the purposes of this essay I will suspend my historical misgivings and grant that Leithart's favorable depiction of Constantine is accurate. I do so because I believe that Yoder and the wider Free Church's notion of a "Constantinian shift"—with its concomitant implications for ecclesiology, ethics, and historiography—stands even if Leithart's portrait of Constantine is true in all of the above regards. The balance of this review essay therefore focuses on Leithart's claim to have successfully dismantled Yoder's interpretation and replaced it with a more viable one.

Yoder on Trial

As he indicates in the preface, Leithart did not intend merely to defend Constantine in this book; his defense of one man's legacy serves as the basis of his prosecution against the legacy of another—the late Anabaptist scholar John Howard Yoder (11). An important part of Yoder's social ethic and ecclesiology is his critique of what he calls Constantinianism, that is, the fusion of church and state most evident in the church's willingness to use the empire or state's coercive power structures—particularly the sword—to assist in the church's mission. According to Yoder, this shift in the church's self-understanding began in the second century, gained momentum under Constantine, thrived under Theodosius, found its culmination in the crusades, and keeps reappearing throughout ecclesial history in new forms. Central to that shift is the fusion of church and society. Unfortunately, Leithart fails to appreciate the true basis for Yoder's Constantinian critique and therefore lodges accusations against him that do not stand under careful cross-examination. I present and evaluate five such accusations below (there are more). Since the first one comprises the central argument of Leithart's book, it receives far more attention than the others. After engaging these accusations, I conclude this essay by raising an important question that those who reject Leithart's proposal must answer if they are to provide a complete alternative to it.

Accusation One: Yoder Is Wrong in Supposing a Constantinian Shift

Leithart's most fundamental accusation against Yoder is that there was no "Constantinian shift" in the Yoderian sense of a fundamental change in the church's self-understanding. Leithart does acknowledge that the church experienced a significant upgrade in social status in the fourth century—thanks to Constantine, Christians went from being a persecuted minority to an acceptable, and eventually preferred, religion in the eyes of the emperor and wider society. He also agrees with Yoder that elements of this shift began before Constantine and culminated after him. But he disagrees that they signaled a substantive departure from New Testament Christianity. Leithart's logic is simple: the church did not change its self-understanding, for there is ample evidence in both the New Testament and late second- and early third-century writings that at least some Christians had always embraced the empire and its sword.

Leithart argues that such evidence is sufficient to undermine Yoder's schema because he believes that it is based on an Anabaptist "fall of the church" historiography that relies on the conviction that the early church for the most part conformed to a pacifist interpretation of the New Testament. For Constantine to truly represent a "fall," Yoder must demonstrate that the early church had actually reached the uniform pacifistic ecclesial heights from which he accuses the later Constantinian church to have fallen. Consequently, all Leithart has to do in order to falsify Yoder's schema is to prove that the evidence is ambiguous and that the early church exhibited a diversity of views as to whether its members could bear the imperial sword (255–260). If he can do this, he believes, Yoder's entire historical paradigm breaks down and his Free Church ecclesiology and pacifist ethics are compromised.

Leithart directs readers to the Gospels, Acts, and a few late second-century documents for such evidence. In Matthew 8:1–13, Matthew 27:54, Mark 15:39, Luke 3:14, and Acts 10–11, he highlights the oft-cited accounts of centurions converted both by Jesus and John the Baptist, neither of whom asked them to quit their jobs. Then, between the New Testament and the late second century, he notes the lacuna in evidence for the church's position. After this time he boasts abundant evidence of Christian participation in the Roman military. For example, Tertullian's polemical antimilitary writings presuppose Christian embrace of military service. Why else would he have had to make his case so emphatically? From all this, Leithart concludes that (a) Christians first endorsed military service in the New Testament; (b) at least some Christians served in the military in the second and third centuries; and (c) this trend increased dramatically in the fourth century after Christians were encouraged to serve in that capacity and when the end of pagan sacrifices and other imperial idolatries made it possible for them to do so without compromising their faith. There was thus no shift in the church's theology, but only in its political position and opportunity (278). Yoder was so blinded by Anabaptist bias, Leithart supposes, that he could not see the evidence in front of him.

Yoder's notion of a shift is further discredited, according to Leithart, by his assessment of the Middle Ages. Leithart argues in chapter 14 that when Yoder illustrates the legacy of Constantinianism he skips from the fourth century to the Renaissance and Reformation, thereby overlooking the medieval period. Moreover, in the several places in which Yoder discusses the Middle Ages, he offers a more nuanced reading that presents the era as being relatively good when compared with the periods before and after. Pockets within the church were "good" insofar as they preserved a strong sense of the church's otherness with relation to the world. By Leithart's reckoning, immediately after Constantine, Eusebius and Theodosius exhibit an unhealthy submission of church to the empire and an unfortunate departure from the way of Constantine, which did not last long. Fortunately, this was corrected by Augustine and therefore finds no subsequent expression in the Middle Ages. The subordination of church to state only reemerges much later among the Protestant nationalist churches. Though Leithart applauds Yoder's critique of these Protestant movements, he interprets the medieval gap in Yoder's Constantinian narrative as another internal inconsistency that undermines his "fall of the church" historiography (323–324). In sum, Leithart accuses Yoder of failing to demonstrate that Constantine represented a shift both away from what came before him and toward what came after him.

But does this accusation hold up under cross-examination? For at least four reasons it does not.

1. Leithart misidentifies the basis of Yoder's historical interpretation

The most significant problem with Leithart's first, and perhaps weightiest, accusation is that he misses the actual basis of Yoder's position and, in so doing, fails to engage his account where it is actually falsifiable. Even if Leithart's New Testament exegesis stood under cross-examination—and I demonstrate below why it does not—he would still be wrong that Yoder's identification of a Constantinian shift depends on a "fall of the church" historiography that requires the early church to have uniformly embraced a pacifist, anti-imperial stance. There is no doubt that Yoder affirms the basic Anabaptist notion of a "fall" within the church, though he nuances his articulation of that fall in numerous places and distances his position from more naïve explanations of the church's fall.[3] Having said that, Yoder bases

---

3. Yoder critically engages restitutionism sporadically through his writings, but some of the most substantial engagements include "Anabaptism and History," in *The Priestly Kingdom*, 123–34; "The Kingdom as Social Ethic," in *The Priestly Kingdom*, 80–101; "Biblicism and the Church," in *The Roots of Concern*, 67–101; *The Fullness of Christ*, 85–105; "Is There Historical Development of Theological Thought," in *Radical Ecumenicity*, 223–35; "Primitivism in the Radical Reformation," in *The Primitive Church in the Modern World*, 74–97; "The Restitution of the Church: An Alternative

his identification of the Constantinian shift as apostasy not on Anabaptist history, but on his interpretation of the entire biblical narrative—especially the Old Testament. The New Testament is not the beginning of Anabaptist pacifism according to Yoder, but the culmination of God's formation of a people that began with Abraham. In over twenty essays devoted to Old Testament themes,[4] Yoder sets forth an interpretation of the biblical story in which God moves his people away from a Constantine-like posture and toward one of nonimperially-aligned service in and to the world. According to this interpretation, the monarchy of Israel represented the original Constantinian-like shift in the shape of God's people and a detour away from the social shape that God bequeathed to his people in Torah.

Nonetheless, God did not abandon his people after they embraced this monarchical or "Davidic" detour (a typological use of David that is sure to frustrate Leithart). Instead, God stayed with them and their kings, worked through a system that he identified as fundamentally flawed, and patiently waited it out. Furthermore, this detour was not retroactively accredited by God on grounds that, like Constantine, David used monarchical resources to minimize external opposition to God's people, healed divisions and unified God's people, submitted to the spiritual authority of religious advisors, offered praise to Israel's God alone, and framed all of his imperial activities as service to God.[5] Even though the Israelite monarchy brought about much good, God regarded it as structural rebellion against his reign and allowed it to crumble under the weight of its own inadequacies. The terrible atrocities that typified Israel's life prior to the monarchy—like those recorded in the book of Judges—take nothing away from

---

Perspective on Christian History," in *Jewish-Christian Schism Revisited*, 133–43; "Thinking Theologically from a Free Church Perspective," in *Doing Theology in Today's World*, 251–65; and "Your Hope is Too Small," in *He Came Preaching Peace*, 123–30.

4. Cf. "The Hilltop City," "Turn, Turn," and "The Voice of your Brother's Blood" in *He Came Preaching Peace*; "Jesus the Jewish Pacifist," and "See How They Go with Their Face to the Sun" in *Jewish-Christian Schism Revisited*, 183–204; "Behold My Servant Shall Prosper" in *Karl Barth and the Problem of War*; " "From the Wars of Joshua to Jewish Pacifism" in *War of the Lamb*; "Generating Alternative Paradigms," in *Human Values and the Environment*; "God will Fight for Us" in *Politics of Jesus*; "If Abraham Is Our Father," in *Original Revolution*, 91–112; "Introduction," in Lind, *Yahweh is a Warrior*; "Noah's Covenant and the Purpose of Punishment" in *Readings in Christian Ethics*; "'Thou Shalt Not Kill,'" in *To Hear the Word*; and "Meaning after Babel," " Biblical Roots of Liberation Theology;" "Creation and Gospel," "Exodus: Probing the Meaning of Liberation," "Exodus and Exile: The Two Faces of Liberation," "Texts that Serve or Texts that Summon," and "'To Your Tents, O Israel'" in various journal articles.

5. This list parallels the reasons Leithart gives for commending Constantine's contributions.

the fact that God interpreted Israel's request for a king like the nations as a rejection of the politics ordained for them in Torah and a culmination of the lesser forms of rebellion that typified Israel's life after their departure from Egypt (1 Sam 8:4–9).

According to Yoder, God separated his people from imperial entanglement and then began to permanently reconfigure them as a people who should never pursue such entanglement again. That process began with the Jewish diaspora of Jeremiah's time and was endorsed by Israel's messiah, who rejected the temptation to revive an "empire like the nations" in favor of a people whose mission was itself diasporic: to fill the earth with communities that reflect God's kingdom as an alternative to the various kingdoms that would preside over the lands in which they lived. This nonimperially-aligned posture was made structurally permanent when God opened this mission to Gentiles and broke down the wall that separated diverse ethnic groups. This means that all Christians from that point forward would have more kinship with fellow believers in other nations than with nonbelievers in the nations or empires in which they lived. To enter their host nations' military apparatus would thus entail a willingness to potentially kill Christians in other nations or empires when they find themselves at odds with their empire or host nation.[6]

My point is this: Yoder's interpretation of Constantine is rooted in a robust reading of the full biblical narrative. This reading establishes the criteria by which he evaluates Constantine's legacy and finds it shifting away from the biblical trajectory. This is evident in Yoder's claim, when discussing the notion that the church had lost its way, that "the first dimensions of the loss to become visible are precisely those traits of early Christianity tied to the Jewishness of the gospel."[7] When the church began marginalizing its Jewish roots, which Yoder sees happening among the early Christian apologists, they lost sight of key lessons that God's people learned from Abraham to Jesus that may have enabled them to resist fusing Gospel ends with imperial means. This loss need not have begun in the second or fourth century for Yoder's position to stand. It could have happened immediately after the revelation of God's purposes in Jesus, just as Israel's golden calf incident happened immediately after God revealed the Decalogue to the Israelites on Mount Sinai. Had Yoder found evidence

---

6. This is only a fraction of Yoder's Old Testament narration. I present and engage its fuller contours with supporting Scriptures briefly in "Politics of YHWH," 71–99.

7. Yoder, "The Jewishness of the Free Church Vision," in *Jewish-Christian Schism Revisited*, 107.

for Christian abandonment of an imperially nonaligned posture in the late first century, he would simply have shifted the beginning of the Constantinian trajectory back a century.

The astute reader might retort that Yoder's biblical narration is only a projection of his Anabaptist or Free Church "fall of the church" historiography. Though this assertion is certainly possible, it is not what we find in Yoder's writings. Instead, we find that the most relevant portions of his Old Testament interpretation, particularly the monarchy, are dependent upon and corroborated by the exegesis of first-rate Bible scholars, including John Bright, Norman Gottwald, Walter Breuggemann, Frank Cross, Gerhard Lohfink, George Mendenhall, Gordon McConville, Millard Lind, Rainer Albertz, and others—the majority of whom are not Anabaptists. Critics of Yoder's thought must therefore be careful not to assume that everything disagreeable about his work must be some sort of naïve reflex of his Anabaptist roots. Anabaptists, too, are capable of a sophisticated interpretation of the Scriptures. Their work, like that of everyone else, must be engaged on its own terms. If Leithart wants to truly engage and falsify Yoder's work, he will have to falsify the pivotal points of his complete biblical narration.

2. Leithart misreads the New Testament

Even though Leithart overreaches in saying that Yoder's position relies upon the pristine purity and absolute pacifist uniformity of the early church, he is right that Yoder's position falters considerably if it can be demonstrated that Roman soldiering was embraced as a viable form of following Jesus within the New Testament itself. Leithart's interpretation of the conversion of Roman soldiers must therefore be seriously engaged.

To begin, none of the four Gospel passages Leithart cites are "conversion" accounts as he calls them. In Matthew 8, Jesus heals a centurion's servant and acknowledges what great faith the centurion demonstrated in believing that Jesus possessed such authority that he could heal from a distance. In Matthew 27:54 and Mark 15:39, the centurion at the foot of the cross confesses that Jesus is the son of God. In Luke 3:14, John the Baptist prepares soldiers for the coming Messiah and kingdom by telling them not to extort money and to be satisfied with their wages. We are not told in any of these passages that these men repented from their sins, received baptism, and from that point forward sought first God's kingdom with their time, energy, and resources. As one who spoke to soldiers before Jesus' ministry, John the Baptist was not logistically capable of converting them to Christianity, but could only prepare them for the Messiah who was to come. All that these accounts demonstrate is that John the Baptist, Jesus, and the early church regarded centurions as people who were capable of great faith. Yet, as far as the Gospels are concerned, this faith never led to conversion. Furthermore, the New Testament furnishes no grounds for assuming, as Leithart does, that if they had actually converted they would have received God's blessing to continue serving in the military.

This case for the nonconversion of Gentile soldiers is strengthened by the apostle Peter's claim, in Acts 15:14, that God first accepted Gentiles as his people with the conversion of Cornelius' household, which took place after Jesus' ascension and Pentecost. Since Cornelius was a Roman centurion, his conversion in Acts 10 is Leithart's strongest evidence. It is important to note, however, that Luke frames this account as the first instance of a Gentile's conversion—not a soldier's conversion. The logic and emphasis of this account is that since God poured his Spirit upon Gentiles in the same manner that he originally poured it upon the Jews (Acts 2), God must approve of the conversion of Gentiles.

The significance of this event cannot be overstated; it signaled an epochal shift in salvation history. This is certainly how the apostle Peter interpreted these events after having been prepared to do so by his thrice-repeated vision of unclean animals. When he saw that Gentiles had received the Spirit just like the Jews, Peter immediately had them baptized. We are never told in this passage, however, what had to change about the life of Cornelius and the various members of his household. We are not told that they repented of anything, not even from worshipping multiple gods, which typified Roman soldiering at that time. This is because the aspects of their former lives that they had to leave behind are not the point of this account. We must not therefore assume that the centurion and his household were sinless and that nothing needed to change about how they lived. Such changes were likely left out of the account lest they detract from what is most important about it: the creation of a new humanity that is neither Jew nor Gentile.

In their New Testament contexts, Leithart's antipacifist prooftexts only tell us that soldiers and Gentiles are persons who were capable of great faith and thus viable candidates for conversion. Without the support of these texts, Leithart's case for continuity between the New Testament and Constantine breaks down and the first-century component of Yoder's narration is left standing.

3. Leithart mistakes Yoder's depiction of the Middle Ages

What about the back end of Yoder's narration? Here Leithart's claim that Yoder cannot locate anything Constantinian in the Middle Ages (321–323) is flatly contradicted by a wider reading of Yoder. I cite one example from Yoder:

> The Roman and Eastern forms of Catholicism, when they speak of one another as "apostate," date that fall from grace with their breach of hierarchical communion with each other. When Magisterial Protestantism sought a date for [the] fall of the church, it was found somewhere after the fifth century, so that the ancient creeds could all be retained. Anabaptism found the root still deeper, at the point of that fusion of church and society of which Constantine was the architect, Eusebius the priest, Augustine the apologete, and the Crusades and Inquisition the culmination.[8]

Far from exculpating the medieval period, Yoder locates within it two events during which Constantinian sensibilities appear to have peaked. He acknowledged, however, that those extreme expressions do not tell the whole story of the Middle Ages and so he clarifies his point, noting that this period contained within it various resources for resisting them. Rather than appreciate Yoder's refusal to interpret this period monolithically—for which Leithart chastises Yoder with reference to Constantine—Leithart abstracts it from Yoder's other statements and marshals it against Yoder's interpretation. Leithart has switched to the role of prosecuting attorney, selectively appropriating evidence so as to engender a guilty verdict over against evidence of innocence.

4. Leithart misunderstands what Yoder means by "Constantinian"

Though Leithart often appears to understand exactly what Yoder means by "Constantinian," the evidence he gives for why Constantine himself was not "Constantinian" in a Yoderian sense fails to falsify Yoder's use of the term. As Leithart tells the story of Constantine's life, he goes to great lengths to demonstrate that Constantine was not a pagan who pretended

---

8. Yoder, "A People in the World," in *Royal Priesthood*, 89. This quote raises an additional point worth noting. As far as Yoder was concerned, a "fall of the church" historiography is not a distinctly Anabaptist practice. Other traditions also employed this trope; they simply located the "fall" at different places.

to be a Christian by applying a thin veneer of Christian religiosity for political gain. Rather, he depicts Constantine as a sincere believer who increasingly strove to order his reign according to Christian principles and to spread the Gospel throughout the world.

Yet the more Leithart's charitable interpretation is upheld, the more Yoder's claim is validated that Constantine represented the significant shift in ecclesial self-understanding that the emperor's name has come to represent. This is because Yoder's definition of Constantinianism is not a statement about the sincerity with which Constantinian Christians use top-down, coercive, worldly power or about the goodness of the ends toward which they wield such power. The shift Yoder labels "Constantinian" is the willingness of God's people to deform their specific God-given identity by merging with worldly power structures and using top-down, coercive, worldly power to accomplish what God has given his people to do without such power.

It is a reversion to the problematic underlying dynamics of "kingship like the nations." Those underlying dynamics did not become wrong for God's people only after they began misusing them; they were always wrong for God's people and always will be. It remains wrong because God set apart a people as a witness in the present world to the world to come—a coming world whose security, justice, and economics are not dictated by human rulers who subsume all aspects of societal life under their imperial jurisdiction and whose citizenry is not constricted by ethnic or geographical boundaries.

So when Leithart argues that the Emperor Constantine was a sincere Christian who used imperial power to heal and unite the church, spread God's truth throughout the world, outlaw sacrificial practices, turn pagan shrines into basilicas, uphold and expand the authority of bishops, and promote believers to positions of worldly power so they may join him in protecting the weak and promoting the good, he is baptizing God's people into an "empire like the nations." That Constantine did all these things with sincere Christian motives, that Christians in his empire extolled him as their champion, that bishops personally escorted him into battle against rival nations, and that the church found a way to incorporate all these developments into its strategy for carrying out God's mission all meant that the days of God-ordained, missional non-alignment with imperial powers were ending. This is certainly an ecclesial shift away from the entire biblical trajectory as Yoder sees it.

Constantine Revisited

Does the fact that Constantine ended the persecution of Christians negate this? Not necessarily. An act can be both good for the church and bad for the church simultaneously. The monarchy is Yoder's precedent. Yes, it stabilized Israel and unified God's people structurally in ways that permanently subdued the Philistine threat, but it also shaped God's people in unhealthy ways that left the biblical historians and prophets framing the rise of the monarchy in negative terms (Judg 9:1–16; 1 Sam 8:1–22; Hos 13:11). This does not mean that we cannot agree with Leithart's claim that Constantine did much good. Yoder frequently noted that the role of kings, according to Scripture, is to use their power to see to it that the good are rewarded and evil punished. To the extent that Constantine did this, he was acting like a king should, but not as a Christian should. Nor does the fact that Constantine "converted" and started using Christian language in his addresses, strove for church unity, and built numerous basilicas negate his role in the Constantinian shift. Yoder's case for a shift is that Christian aims are now pursued with all sincerity using imperial means. This is precisely the fusion of church and state that Yoder decries.

Accusation Two: Yoder is Constantinian in His Historical Methodology

Having engaged Leithart's most fundamental accusation at length, I now briefly address four remaining accusations, which are in some ways connected to the first. To begin, in good polemical form Leithart turns the tables on Yoder by arguing that he—and not Constantine—is the true Constantinian (317–321). He claims that Yoder exhibits historiographical, methodological, and epistemological Constantinianism by denying Constantine a carefully nuanced, sympathetic reading and by accepting the biased accounts of cynical historians. Instead of following his best historiographical insights and keeping an open-handed view of history (319), Yoder supposedly seizes the levers of history and forces Constantine into his predetermined Anabaptist "fall of the church" grid.

This accusation does not stand, of course, if Yoder is right about the Constantinian shift and if his interpretation of history is based less on a rigid sectarian revision of history and more on a robust interpretation of Scripture. When Leithart speaks of Yoder's best historiographical insights, I suspect he is speaking about the methodological approach Yoder champions in *The Jewish-Christian Schism Revisited*.[9] Yet in that work what

---

9. Yoder, "It Did Not Have to Be," in *Jewish-Christian Schism Revisited*, 43–63.

Yoder means by maintaining an "open" disposition toward history is not exhibiting openness to interpreting developments that one deems unfaithful according to biblical standards as if they were viable expressions of faithfulness. It means not assuming that the way things turned out is the way they had to turn out. For example, that Christians and Jews eventually parted ways, Yoder argues, does not mean that it was inevitable that they would do so. With reference to Constantine, an open view means that Constantine did not have to use imperial power to advance the Gospel, but could have done otherwise. Yoder is not betraying this historiographical insight if he is right about the biblical story and if Constantine was truly instrumental in the ecclesial shift that Yoder names after him.

This accusation also falters if it can be demonstrated that Yoder was more nuanced in his use of the term "Constantinian" than Leithart allows. Though Leithart frequently acknowledges that Yoder qualifies his use of the term, he nonetheless perseveres in his accusation that Yoder denied Constantine a nuanced reading. However, as the following quote demonstrates, Yoder could hardly have nuanced his reading of Constantine's role in the "fall of the church" any further without abandoning his conviction that Constantine did, in fact, play a part. "It is also important to note," writes Yoder,

> that the beginning dilution of messianic specificity began at the very beginning of Christianity and began to be spelled out intellectually in the second century. This should protect us from the oversimple notion that the big turn did not come until the fourth century. Yet, it is clear that the largest portion of the later case for primitivism arose then. Between the third century and the fifth, the relationship between the church and the world was profoundly redefined, in ways that raised the notion of restoration to a qualitatively new level. We look to that change, then, as representative, prototypical, but not as the whole for the reason renewal would be needed.
>
> It is a mistake to think that the change associated in legend with the name Constantine has to do principally with the relationship of church and state. For the sake of my present assignment, I shall be pursuing the church-state theme, but that is only one facet, and perhaps not the most important, of what was transformed.
>
> It is also a mistake to focus our interpretation of the change, as legend has done, on the man Constantine, as if he were the only major actor. Constantine was in fact a larger-than-life figure; the orders he gave did in fact reverse the course of history

> with regard to the place of Christianity in the empire. Yet his coming to be seen as a savior figure, as an inaugurator of the millennium, was not his work alone. He was decisively abetted by the mythmaking capacities both of popular culture and of Eusebius of Caesarea. Some of the systemic changes that Constantine as a mythic figure symbolizes for the historian (such as Christians' believing that God favored the empire against its enemies) had begun before he came along, and some (like the legal prohibition of the pagan cult or of the prosecution of Christian dissent) took a century after him to be worked through. So when his name is used as a mythic cipher it would be a mistake to concentrate on his biography.[10]

Clearly, Leithart's presentation of Yoder's use of the term Constantinian and his view of the church's "fall" is not as nuanced as it should be.

Throughout *Defending Constantine*, Leithart attributes Yoder's misunderstanding of the church's fall to his Anabaptist historiography, but as this quote and other writings demonstrate, the core problem for Yoder was the church's quite early "dilution of messianic specificity."[11] When the church began severing its Jewish roots, it began to lose its sense of continuity with Old Testament Israel, which rendered it vulnerable to being transplanted into alien soil as opposed to speaking and living out the Gospel in many cultures in contextually appropriate ways that are true to its biblical roots.[12]

Even so, since Yoder strove to be a careful historian, should he not have identified Theodosius or Eusebius as the namesake of this shift in ecclesial self-understanding? Theodosius went much further than did Constantine to subordinate Christianity to the empire, and Eusebius narrates this shift more charitably than any other figure in world history. For biblical reasons, the answer is no. The author/editors of 1 Samuel through 2 Kings, often called the Deuteronomistic historian(s), undertook the challenging task of bringing into a coherent framework an unwieldy account of over forty kings who reigned over two closely related kingdoms. To simplify matters, they chose two representative kings to serve as reference points. David represents kings who observed right worship of Israel's God (by bowing to God alone and disallowing high places to compete

---

10. Yoder, "Primitivism in the Radical Reformation," in *Primitive Church in the Modern World*, 81–82.

11. Ibid., 81.

12. See Yoder, "It Did Not Have to Be," in *The Jewish-Christian Schism Revisited*, 43–63.

against God's sanctuary) and Jeroboam represents idolatrous kings (by bowing to other gods and sponsoring illicit high places). These choices were appropriate because David was the first king to worship God properly and because Jeroboam sponsored the golden calf tradition that led to rampant idolatry in Israel. Yet David is not identified as Israel's best king; Josiah is (2 Kings 23:25); and Jeroboam is not identified as Israel's worst king; Manasseh is (2 Kings 21:9–17). Why, then, did the biblical authors not choose the kings who most identified the spirit of their typologies? Perhaps because, for the purposes of theologically instructive historiography, the earliest, most public, and transitional representative is the most appropriate.

Accusation Three: Yoder Is Constantinian in the Emphasis He Places on an Emperor

Yoder is also Constantinian, Leithart argues, insofar as his narrative places so much emphasis on Constantine that it makes him the central and most determinative figure in world history. A truly non-Constantinian historiography, Leithart continues, would dispatch Constantine quickly and recount world history primarily in light of God's more determinative, future kingdom, as Augustine does in *The City of God*.

As Hauerwas notes in his Christian Century review of Leithart's book,[13] Yoder would certainly not want his chosen historiographical foil to play an inordinately large role in the meaning of Christian history. To do so could give the appearance that the powers and principalities could wrest control of world history from God. Yoder would want to avoid that appearance because God's control of world history is the basis of his commitment to nonviolence. For Yoder, Christians need not wield the sword precisely because God is able to control the direction of world history without their help.[14]

It is absolutely clear that Yoder's historiography is inseparable from his conviction that God's people—to the extent that they faithfully carry out their part in God's saving purposes that culminate in Christ—bear the meaning of world history and that God's formation of that people began not with a supposedly pristine early church, but with Old Testament Israel. For the sake of convenience, I set forth a distillation of Yoder's historiography—which may be called an "ecclesial" historiography insofar

13. Oct. 13, 2010.
14. Yoder, *Politics of Jesus*, chap. 10.

as it focuses on the changing shape of God's people throughout world history—in terms of five stages. I intend these stages to show the wider scope of Yoder's historiography, which becomes visible when one reads more widely in Yoder's material than many scholars have or take time to do.[15]

1. Formation of a People: from Abraham to Judges
2. Deformation of a People: from Monarchy to its Collapse
3. Re-Formation of a People: from Jeremiah to the Early Church and Centering on Christ
4. Re-Deformation of a People: from the Apologists through the Reformation[16]
5. Re-Re-Formation of a People: from the Radical Reformation through the Contemporary Free Church Tradition

There are multiple ways to quibble with this historiography, especially if one were not favorably disposed toward the Free Church tradition. It is certainly not comprehensive and it requires a fair number of explanations and disclaimers that space does not allow me to discuss here at length. For instance, Yoder's conviction that the Radical Reformers' break from the church-empire merger is more faithful to Christ's intentions for his people does not lead him to assert that God has withdrawn from ecclesial traditions that strove to maintain that merger as long as possible or to suggest that those who advocated separation from the empire have not departed from God's intentions in other important ways. Nor does it imply that God's purposes came to a screeching halt during stages 2 and 4 (above) or that God did not raise up giants of faith and theology during those eras. Deformation is not the whole story, but the prevailing sociological or ecclesiological form. The sole purpose of this skeletal outline is to make explicit for those who have not read Yoder widely that Constantine or the "specter of Constantinianism" is not the center of Yoder's historiographical framework. Yoder may be faulted for a lot of things, but failure to make

---

15. The sheer volume of Yoder's literary corpus is intimidating enough to drive most scholars away. It is to Leithart's credit that he consulted at least thirteen of Yoder's works. The online searchable Yoder index (www.walkandword.com/yoder/) should facilitate Yoder research.

16. Yoder does not fault everything about the early apologists. With regard to ecclesiology and historiography, he faults them for severing the Jewish roots of Christian faith in their efforts to speak to the Greco-Roman world. Likewise, Yoder lauds much about the Reformation and claims to be a direct heir of it, but not without observing that key components of Christendom ecclesiology were not sufficiently challenged by the magisterial reformers.

Christ the center of his thought and his historiography should not be one of them. It is understandable, however, that those who read Yoder's work primarily with an eye toward his treatment of Constantine may deduce that he plays a disproportionately large role in Yoder's thought.

A careful reading of Yoder shows that Christ brought about the most fundamental change in world history and that a Christological reading of the biblical narrative is the key to whether Constantine was a departure from Christ's work or a culturally appropriate extension of that work. If Yoder's biblical narration is correct, Constantine is a departure and Leithart is making a monumental mistake in trying to reclaim him as a promising role model.

Accusation Four: Yoder is a Poor Exegete of Jeremiah and Ezra

Leithart joins a host of scholars in accusing Yoder of poorly interpreting the shifts represented by Jeremiah and Ezra.[17] Yoder makes Jeremiah out to be the harbinger of permanent diasporic existence for God's people, despite the fact the Jeremiah himself hopes for and anticipates a return to Jerusalem. Then, when Ezra and Nehemiah take leading roles in that return, Yoder dismisses them as politicking elders who are trying to recapture the golden days of the monarchy, which God brought to a decisive end. Leithart calls this bad scholarship, even anticanonical, and shows that Yoder is inconsistent inasmuch as he claims Daniel, Joseph, and Esther as examples of diasporic flexibility, but not Ezra and Nehemiah (296). Why not just say that different circumstances required different responses?

Several scholars have objected to Yoder's thesis of a Jeremianic turn on grounds that Jeremiah could not possibly have imagined himself to be heralding the end of palestinocentric existence and the beginning of diasporic mission.[18] Yet for Yoder, what Jeremiah imagined is not the point. Yoder is neither a professed Jew who reads Israel's history primarily in light of subsequent rabbinic development, nor an Old Testament scholar who locates the text's full meaning in authorial intent. He is a Christocentric biblical realist who reads all of Scripture and history in light of the

---

17. Yoder does this most forthrightly in "See How They Go with Their Face to the Sun," 183–202.

18. Ochs, "Commentary," in *Jewish-Christian Schism Revisited*, 204; Cartwright, "Afterword," in *Jewish-Christian Schism Revisited*, 218–19, 223; Goldingay, *Israel's Gospel*, 764 n. 86; Kissling, "John Howard Yoder's Reading of the Old Testament and the Stone-Campbell Movement," 137–44; and Weaver, "John Howard Yoder's 'Alternative Perspective' on Christian-Jewish Relations," 299 n. 14.

Constantine Revisited

definitive revelation of God's purposes in Christ and his church. Several canonical developments shed important light back onto the book of Jeremiah such that the significance of his ministry was greater than what he realized. For example:

- When the Messiah came, he distanced himself from the Jerusalem establishment (John 2:13–21).
- Jesus did not reconstitute Israel as a palestinocentric community but prepared his people to be scattered across the world by his Spirit (John 4:21–24; Acts 1:8).
- Jesus unmasked the powers' claims to be benefactors and self-consciously adopted the suffering servant posture (Luke 22:25–27).
- Jesus proclaimed a kingdom whose citizens were committed to peacemaking, enemy love, and transnational disciple-making (Matt 5:38–48, 28:19).
- Previously scattered Jews as far back as Jeremiah formed synagogues throughout the world that became central to the church's missionary expansion (Acts 9:17, 14:1, 17:1–3).
- The earliest Christians viewed themselves as aliens, exiles, strangers, and dispersed ones (Jas 1:1; 1 Pet 1:1, 2:1) whose citizenship is in heaven as opposed to Rome or Jerusalem (Phil 3:20).[19]

For Yoder, these developments must not be ignored when assessing Jeremiah's legacy. The strength of his position lies not in sixth-century prophecy and history, but in the first-century revelation of God's purposes through the Messiah, the Holy Spirit, and the church. From Yoder's perspective, we ought to ask not only what Jeremiah thought he was saying to sixth-century Jews, but also what God is saying through him to post-Pentecost Christians. Leithart makes a similar move when he grants that Constantine was accomplishing more for God's purposes than he may have realized (331).

Yoder's interpretation of Ezra and Nehemiah is less defensible. Several observations should be made, however, before scholars pass judgment on a few lines from one essay in a section titled "Further Testing."[20] First, it should be noted that Yoder was not suggesting that the canonical books

---

19. I make this point also in *Politics of Yahweh*, chap. 9; and "Biblical Warfare Revisited: Extending the Insights of John Howard Yoder," 167–84.

20. Yoder, "See How They Go with Their Face to the Sun," in *Jewish-Christian Schism Revisited*, 193–94.

of Ezra and Nehemiah were wrong in any way. Bible books often record events during which God's people perform various acts in God's name and for God's glory but against God's will (e.g., Judg 11:29–40). Yoder was simply testing the possibility that the books themselves were presenting these post-exilic reformers ambivalently. Charges that his critiques were anticanonical, then, are overstated.

Second, Yoder's questions about the legacy of Ezra and Nehemiah were open questions for him. This is likely why he placed them in a section that he called "Further Testing." Yoder had not found a satisfactory way to integrate the return from exile into his overall biblical narration, so he started a conversation that he would not live to finish. His inability to finish it does not mean his overall narration crashes on its inability to deal with Israel's rebuilding and refortification. As I argue elsewhere, it could be emphasized that, whereas it was crucial that many Jews scatter throughout the world in preparation for the Gentile mission, it was equally important that a certain number of Jews retain their identity as Jews in the Promised Land so that the Messiah could fulfill the prophecies regarding the gathering and sending of God's people "from Jerusalem" (Lk 24:46–47).[21] Although this oversight on Yoder's part weakened his narration and has rightly elicited criticism, it does not compromise his fundamental thesis that, from the beginning, God had been shaping his people in preparation for the transethnic, transnational missionary work of the church.

This still does not answer the question of why Yoder spoke so favorably about Joseph, Esther, and Daniel, despite the fact that they occupied influential positions in world empires. One reason could be that these individuals were taken into imperial custody, presumably against their wills: Joseph was sold as a slave, Esther was taken into a pagan king's harem, and Daniel was exiled from his homeland. God nonetheless used their reluctant placement within a pagan empire to serve his sovereign purposes. Thus, Daniel goes out of his way to show that he is not one of the king's minions in Daniel 1, and Joseph and Esther only learn in retrospect that God was planning to use their captivity for his providential purposes (both of which involved saving God's people from extinction). These exiled Jews found themselves in places they did not strive to be, and they made no effort to make those empires Jewish by converting them to Torah or by recruiting them to serve the unique purposes for which God set apart his chosen people.

---

21. I make this point in much greater detail in *Politics of Yahweh*, chap. 9.

Constantine Revisited

Accusation Five: Yoder Is Blind to How Jesus Is Relevant to Governing Authorities

Toward the end of his book, Leithart begins sketching his constructive proposal for how Christians ought to relate to empire in a fallen world. He supports it with an intriguing interpretation of the biblical story wherein God's people "grow up" throughout Scripture and are given greater responsibility (333–337). Whereas in the Old Testament God fought for his people, according to Leithart, by the New Testament God's people are commissioned to join the fight. Of course, the spiritual weapons God gives them are superior to those of the world. However, in a move that is intended to overturn the pacifist interpretation of the New Testament, Leithart explains that "if the Lord lets Christians wield the most powerful of spiritual weapons, does he not expect us to be able to handle lesser weapons? If he has handed us a broadsword, does he not assume we know how to use a penknife?" (336) My point here is not to critique Leithart's problematic a fortiori argument, but to engage what he does with the specific teachings of Jesus. Rather than deny the relevance of Jesus' radical demands to imperial life, he enumerates nine ways that they apply to rulers (338–339):

- Turning the other cheek teaches emperors not to wage war for purposes of retaliation and defense of honor.
- Rulers should learn to settle disputes quickly with their adversaries in order to diffuse disputes before they escalate.
- Rulers should not look at women lustfully, but should stick to their jobs and be faithful to their wives.
- Rulers should be honest and speak the truth even when it hurts.
- Rulers should not perform acts of charity simply to be seen by others.
- Rulers should love their enemies, do good to all, and punish offenders only out of love for both victims and their persecutors.
- Rulers should not worry excessively about budgets, but store up heavenly treasure through acts of charity.
- Rulers should exercise authority as those who will be called to account regarding how well they treated the naked, hungry, and imprisoned.
- Rulers may even be asked to endure a cross for the sake of righteousness.

The "politics of Jesus," according to Leithart, is thus highly relevant to the politics of empire. But Yoder allegedly cannot grasp this because his "pacifism blinds him and keeps him from seeing that the whole of Jesus' teaching and activity is abundantly instructive to rulers" (338).

This accusation is perhaps easiest to dismiss. Yoder agrees with Leithart not only that Jesus' teachings are relevant to all people, but also that Christians have a responsibility to proclaim the implications of Christ's lordship to all people, including rulers. Conspicuously absent from Leithart's bibliography is Yoder's most complete statement of the church's relationship to the state: *Christian Witness to the State*.[22] Yoder explains there, in his capital punishment writings,[23] and among his scattered remarks about vocation,[24] that the way of Christ is relevant to all aspects of life. No public sphere is free from his reign; all are subject to him as he sits enthroned at God's right hand. The way of Christ is relevant not only to church life, but also to banking, housing, practicing medicine, and governing. So Yoder and Leithart actually agree that the way of Christ is relevant to all vocations and that Christians are best positioned to proclaim what it looks like there. They disagree about whether participation in certain vocations is consistent with Christian faith.

An Interesting Question Raised by Defending Constantine

A thorough, though far from exhaustive, cross-examination has cast a long shadow of doubt over the notion that Leithart has exposed a fundamental flaw in Yoder's ecclesiological, ethical, and historical project. But Leithart nonetheless raises an interesting question that those who disagree with him must answer: what should an emperor like Constantine have done after being converted? Should he have quit his job? The apostle Paul teaches in 1 Corinthians 7 that believers should remain in the stations in

---

22. Yoder, *Christian Witness to the State*.

23. These works have been gathered for publication as *End of Sacrifice*.

24. Yoder's doctrine of vocation is scattered throughout his writings: *Body Politics World*, 25–27 and 52–53; *Christian Witness to the State*, 20–21, 27–28, 56–57, and 88; *Discipleship as Political Responsibility*, 45; *For the Nations*, 184–86 and 233–35; *Fullness of Christ*, 39–40; "I Choose Vocation," 6–7; *Original Revolution*, 118–21; *Politics of Jesus*, 8–9; *Priestly Kingdom*, 83, 109–10, 138–39, 162, and 210; and *Royal Priesthood*, 56–64, 80–82, 94–95, 113–14, and 117. I summarize Yoder's doctrine of vocation in "Kingdom Work: John Howard Yoder's Free Church Contributions to an Ecumenical Theology of Vocation," 149–72.

which they were called. Zacchaeus did not quit his job upon conversion, but reformed it radically in light of Christ. Should Constantine have attempted to do the same? Is there evidence in *Defending Constantine* that this is what Constantine did? Removing false worship from imperial life was a move in the right direction, but using imperial power to preempt the freedom God gave pagans to be pagan is a different matter. One wonders, however, whether Zacchaeus was able to keep his job. What happened to him when his superiors came calling and he was not able to pass along their customary cut? Was he praised, fired, imprisoned, or executed? What would have happened had Constantine used his position to accomplish the more moderate role that God has ordained for the state according to Scripture? We will never know, because that is not what happened. That may not have happened because, as Leithart notes, most of the bishops and leaders who maintained their integrity amid persecution had been martyred before Constantine's time (29), and the church was not as strong as it could have been to give Constantine proper instruction about his role.

In *Defending Constantine*, Peter Leithart gives us a lot to think about and perhaps even "fight" about. In bringing fresh perspectives to stale conversations, he has invited us to revisit the biblical and historical evidence to verify if it really says what we have always thought it says. In doing this, he has done the academy and the church a great service.

2 "Converted" but Not Baptized

Peter Leithart's Constantine Project

ALAN KREIDER

DEFENDING CONSTANTINE: THE TWILIGHT *of an Empire and the Dawn of Christendom* is a formidable book. In it, Peter Leithart draws upon a wide reading of both historical and theological sources. He thinks robustly, organizing the historical and theological materials into fresh categories. He writes colorfully and with rhetorical flair. Leithart is self-confessedly polemical, proudly and pugnaciously so. Among conservative American Reformed theologians he is a creative mind who, in this book, gives extended treatment to the Mennonite theologian John Howard Yoder.

Leithart is right to subject Yoder's work to critical analysis. Yoder was a church historian by training, but his interests were wide. He wrote essays and books on matters theological, biblical, ethical, and ecclesial, about all of which he thought historically. Like all historians, Yoder thought not simply in terms of events and texts, but also in terms of periods and paradigms. But unlike many thinkers, Yoder was not content simply to accept the dominant paradigms of his professional peers; he challenged them and proposed alternatives that shifted the terms of the discussion. For Yoder, whose thought was shaped in Europe amid the ruins of World War II, a triumphalist progressive reading of Western Christian history simply did not make sense. In this setting, a "Constantinian shift"—a change of direction so fundamental that he used the terms "fall" and "apostasy"—made sense.[1] In hundreds of essays he inhabited this paradigm, frequently

---

1. In using these terms, Yoder recognized that he was aligning himself with a tradition that went back to the Middle Ages. See Yoder, *Christian Attitudes to War, Peace, and Revolution*, 59–60.

discussing its implications. But Yoder never systematically examined the ancient evidence for the "Constantinian shift," so others need to do the historical reality-testing. As we shall see, Leithart begins to do this testing, but his main concentration is elsewhere—on rehabilitating Constantine the man and critiquing what Yoder called "Constantinianism." In this, Leithart at times sheds some new light on the issues. Leithart has read a lot of Yoder's writings, and his own writings display a breadth of interest that is almost Yoderian.

As Yoder often observed, we learn through conversations.[2] Dialogue is essential. All sides of a debate often bear elements of the truth that, if not equal in validity, are nevertheless necessary. To give voice to all sharpens our understanding and points to wisdom that any one person in isolation may ignore. So Leithart's book, weighty though it is, inevitably requires a rejoinder. Conversations must go on, and alas Yoder cannot take part. How intriguing it would be to read his response to *Defending Constantine*! So it has come to others to carry on the Anabaptist side of the conversation. I do so not to defend Yoder, nor to represent what others in the Anabaptist tradition think. Rather, in this essay I present my own point of view, as a historian in the Anabaptist tradition whom John Yoder, in his apostolic mode, many years ago beckoned into the study of early Christianity. To think responsibly about what he called the "Constantinian shift" Yoder knew that he needed the help of others.

In this paper I will start by looking at some contributions that I believe Leithart makes to the discussion. Second, I will consider a topic in which Leithart was intensely interested—Christian attitudes toward and participation in warfare in the early centuries and into the fourth century. Third, I address topics that apparently did not interest Leithart very much in this text—baptism, including the baptism of Constantine and the "baptism of Rome" that Leithart believes Constantine accomplished. Finally, I will turn to the impact of Constantine upon mission within the Roman Empire.

As I proceed, I will contend that in area after area there were numerous shifts between the Christianity that preceded Constantine and the Christianity that came in his wake. These shifts, I will argue, fit into two patterns or gestalts.[3] In the first five centuries of Christianity in the

---

2. Yoder, *Body Politics*, 47–70; Yoder, *Priestly Kingdom*, 22–29.

3. A "gestalt" is "a structure, configuration, or pattern of . . . phenomena so integrated as to constitute a functional unit with properties not derivable by summation of its parts." *Merriam-Webster's Collegiate Dictionary*, 525.

Roman Empire there was a movement from one gestalt—"Early Christianity"—to a second gestalt that took several centuries to take shape, and that many people, including Leithart in the last word of his book title, call "Christendom." Did this gestalt-shift indeed take place, and, if so, how was the shift related to the emperor Constantine I?

Leithart's Contributions

Leithart's professed aims are disarmingly modest: to provide "a fairly fair account of Constantine's life and work" (10). In contrast to Yoder, who he claims is interested in Constantine as an idea ("Constantinianism"), Leithart's project focuses on Constantine the man (29). He paints a portrait of an emperor claimant who, at crisis points in AD 310 and 312, through dreams and visions "experienced a religious conversion" (96). From these experiences onwards, Leithart says, Constantine was a self-consciously Christian emperor whose mission it was to convert the Roman Empire to Christianity. This required him to work ceaselessly for unity, for, as emperors had long known, the safety of the empire depended upon a unified people offering right worship. Constantine's concern for unity required him to take vigorous measures against heretical and schismatic Christian groups. As to pagans, Leithart argues that Constantine was a "Lactantian Christian," following "a policy of tolerant concord" but using favors, iconography, and the despoiling of pagan shrines to pressure pagans to convert (110). Constantine's fierce statements against the Jews were counteracted by Augustine, who, a century later, rejudaized the faith (136). Similarly, the brutality of punishment that Constantine's laws stipulated was mitigated by spotty enforcement and did not detract from a general "Christianization of law" (232). Constantine appointed Christians to imperial offices; together with the growing number of aristocratic bishops they created a Christian governing class. Constantine granted privileges to the bishops and lavished resources on the church, building elaborate basilicas and creating a new Christianized capital in Constantinople. As Christians participated in military service and supported the empire, Constantine's reign marked an intensification of attitudes and behaviors that were already present. To express Constantine's main contribution Leithart draws on one of the potent words in Christian vocabulary—baptism. With Constantine came the baptism of Rome and then the baptism of the Roman Empire. This baptism involved the empire dying to something old—pagan sacrifice—and being reborn as a Christian society animated by something new—the bloodless sacrifice of the eucharist. Constantine died in 337, within weeks of his own baptism.

In researching *Defending Constantine* Leithart has read widely in the historical literature dealing with Constantine and his setting in late antiquity. In my view, he makes some valuable points. Leithart gives a detailed account of the persecution under Diocletian, and contends—with some justice, I believe—that Yoder and other Anabaptist writers have paid insufficient attention to the persecution's horrors and to the gratitude that Christians had when the emperor, Constantine, legalized their existence (28). Leithart further points out that at times, in current-day Anabaptist circles, the rhetoric of anti-Constantinianism has led to a lack of sympathetic engagement with the European Middle Ages.[4] And he puts his finger on several tendencies in Yoder's writing that I also find distressing. One of these is Yoder's inclination to equate Eusebius and Augustine (180), whereas, as many scholars have pointed out, Augustine in his mature writings explicitly distanced himself from Eusebius. A second occurs in the passage in which Yoder links Constantine with Charlemagne as emperors who required "that every European must be Christian."[5] And underlying Leithart's critique of Yoder is a challenge: does Yoder take the details of history seriously, or is he so misled by his pacifist commitments and Anabaptist presuppositions that he cannot understand history? "If [Yoder] got Christian history wrong," Leithart comments, "that sets a question mark over his theology" (254). Of course, that challenge can go the other way. Is Leithart influenced by *his* presuppositions? Does *he* get history right? If so, or if not, what does that say about *his* theology?

Military Service

The debate about whether believers prior to Constantine were antimilitarist is an old one. The correct answer of those who told the story of the Christendom churches has been, "The church was never pacifist." Scholars primarily from the "heretical" traditions—Anabaptists, Quakers, and others—have maintained that the early Christians resisted military service. But things are messier than that. Indeed, there have always been scholars from the Christendom ecclesial traditions who maintained that the

---

4. One might note that many Christian traditions have difficulty connecting with Christians prior to the point at which their heroes enter the scene; even Reformed Christians have not always sympathetically engaged with the Middle Ages.

5. Yoder, *Royal Priesthood,* 254; Leithart, *Defending Constantine,* 112.

position of the pre-Constantinian church—of the magisterium as well as the theologians—was antimilitarist.[6] So in viewing the decision of the Church to justify lethal military service as paradigmatic of a Constantinian "shift," John Yoder was not innovating. And Yoder's case is compelling enough to cause Leithart to devote no fewer than twenty-five pages—an entire chapter of his book—to this issue.[7]

What is Leithart's case? Leithart maintains that he does not need to disprove that some Christians were pacifist before Constantine. Instead, Leithart simply needs to prove that before Constantine there was "diversity and ambiguity" and that after Constantine there was also "diversity and ambiguity." Leithart contends that unlike himself, Yoder must prove that there *was* a change, and that if he fails to do so, he is "wrong" (278).

Leithart proceeds to make a case for "diversity and ambiguity." He observes that "we do not know whether the church of the first two centuries was pacifist in practice" (261). But in the late second century things clarify. Beginning with the "Thundering Legion" of the 170s, Leithart cites evidence that there were Christians in the Roman legions, in varying numbers depending on the locality. This military service was not, *pace* Yoder, primarily a part of the civil service; it was engaged in the full range of activities of the legions. Of course, there was "a small, articulate minority" of intellectuals (259) who opposed this participation; these intellectuals are the authorities that pacifists like Yoder quote. But there were other thinking Christians who disagreed with the intellectuals. Here Leithart points to Christian men in North Africa, evidently legionaries, with whom Tertullian debated in his treatise *On Idolatry*.[8] Tertullian countered them by appealing to the teaching of Jesus, who, in disarming Peter, unbelted every soldier. But, Leithart argues, it was not primarily the soldiers' killing that offended Tertullian and the other antimilitarist Christians; it was the idolatry—the pagan worship—that was an unavoidable part of military life. Leithart assumes that there were "countless, nameless and forgotten local pastors" who gave the eucharist to "converted soldiers" (261). Constantine, by depaganizing the Roman military, changed things for Christian soldiers. Constantine eradicated sacrifice from the army camps and changed the military flag to the Christian cross. In their military assemblies troops now needed to say only an unoffensive monotheistic prayer, and

---

6. Fritz, "Service Militaire," cols. 1972–1981; also the Reformed scholar Hornus, *It is Not Lawful for Me to Fight*.

7. Leithart, "Pacifist Church?" 255–78.

8. Tertullian, *De Idololatria* 19.

on Sundays they were free to worship in Christian churches. So, Leithart contends, "many Christians [now] found military service a legitimate life for a Christian disciple" (273). Already in the Council of Arles of 314, the bishops gave their ambiguous blessing to Christians in the legions by forbidding them to lay down their arms, at least in peacetime. By the fifth century Christians were widespread in the Roman military, but Augustine of Hippo, picking up earlier Christian themes, ensured that the soldiers would maintain the love of enemies in wars waged with benevolent purpose for the sake of peace. Thanks to Augustine and the theologians "responsible for . . . mainstream Christian views on war," Christian attitudes to war have continued to be ambiguous right to the present (278).

An Ecosystem of Peace

Leithart states his position well. But five flaws distort it. First, Leithart's focus is narrow. His interest extends only to early Christian texts that deal explicitly with military service; he ignores texts that illuminate the Christians' daily practices, liturgical life, and pastoral vision. So he fails to comprehend the early Christian attempt to establish what one could call an ecosystem of peace, which fostered the Christians' approach to many issues, including military service.[9] Samples of this ecosystem are:

- Clement of Alexandria, who around 200 urged Christians, when buying signet rings, to avoid rings with swords and bows, for "we are a people of peace."[10]
- The bishop of the Syrian church of the *Didascalia Apostolorum* of about AD 250, who was ordered to "preach peace" and preside over a liturgical peacemaking process leading to peace in community. "We do not call them brothers until there is peace between them."[11]
- The great theologian Origen, who, in a letter to the historian Julius Africanus, referred to Isaiah and Micah's famous "swords into ploughshares" passage as a thematic text, probably taught in catechesis, for the Christian communities. So Origen could say confidently,

---

9. Ferguson, "Love of Enemies and Nonretaliation in the Second Century," 92.

10. Clement of Alexandria, *Pedagogue* 3.5.57. For comment, see Finney, "Images on Finger Rings and Early Christian Art," 185. Finney adds, "images of behaviors incompatible with Christian morality are off limits" (186).

11. *Didascalia Apostolorum* 2.57, 2.49.

"Who of all believers does not know the words in Isaiah?"[12] Indeed, this passage was one of the Old Testament texts cited most widely by the Christians of the early centuries.[13]

- The apologist and catechist Justin, writing in mid-second-century Rome, who saw peace as one of four changes that came with Christian conversion.[14] Referring to the Isaiah/Micah text as a key to the early Christians' self-understanding, Justin confessed: "And we who delighted in war . . . have in every part of the world converted our weapons of war into implements of peace—our swords into ploughshares, our spears into farmers' tools." As a result their culture would be different—they would "cultivate piety and justice" and be converted into lovers of their enemies.[15]

- Bishop Cyprian of Carthage, in whose Sunday services the kiss of peace preceded the eucharistic meal, giving Christians who were at odds with each other the opportunity to be "peacemakers." This was important, because Cyprian viewed "peace and brotherly agreement" as the Christians' "greater sacrifice."[16] To the catechists who were preparing candidates for baptism, Cyprian issued instructions to inform the candidates that their behavior would henceforth be unusual: "the believer ought not to live like the Gentiles . . . [and] that the example of living is given to us in Christ."[17] Cyprian, like other early Christian leaders, was preparing his community to be an ecosystem of peace.

None of these elements of an ecosystem of peace proves that the Christians of the early centuries were pacifist. However, almost all of these elements either disappeared in the centuries after Constantine or mutated so that their meanings changed fundamentally.

---

12. Origen, *Letter to Julius Africanus* (ca 240) 15.

13. Lohfink, "'Schwerter zu Pflugscharen': Die Rezeption von Jes 2, 1–5 par Mi 4, 1–5 in der Alten Kirche und im Neuen Testament," 184–209.

14. Kreider, *Worship and Evangelism in Pre-Christendom*, 15; and Kreider, *The Change of Conversion and the Origin of Christendom*, 2–7.

15. Justin, *Dialogue with Trypho* 110; 1 *Apol* 14–15.

16. Cyprian, *Lord's Prayer* 23.

17. Cyprian, *Ad Quirinum* 3.34, 3.39. For an analysis of Cyprian's catechetical program, see Alexis-Baker, "*Ad Quirinum* Book Three and Cyprian's Catechumenate," 357–80; also Ferguson, "Catechesis and Initiation," 29–32.

Christians Who Refused to Kill

Second, Leithart, blinkered by his concentration on texts dealing with military service, fails to acknowledge the many early Christian texts that repudiate all forms of killing humans. He recognizes that the Christians opposed the "spectacles" (lethal combat in the arenas); he acknowledges that they prohibited the exposure of infants and abortion (202, 218, 228). But he does not see that these prohibitions are part of a systematic repudiation of killing. To many early Christians capital punishment and killing in warfare were as reprehensible as killing in the womb or the arena. Unlike Leithart, "Unlettered people, tradesmen and old women" could see this, and they rejected lethal violence in all its forms: "we are altogether consistent in our conduct."[18] The theologian Origen could see this: Christ "did not consider it compatible with his inspired legislation to allow the taking of human life in any form at all."[19] The philosopher Lactantius could see this: "It is always unlawful to put to death a man, whom God willed to be a sacred animal . . . [It is] not lawful for a just man to engage in warfare, since his warfare is justice itself, nor to accuse any one of a capital charge . . ."[20] In these and many other passages,[21] Christian writers comprehensively repudiated killing, anticipating what Joseph Cardinal Bernardin in his *Consistent Ethic of Life* called the "seamless garment."[22]

The Church Orders

Third, Leithart ignores the church orders.[23] These are a genre of ancient texts—from the early *Didache* through the late-fourth-century *Apostolic Constitutions*—that purport to be handbooks for leaders, assisting them in regulating the worship, communal life, and ethics of Christian communities. In the second half of the twentieth century, the church orders

---

18. Athenagoras, *Legatio* 11, 34–35.
19. Origen, *Contra Celsum* 3.7.
20. Lactantius, *Div Inst* 6.50.15–17.
21. Arnobius, *Adv Nat* 1.6; Cyprian, *De Patientia* 14; Justin, 1 *Apol* 39; Tertullian, *Apol* 37.
22. Bernardin, *Consistent Ethic of Life*, 13. See also Arner, *Consistently Pro-Life*.
23. For a critical survey of the church orders, see Bradshaw, *Search for the Origins of Christian Worship*, chap. 4. For studies that recognize their importance in studying the early church's approach to military service, see Yoder, "War as a Moral Problem in the Early Church," 101–2; Hornus, *It is Not Lawful for Me to Fight*, 158–68; Kreider, "Military Service in the Church Orders," 415–42.

have come into their own as historical sources; they have been published in numerous editions and studied intensively. The church orders are difficult sources. As "living literature" they were composed by various writers, possibly at differing times and places.[24] But they are important for our purposes here for two reasons: because four of them deal specifically with Christian approaches to military service; and because they are cumulative, with later orders revising the earlier ones. So they enable us not only to get insight into the life of the early Christian communities, including their approach to military service; they also enable us to trace changes in these communities across time, from the second to the late fourth centuries; and they enable us to see whether, possibly, these changes were sufficient to constitute a "shift."

To see what the church orders tell us about the Christian leaders' approach to military service, let us look at four such documents, beginning with the *Apostolic Tradition*, chapter 16, dating possibly from the early third century in North Africa and Rome.[25]

> Church Order 1, Apostolic Tradition 16 *(mid-3rd c.)*: A soldier who has authority, let him not kill a man. If he is ordered, let him not go to the task nor let him swear. But if he is not willing, let him be cast out. One who has the authority of the sword, or is a ruler of a city who wears the purple, either let him cease or be cast out. A catechumen or faithful [person] if he wishes to become a soldier, let them [sic] be cast out because they despised God.[26]

The context of this passage is significant—the provision of guidance for church leaders about admitting people to the church's three-year catechumenate. Instead of welcoming interested persons eagerly, the *Apostolic Tradition* instructs the teachers to scrutinize the applicants, questioning them and their sponsors about their professional life and their state of life. The scrutiny is intended to discover whether the candidates will be teachable, whether they will be willing to be formed into the values of the Christian community, "whether they are able to hear the word" (*AT* 15). So the teachers inquire whether the candidates are involved in professions

24. Bradshaw, *Search for the Origins of Christian Worship*, 91–92.

25. Bradshaw et al., *Apostolic Tradition: A Commentary*, 93; Johnson, 100–101.

26. I cite the English translation of the Sahidic (Coptic) rendering of the Greek original; parallel translations in Arabic and Ethiopic have small but significant differences—*The Apostolic Tradition: A Commentary*, 88. The Arabic and Ethiopic renderings were even more severe than the Sahidic, and thus possibly older. See Eoin de Bhaldraithe, "Early Christian Features Preserved in Western Monasticism," 170–72.

that involve behavior that is contrary to the Christian community's way of life—illicit sex (brothel-keepers, prostitutes); idolatry (sculptors, pagan priests, diviners); and killing (charioteers, gladiators, and soldiers). Note several things:

a. The *Apostolic Tradition*'s concern about soldiers is not whether they will engage in idolatrous acts that are an unavoidable part of military life. It is rather concerned about whether they will kill—if they are ordered to kill, they shall resist the order. If they fail to resist and do take life, they are to be cast out of the catechumenate.

b. Soldiers may be admitted to the catechumenate if they agree not to kill; so the text assumes that it is possible to be in the military without killing, doing the many civil service tasks (e.g., scribes, messengers, accountants) that the third-century legions were charged with doing.[27] It also assumes that it is possible to be in the military without engaging in its idolatrous worship.

c. People already admitted to the catechumenate or already baptized may not become soldiers; if they do so, they are to be cast out of the catechumenate or excommunicated. They have despised God.

John Helgeland, whose research Leithart follows, gives little attention to chapter 16 of the *Apostolic Tradition*. This passage, he contends, is "very brief"; its meaning is unclear; and its "chief objection" was the military oath.[28] Clearly the text did not pique Helgeland's curiosity. Further, Helgeland ignores three subsequent church orders that embed the *Apostolic*

---

27. MacMullen, *Soldier and Civilian in the Later Roman Empire*, 155–57, 176; Secrétan, "Le Christianisme des premiers siècles et le service militaire," 345–65; Rordorf, "Tertullians Beurteilung des Soldatenstandes," 109–10. This would make sense of the position worked out by the bishops at the Council of Arles (314), in which Christians in the legions were forbidden to lay down their arms in time of peace; but presumably were allowed to lay them down in time of war, when they might have had to use them lethally—Dörries, *Constantine the Great*, 112, whom Leithart cites on 275, gets this right.

28. Helgeland, "Christians and the Roman Army from Marcus Aurelius to Constantine," 752. See also Helgeland et al., *Christians and the Military*, 36, which, following Dom Gregory Dix's edition, puts articles 17–19 (Dix's numbering) "in the context of idolatry," translates as "execute" the Sahidic word (Latin *occidere*) that Bradshaw, Stewart-Sykes, Botte, and Cuming translate as "kill," and contends that "the train of thought before and after rules out the taking of life in combat as its meaning." Helgeland, Daly, and Burns do not mention the three later church orders that revise this clause: the *Canons of Hippolytus*, the *Testamentum Domini*, and the *Apostolic Constitutions*.

Tradition and alter it in ways that reflect the changing circumstances in the fourth century. Let us look at these in turn.

> *Church Order 2, Canons of Hippolytus 13–14 (Egypt, ca. 336–340)*: Concerning the Magistrate and the Soldier they are not to kill anyone, even if they receive the order: they are not to wear wreaths. Whoever has authority and does not do the righteousness of the gospel is to be excluded and is not to pray with the bishop. Whoever has received the authority to kill, or else a soldier, they are not to kill in any case, even if they receive the order to kill . . . A Christian must not become a soldier, unless he is compelled by a chief to bear the sword. He is not to burden himself with the sin of blood. But if he has shed blood, he is not to partake of the [eucharistic] mysteries, unless he is purified by a punishment, tears, and wailing.[29]

a. In the *Canons of Hippolytus*, killing remains the church order's central concern. Even at the end of Constantine's reign, by which time obligatory pagan worship in the legions had long been abolished, the church order commanded the catechumens not to kill, even if they were ordered to do so. Further, in the late 330s, at the very end of Constantine's reign, the *Canons of Hippolytus* forbade Christians to join the legions unless they were forced to do so at sword-point.

b. Christians at times did shed blood, possibly at times because they were compelled to do so. If they killed, they were to be excluded from the eucharist until they completed a penitential discipline.

> *Church Order 3, Testament of our Lord 2.2 (Asia Minor? second half of 4th c?)*: If anyone be a soldier or in authority, let him be taught not to oppress or to kill or to rob, or to be angry or to rage and afflict anyone. But let those rations suffice him which are given to him. But if they wish to be baptized in the Lord, let them cease from military service or from the [post of] authority. And if not let them not be received. Let a catechumen or a believer of the people, if he desire to be a soldier, either cease from his intention, or if not let him be rejected. For he hath despised God by his thought and, leaving the things of the Spirit, he hath perfected himself in the flesh, and hath treated the faith with contempt.[30]

---

29. English translation by Carol Bebawi, in *Canons of Hippolytus*, 18.

30. English translation in *Testamentum Domini*, 118. I accept the dating and geographical locating of this text by Sperry-White, *Testamentum Domini*, 6.

The *Testament of our Lord* instructed catechumens approaching the church to behave according to John the Baptist's admonitions in Luke 3:14 (contentment with wages, no oppression or robbery); but it intensified this instruction by prohibiting killing or being angry. A catechumen or believer who joins the military was to be excluded. Before being baptized catechumens were to leave the military.

> *Church Order 4, Apostolic Constitutions 8.32.10 (Syria, ca. 385):*
> If a soldier come, let him be taught to do no injustice, to accuse no one falsely, and to be content with his allotted wages; if he submit to those rules, let him be received; but if he refuse them, let him be rejected.[31]

a. The *Apostolic Constitution*, the final reworking of the *Apostolic Tradition* dating from the end of Constantine's century, drops the *Apostolic Tradition*'s clause that prohibits soldiers who want to become catechumens from killing.

b. It makes John the Baptist's counsel in Luke 3:14 the standard rule governing the behavior of Christians in military service; if soldiers refuse these rules, they were not to be admitted to the catechumenate.

These four church orders clearly indicate that in the two centuries from AD 200 to 400 Christians made authoritative pronouncements about the participation of believers in military service. They were silent about the possibility that Christians in the legions might engage in idolatrous practices. Instead, they were concerned that Christians in the military might be ordered to kill people, and three of the four church orders forbade it.

The Magisterium

But how authoritative were the church orders? Do they enable us to approximate a position of those responsible for the church's teaching and pastoral oversight, of the "magisterium" (to use an anachronism)? According to Paul Bradshaw, the authors of the church orders may have been "indulging in an idealizing dream—*prescribing* rather than *describing*." Bradshaw also acknowledges that there was in these sources "undoubtedly some foundation based on the reality either of local tradition or influences from other churches."[32] Alistair Stewart-Sykes, writing about the *Apostolic*

---

31. *Constitutions of the Holy Apostles*, 495.
32. Bradshaw, *Search for the Origins of Christian Worship*, 95–96.

Tradition, sees it as a product of disputes in third-century Rome, which was attempting to construct "a social (or ecclesial) reality" around which Christians could unite, and whose material, particularly concerning the catechumenate and baptism, is "genuinely descriptive because of the extent to which it coheres with later practice."[33] Of course, as Bradshaw and Stewart-Sykes agree, the church orders must be tested by other sources. Stewart-Sykes proposes one—coherence with later practice. Leithart proposes another source of authority—"the countless, nameless and forgotten local pastors" (259). These are by definition an irretrievable source, and thus possibly a mouthpiece for one's own prejudices. But as it happens, one of these pastors was not quite forgotten. Theotecnus was bishop of Caesarea in 260 when Marinus, a Christian centurion, was "outed" by fellow soldiers when he refused to sacrifice to the emperors. A military judge condemned Marinus, but gave him three hours to reconsider. Theotecnus heard about the judge's decision, sought out Marinus, and led him by hand to the church where he placed Marinus directly in front of the altar. Theotecnus pulled Marinus's cloak aside and pointed to his sword. Then he placed "a copy of the divine Gospels" before Marinus, and "asked him to choose which he preferred." Marinus chose the Gospels, whereupon Theotecnus sent him "in peace" to face execution.[34] For this local pastor, the "divine Gospels" trumped the sword. In the case of other pastors this may not have been the case. Considering the pastoral impact of the church orders, Christine Mühlenkamp speculates that when dealing with ethical issues many pastors may have constructed a "soft boundary" between the Christian community and pagan society, in contrast to the "hard boundary" they constructed in cultic/religious issues.[35]

It is unknowable how authoritative these four church orders were. But their substance is distinctive and their extension across time, geography, and languages is impressive. All the church orders attempt to screen potential catechumens for their capacity to hear "the word" of the teachers that will form them, in catechesis, to be Christians. All of them recognize that military service will affect the capacity of candidates to participate in a process of resocialization.[36] Across the fourth century, it is clear that the resocialization was becoming less rigorous; and one critical indicator of this loss of rigor is the nuancing of the approach to killing. Three of

33. Stewart-Sykes, ed. *Hippolytus, On the Apostolic Tradition*, 50.
34. *The Martyrdom of St Marinus* 241–43.
35. Christine Mühlenkamp, "'Nicht Wie die Heiden,'" 204.
36. Meeks, *Origins of Christian Morality*, 163–64.

the four church orders focus on killing as something that is incompatible with the Word; but the fourth construes the Word to refer to John the Baptist's Luke 3:14 injunctions to soldiers about discontent, injustice, and false accusations. These were matters of spiritual import that had to do with the way of living taught and embodied by the Christian church. The four church orders record changing responses to external circumstances, across a century and a half. Thus, the *Canons of Hippolytus* introduced penance for Christians who killed, which Basil of Caesarea's *Canonical Epistle* refines.[37] The *Testament of our Lord* introduced Luke 3:14 as the standard, but for catechumens rather than baptized believers.

Only with the *Apostolic Constitutions*, a considerable time after the *Apostolic Tradition* and half a century after Constantine I's death, did the church orders rescind the prohibition of killing. In many ways, the community governed by the *Apostolic Constitutions* was still a counterculture; but it was a community whose members could at last be soldiers who killed.[38] With reference to killing, the church orders document a shift that Leithart, apparently unaware of these sources, was unable to see.

Christians in the Legions

Fourth, Leithart's view of the entry of Christians into the legions is wishful. "When the emperor expunges sacrifice from the army and changes the standard to a Christian cross," he states, then "many Christians" wanted to serve in the military (271). Indeed, "many Christians found military service a legitimate life for a Christian disciple" (273). Studies of the fourth-century Roman legions simply do not bear out these statements. At the end of the fourth century, only a few troops, the emperor's personal bodyguard, carried the *Chi-Rho* shield.[39] The army was flexibly conservative, motivated by desire to be successful militarily but not by religious zeal of any sort. Throughout the century its commanders were interchangeably pagan, Nicene, and Arian, chosen for military effectiveness and not by creed; and most of the troops, recruited in rural areas where Christianity

---

37. Basil, *Ep* 188.13.

38. On countercultural aspects of the *Apostolic Constitutions*' approach to conflict, see Kreider, "Peacemaking in Worship in the Syrian Church Orders," 183–87; on the church's fear of the army, see *Apostolic Constitutions* 8.12—we pray "for the whole army, that they may be peaceable towards us . . ."

39. Elton, "Warfare and the Military," 336.

had made little progress, continued to be pagan.[40] From 416 all soldiers were to be Christians, but members of heretical groups were allowed to serve;[41] and the "conversion" of the legions was very gradual.

Continuity in Patterns of Military Service?

Fifth, Leithart argues that between the third and fifth centuries there was a continuity in Christian approaches to military service. There is some truth to this, but he misconstrues it. Following David Hunter, Leithart states that Christians such as Augustine, who justified participation in warfare for a "just" cause, were in "fundamental continuity with at least one strand of pre-Constantinian tradition."[42] This is correct: one can document Christians in 210 who presented arguments similar to those that Augustine offered two centuries later. The question is—who were these Christians and what was their ecclesial status?

We have seen that around the year 210 the North African theologian Tertullian was engaged in debate with Christians who were serving in the military and were unapologetic about it. Tertullian deployed against them some of his crisp phrases: There is "no agreement between the divine and the human sacrament. . . . One soul cannot be due to two masters." But Tertullian was disconcerted when he found that the soldiers were also developing their own point of view. According to his report they were thinking of biblical stories in which they found precedents for their military service: Moses carried a rod; Aaron wore a buckle; John the Baptist wore leather; Joshua led a line of troops; the Israelite people warred; the centurion of Matthew 8 believed; and John the Baptist (in Luke 3:14) gave to the soldiers who came to him "the formula of their rule." Tertullian was incensed by the soldiers' arguments; he accused them of "sporting with the subject." To him it was clear that Christ had taken away the sword from all Christians. "How will a Christian war, nay, how will he serve even in peacetime, without a sword, which the Lord has taken away?" Christ, in disarming Peter, has disarmed every soldier.[43]

We go forward to 419, still in North Africa, where Augustine of Hippo was corresponding with Boniface, Count of Africa. Augustine

---

40. Tomlin, "Christianity and the Late Roman Army," 45.

41. *Codex Theodosianus* 16.10.21 (416); 16.5.56 (428).

42. Hunter, "Decade of Research on Early Christians and Military Service," 93; cited by Leithart, *Defending Constantine*, 259.

43. Tertullian, *De Idololatria* 19.

urged Boniface not to "think that it is impossible for anyone to please God while engaged in active military service." Where did Boniface get that idea? Might it have been a deep part of the early Christian tradition?[44] In any event, Augustine attempted to dissuade Boniface from his scruples by providing a succession of biblical *exempla* similar to those that the legionaries offered to Tertullian: David, and other righteous men in the Old Testament; the faith-filled centurion; and John the Baptist, "the friend of the bridegroom," who told the soldiers (in Luke 3:14) to do no violence and be content with their wages. At this point Augustine altered his idiom and drew from the Ciceronian well: "Peace should be the object of your desire; war should be waged only as a necessity."[45]

Boniface, perhaps swayed by Augustine's reasoning, stayed in the imperial service. The arguments that Augustine used were in part a recent addition to Christian ethics (the just war ideas), but in part they were old, having been aired in North Africa over two centuries earlier. So there was continuity. But who was it that used the arguments? In 210 it was Christian laity, probably soldiers, who appealed to Joshua, the centurions, and Luke 3:14, while the leading theologian in the province, Tertullian, articulated the position of the church to correct them. In 419 it was the leading theologian in the province, Augustine, who appealed to the same biblical passages to justify military service in a church that was rapidly becoming society-encompassing. Over this period much had changed: the church orders had become more accepting of conventional values, Christian approaches to killing had changed, and the church's ecosystem of peace had been degraded. So Augustine was in continuity, not with the deep Christian moral tradition, but with the argument of the laity in the legions.[46] This represents a shift—a shift from the gestalt of early Christianity to another gestalt—Christendom.[47]

---

44. See the similar reactions of the aristocratic Volusian (Jesus' "preaching and doctrine are not adaptable to the custom of the state") with Augustine's rejoinders. Augustine, *Ep* 136.

45. Augustine, *Ep* 189, to Boniface.

46. If a century from now diocesan bishops and ethicists at the Gregorian University provide thoughtful justification for artificial birth control, there will be a similar example of continuity, in which theologians and hierarchs eventually bless the views and practices of lay people and make it the church's position. Continuity, in which change filters upwards, is nevertheless a shift.

47. Yoder saw the change regarding war in a large, gestalt-like context: "What has changed is . . . the entire setting in which doing God's will can be thought about." Yoder, "War as a Moral Problem," 104.

Baptism

Constantine's Conversion

A second gestalt shift has to do with baptism, a subject that evidently does not interest Leithart in this book. It takes him 298 pages to get to Constantine's baptism, and then he devotes only slightly more than a page to it. In view of his professed interest in Constantine the man, why is Leithart so uninterested in Constantine's baptism? Why does he give more space to the medieval *Acts of Sylvester*, which gives a legendary account of Constantine's baptism, than he does to Eusebius's *Life of Constantine*, which gives a streamlined but liturgically credible account of the actual events (298–300)?

In other ways, however, Leithart gives remarkable prominence to baptism. Not to the rite and its preparatory catechesis, and not to the actual baptismal practice of the fourth-century churches—to these he pays no attention at all. No, Leithart is interested in the idea of baptism, not its ritual embodiment or even its sacramental theology. In *Defending Constantine* baptism functions without a rite, without an "effective sign," and without faith. It is a symbol of Christianizing change. And in Leithart's prose baptism makes for arresting rhetoric. The baptismal theme takes on many forms. Thus, Leithart tells us that in 312 at the battle of the Milvian Bridge "Rome had been baptized in the Tiber" (69). Later, he informs us that Rome's baptism involved the baptism of public space, the baptism of the aristocracy, the baptism of historical writing, and, not to be too modest about it, the baptism of the entire Roman Empire (125, 227, 250, 324). In this baptism, "*something* happened, some border was crossed . . . [and] this something made things Christian" (324; italics Leithart's). Like all baptisms, of course, this baptism was only a beginning. "It was, like every baptism, an infant baptism" (324). So of course the baptized cities, persons, and empire need teaching or *paideia* (204). But the baptisms set a new trajectory—in this case, into a world without sacrifice. So Leithart entitles his final chapter, the longest in the book, "Rome Baptized." Underneath this grand talk about baptism, what was happening on the ground? As best we can tell, what was Constantine's baptism like? And what was going on when Rome was "baptized," or the Roman aristocracy was "baptized"?

For Constantine's baptism, Leithart sets the scene. While advancing on Rome in 312, Constantine, an ambitious claimant of the imperial throne, had "mystical experiences." On the eve of a battle Constantine had a vision of a cross of light in the sky upon which he saw the inscription, "Conquer by this."[48] "For fourth-century Christians," Leithart asks, "how can that be anything other than a sign of conquest by the cross?" (78) This vision presaged Constantine's victory over his rival Maxentius and his conquest of Rome. The following year Constantine legalized Christianity and by 324 he had become sole emperor by defeating his rival Licinius. What Constantine experienced in 312, Leithart claims, was "a religious conversion" (96).

What impact did Constantine's "conversion" make on his life? According to Eusebius, Constantine put "the trophy of the cross" on his battle flags; because of its apotropaic powers, he always used the "saving sign" at the head of his armies for protection. Constantine felt that he needed help to understand his experience, so he summoned Christian priests, asking who this god was and what the vision might mean. His consultants talked about "the Only begotten Son of the one and only God," and "began to teach him the reasons for his coming." In some detail they explained the "story of his self-accommodation to human conditions." Constantine listened. But then, at the point at which Christian catechesis would customarily begin, the teachings were broken off. Eusebius seems to indicate that it was Constantine who decided to end them: "he made up his mind."[49] But why did Constantine decide this? Was it because he as emperor was too busy? Was he unable to adjust his life to the church's well-established convictions? Did the churchmen precipitate the decision by deciding that they, although attracted by the idea of having Constantine in their midst, were not persuaded by his radical transformation of the cross from a gesture invoking the Spirit's protection of the individual into an instrument of military conquest?[50] Were bishops unwilling to change their ethical standards even for the emperor? What a pregnant moment! What if Constantine, in response to the bishops' initial catecheses, had submitted himself to the Christians for teaching and apprenticeship? What if he, like all catechumens, had made initial steps into a society that was not replicating or validating the dominant societal structures, but querying them and

---

48. Eusebius, *Life of Constantine* (henceforth *VC*) 1.28. I always cite this work in the edition of Cameron and Hall, *Eusebius*. For an earlier, somewhat different report, see Lactantius, *De Mortibus Persecutorum* 44. Leithart's pages (73–79) that harmonize the two accounts by positing two separate incidents (in 310 and in 312) reflect recent scholarship and may be correct.

49. *VC* 1.32.3.

50. For elements in this shift in the use of the cross, see Heid, "Kreuz," cols 1123–1130.

inventing alternatives to them? Of course, if Constantine had entered the Christian community a rival might have killed him. But is it better for a Christian to kill other people, as he himself did,[51] than to be killed by them? Earlier Christians had said to those who threatened them, "You can kill us, but you cannot do us any real harm."[52]

According to Eusebius, Constantine decided it was safer to be self-taught. He would study by himself in his palace. He would have no teacher, no sponsor who would teach by embodiment as well as conversation; he would "personally apply himself to the divinely inspired writings."[53] He would be a Christian autodidact. He would have priests in his entourage to advise him, and he would foster due rites and fight heresy. But he would not be baptized. So, according to standards of the early church that were still operative, Constantine had not been converted.

What then are we to make of Constantine's "religious conversion" of 312?[54] This expression is anachronistic. According to the teachings of the Church conversion could not have been merely the result of a vision; nor was it just "a moment of psychological conviction."[55] Conversion was more serious than that. It was the fruit of a journey of change that culminated in baptism. According to Robert Finn, "the task of conversion was to reshape an entire way of living and system of values."[56] Wayne Meeks calls this journey "the resocialization into an alternative community."[57]

This journey was time-consuming and humbling. According to the church orders, which fit well with other evidence from Origen and Cyprian, a person who wanted to become a Christian, or who had had a mystical experience, would come to the Christian teachers and ask to become someone who was taught—a catechumen. As we have seen, admission to the catechumenate was not automatic. The church leaders examined the candidates to see if they were living in a way that would allow them to hear

51. Leithart, *Defending Constantine*, 227 ("scandalous exercise of power by Constantine" in killing his wife, Fausta, and son, Crispus), 230. Cf. Ramsay MacMullen's estimate: "The empire had never had on the throne a man given to such bloodthirsty violence as Constantine." *Christianizing*, 50.

52. Justin, 1 *Apol* 2.

53. *VC* 1.32.3.

54. Leithart, *Defending Constantine* 96, quoting Barnes, *Constantine and Eusebius*, 275. Barnes is an eminent ancient historian who has often said this kind of thing.— e.g., "Conversion of Constantine," 372; "Constantinian Reformation," 46.

55. Barnes, *Constantine and Eusebius*, 43.

56. Finn, "It Happened One Saturday Night," 609.

57. Meeks, *Origins of Christian Morality*, 26.

the word. Or were they living in ways that enmeshed them in idolatry, immorality, or violence? If so, they must go away, change their behavior, and apply again. The church was confident enough in the truth of its teachings and in its numerical growth that it did not have to water down its requirements. When the catechumens began to receive instruction, they left an old world, marked by spiritual bondage and addictive behavior, and entered a new, liminal world learning and unlearning.[58] The great third-century catechist Origen compared the entry into the catechumenate to the Israelites crossing the Red Sea, leaving the bondage of Egypt for the liminal space of the Wilderness.[59] There, often daily and over a substantial period of time, the teachers gave the candidates a new narrative (the stories of Israel and Jesus) and a new way of living characterized by Jesus' teachings in which they experienced a freedom that the old order had denied them.[60] Sponsors embodied the Christian way so that the candidates, who were their apprentices, could imitate their lives; the sponsors also observed and encouraged the changing behavior of their charges.

When the candidates seemed ready, the sponsors brought them to the teachers who examined them and their sponsors to find out whether the candidates had lived like a Christian. In Egypt, late in Constantine's reign, the questions included: "[Have you] hated vainglory, despised pride, and chosen for [yourself] humility. . . . Are you in two minds, or under pressure from anything, or driven by convention?"[61] If the bishop was satisfied with their answers, the candidates were admitted to final instruction in which they learned to pray the Lord's Prayer and to understand the Creed. The journey of conversion came to completion in baptism, the watery rite in which the candidates left the liminal space and crossed the Jordan into the promised land.[62] The baptism was ritually memorable, with exorcisms, anointings, and a threefold immersion in lots of water. As Origen graphically put it, the Egyptians (the rulers of this world) are hot on your heels and want you to go back into their slavery. "But you descend into the water, you leave it safe and sound. Washed from the stains of sin, you come up again a 'new man,' ready to 'sing a new song.'"[63] There is jubilation as the congregation embraces the baptizands, enveloping them in a

58. See Kreider, "Journey of Conversion," chap. 3.
59. Origen, *Hom on Exodus* 5.5.
60. Kreider, *Worship and Evangelism in Pre-Christendom*, 21–26.
61. *Canons of Hippolytus* 16.
62. Origen, *Hom on Joshua* 4.1.
63. Origen, *Hom on Exodus* 5.5.

new family in which they are brothers and sisters; prays with them; kisses them; shares the eucharist with them; and with special food—milk and honey—symbolizes that the candidates have entered a new world. They will now live by different convictions and be animated by a different story. Then, and only then, are the candidates converted. Outsiders look at the new believers and want to imitate them and become Christian, because "the progress of those who have been illuminated is high and better than the common behavior of people."[64]

So was the unbaptized Constantine then a Christian? Leithart calls him "a seriously Christian ruler" (82); indeed, "not just a Christian; he was a *missional* Christian" (88). Leithart is often convincing when he sees Constantine attempting, according to his own lights, to rule in Christian ways. He rightly emphasizes Constantine's role in the Council of Nicaea, with its attempts to determine orthodox doctrine and the date of Easter so there would be *homonoia* (concord) on matters religious.[65] Leithart devotes pages to Constantine's acts of benevolence toward the church, his lifting of tax burdens from churchmen, his building projects in Rome, Constantinople, and Jerusalem. Further, Leithart discusses Constantine's legal reforms, his attempts to improve justice for women and poor litigants. Leithart acknowledges MacMullen's evidence for the growing use of torture and capital punishment under Constantine, and observes that "many of his decrees suggest a horror show." But he argues that it is not clear whether the prescribed punishments were enforced.[66] In all of this, Constantine was exploring ways to rule as a new kind of Christian—self-taught, solitary, and unbaptized. He wanted at the same time to be Christian and emperor, without deconstructing his old world and being resocialized into a new world. He wanted to set his own terms.

As to Constantine's religious life, his position was anomalous. He did not belong to the church. He could invite the bishops to his palace and receive them at his splendid table.[67] But they could not invite him to their awesome table to receive the eucharist.[68] So Constantine, instead of

64. *Canons of Hippolytus* 19.

65. VC 3.20.3.

66. Leithart, *Defending Constantine*, 198–200, commenting on MacMullen, "What Difference did Christianity Make?" 322–43.

67. VC 3.15.

68. In third- and fourth-century Christian worship services, only catechumens and baptized believers were admitted to the service of the Word; and the eucharist began only after the unbaptized catechumens departed. Kreider, *Change of Conversion*, 22–26; Finn, *From Death to Rebirth*, 191–93, 201–3.

gathering with the faithful on Sundays, engaged in private worship in his imperial quarters, where "the body of persons assembled ... was in all aspects a church of God" —without the eucharist, to which the church could not admit him.[69] According to Eusebius, when at home, Constantine shut himself into places in the imperial palace where he "would converse with his God alone."[70] On his final campaign against the Persians, Constantine took bishops along with him to "fight at his side with supplications ... to God the giver of victories" in a tent "to form the church."[71] Clearly Constantine continued to engage in self-catechesis. In his *Oration to the Assembly of Saints* (possibly of 325), Constantine was able to discourse learnedly about Christianity. "We have," he insisted, "received no aid from human instruction"—a claim no early-fourth-century Christian could or would make![72] The content of the address is that of a thoughtful, intellectually gifted man who had not received catechesis. He differentiates himself from the "saints" whom he is addressing: "Compare our religion with your own. Is there not with us genuine concord, and unwearied love of others?" Constantine knows that his behavior has been objectionable to many of his hearers, and he is defensive: "surely all men know that the holy service in which these hands have been employed has originated in pure and genuine faith towards God...."[73]

In 337 an illness persuaded Constantine that his death was approaching, so he sacrificed his two-mindedness and approached the churchmen in order to "purify himself from the offences which he had at any time committed."[74] In the words of Averil Cameron and Stuart Hall, "Constantine becomes a catechumen."[75] In the account that follows, all of the traditional elements of the baptismal journey were present, telescoped by the time pressure of Constantine's illness. Constantine knelt on the floor before the churchmen, confessed his sins, and, for the first time, was prayed for, accompanied by the laying on of hands. Constantine told the

69. *VC* 1.17.3.
70. *VC* 4.22.1.
71. *VC* 4.56–57.
72. Constantine, *Oration* 11.
73. Ibid., 25–26.
74. For Constantine's journey of conversion, see *VC* 4.52–64.
75. *Eusebius: Life of Constantine*, 340. Almost a century ago Pierre Batiffol advanced the idea that Constantine became a catechumen just before his baptism.—"Les Étapes de la conversion de Constantin," 264. More recently, a world authority in fourth-century Christian initiation came to the same conclusion.—Yarnold, "The Baptism of Constantine," 98.

bishops that he had long "thirsted and yearned to win salvation in God . . . [and to be] hereafter numbered among the people of God." Constantine was tired of praying by himself. In the future he wanted to "meet and join in the prayers with [the people] all together." And he resolved to live according to "rules of life which befit God." The churchmen responded by providing as much "preliminary instruction" as time permitted, and then performed the "customary rites" (evidently of exorcism, baptism, and anointing) by which Constantine was "initiated by rebirth in the mysteries of Christ." Constantine's experience of the baptismal liturgy was profound. He exulted in the Spirit, "awestruck at the manifestation of the divinely inspired power." And he responded to this experience ethically. Like the early Christians he refused any longer to wear the purple robe that signified wealth and dominance. And he sang a new song full of praise for what God had done: "I know that *now* I am in the true sense blessed, that *now* I have been shown worthy of immortal life, that *now* I have received divine light."[76] Not previously. Finally, in the last days of his life, Constantine became a Christian, twenty-five years after what Leithart calls his "conversion."[77]

This is an unsettling thought. According to Jesuit liturgical scholar Edward Yarnold, it is "startling." "It implies, for example, that Constantine presumed to sit among the bishops at the council of Nicaea and direct their deliberations when he was not even a catechumen."[78] That Constantine was committed to using the Christian Church as a means of bringing about concord, *homonoia*, in the Roman Empire makes sense.[79] It also makes sense that Constantine therefore saw his task as promoting the Christian Church, whose membership at his accession was at most 10 percent of the empire. His granting of privileges to churchmen, building

---

76. *VC* 4.63.1; italics mine.

77. Of Constantine's baptism, Leithart writes (300): "Constantine seemed to believe there was a basic incompatibility between being an emperor and being a Christian, between court and church, warfare and prayer, the purple and the white. It would be an ironic conclusion: Constantine, the first anti-Constantinian. Constantine the Yoderian." On the contrary, how much more accurate it would be to rewrite this Leithart passage as follows: "*the church* believed that there was a basic incompatibility between being an emperor and being a Christian, between court and church, warfare and prayer, the purple and the white." Thus Constantine, in affirming the church's teaching and the ethical dimension of baptism by rejecting the purple, was far from being the first anti-Constantinian; he was simply becoming a Christian.

78. Yarnold, "Baptism of Constantine," 98.

79. MacMullen, *Constantine*, 165: "[*Homonoia*] is the key to his whole Church policy."

monumental structures, excoriating schismatics, and persecuting heretics also makes sense. But he was not doing these things as a Christian. And if, as Leithart puts it, Constantine was involved in "baptizing Rome," he was doing the baptizing as an unbaptized person.

What then do Leithart's baptismal phrases mean? Leithart assures us that he is interested in studying the fourth century as a historian, but for him baptism "has become more an idea than [reality]."[80] So Leithart brandishes baptismal phrases as slogans: "Rome had been baptized in the Tiber" (69); "He [Constantine] had baptized public space"[81]; "The baptism of the aristocracy." I propose in light of recent scholarly research to look at these slogans—*the baptism of Rome* (including the baptism of public space) and *the baptism of the aristocracy*. In both cases we shall see that reality—what actually was happening on the ground—was more intriguing, credible, and complex than Leithart's slogans would indicate.

The Baptism of Rome

"The baptism of Rome." According to Leithart, this happened already in 312 when Constantine, after his victory at the Milvian Bridge, entered Rome with his troops carrying the *labarum*—the cross-bedecked battle standard. Begun in victory, this "baptism" of Rome continued through Constantine's building policy. Constantine was "a great builder of churches, *Christian* churches," not least in the imperial capital of Rome (121, italics Leithart's). These were large buildings, whose basilica form and splendid ornamentation communicated Christianity's triumph in the Roman world. The buildings replaced domestic structures, where Christian churches had earlier met, because "domestic spaces could no longer house the crowds," and because Constantine's Christianity was to be public, not private. According to Leithart, through commissioning monumental buildings Constantine "baptized public space" (125).

To some extent this picture is true. Constantine did indeed sponsor an elaborate and expensive building program in Rome. Already in 313 Constantine began construction of a large basilica, St John Lateran,

---

80. This is what Leithart says Yoder and others have done to Constantine, "who has become more an idea than a man." *Defending Constantine*, 29.

81. Generally when Leithart refers to the Constantinian baptisms (of Rome, the aristocracy, historical writing, the empire) he uses the passive voice and indicates no agent. But here (125) Leithart uses the active voice and sees Constantine as the baptizer, which I find theologically and liturgically astonishing.

completed in 319. In subsequent years he built seven more basilicas—an impressive statement of the importance of the church to his program for the empire.

But the picture is more complicated than this. For example, consider the location of the eight basilicas. One of them, St John Lateran, was built just inside the city walls where it served as "the first building in Rome to be specifically designed for the needs of the Christian community."[82] The other seven were scattered outside the walls, six of them around the southern and eastern edges of the city and one of them—St. Peter's—in the northwest. Significantly, all of them were built on private imperial property. None of them was built in city center, the historical and ceremonial showplace area with its capitol, administrative buildings, forums, and great temples. Constantine was proud to build in the public center of Rome; he erected the baths on the Quirinal, his triumphal arch, the Basilica Nova, and the colossal statue of himself, crowned by his six-foot-high head. But he built no church there.[83] Private patrons renovated existing house churches, and in 336 Pope Mark constructed San Marco, the first papal construction in central Rome. But visually these efforts were modest, hardly rivals to the venerable structures that the pagans were rebuilding and restoring.[84] According to Richard Krautheimer, "The Roman Forum in particular seems to have remained a pagan preserve." And the new churches around the city's fringe "were hardly visible to Rome's casual visitor."[85] Why not visible, if Constantine was baptizing Roman public space?

Because of pagan opposition. The religious and administrative center of Rome was controlled by the senatorial aristocracy, and these aristocrats during Constantine's reign were "overwhelmingly pagan" in their sympathies.[86] Constantine had already offended them in 312 when he entered Rome with the *labarum*.[87] So, to avoid offending these locally dominant figures, Constantine built his huge basilicas on less visible lands that he, not the Senate, controlled.

82. Curran, *Pagan City and Christian Capital*, 96.
83. Krautheimer, "Ecclesiastical Building Policy of Constantine," 545.
84. Cameron, *Last Pagans of Rome*, 50.
85. Krautheimer, *Rome, Profile of a City*, 312–1308, 30–35.
86. Krautheimer, "Ecclesiastical Building Policy," 531. By the 350s and 360s, Christianity began to make inroads into aristocratic circles, especially among women. Cameron, *Last Pagans*, 187.
87. Krautheimer, *Rome, Profile of a City*, 31.

Constantine Revisited

Further, of the eight basilicas that Constantine constructed, only one—Saint John Lateran—was constructed primarily for services of eucharistic worship. Even St. Peter's, which was adaptable to eucharistic worship, was "founded by Constantine primarily as a covered cemetery and funeral hall" on the site of the martyr's tomb.[88] The other six basilicas were huge U-shaped structures, covered cemeteries with table-like graves similar to those on which for centuries Romans had funerary feasts on anniversary days, months, and years. Christian Romans also celebrated feasts at graves, but they liked to bury their dead near the graves of martyrs (*ad sanctos*), which they believed would be spiritually beneficial to them. Depending on the family, these feasts had more or less relationship to the Christian faith; they were often occasions of intemperance and inebriation.[89] One basilica for eucharistic worship; six for *refrigeria*, or funerary feasts; and one (St. Peter's), a hybrid. What an odd way for Constantine to balance his building projects, the monumental face of his "baptism" of Rome.

Constantine built in this way because he was facing not only the opposition of Roman aristocrats; he also was facing the footdragging of the Roman populace. And this footdragging did not happen only in Rome. Leaders in many parts of the empire encountered similar opposition to their attempts to Christianize recalcitrant locals. In 395 Augustine, newly appointed as bishop of Hippo, attempted to forbid locals from filling "the whole space of a great basilica . . . with their mobs of feasters and drinkers."[90] Riots ensued, because the people had been feasting and drinking at tombs for centuries. The reason the bishops had let these observances into the churches in the first place is intriguing. According to Augustine, it was because "with the advent of peace," when Constantine came to the throne and persecutions ended, many pagans were put off Christianity by the church's disapproval of their pagan feasting and drinking. So bishops decided to *inculturate*—to insert Christian values into Roman culture by allowing Christian feasting and drinking "in honor of the holy martyrs." Pagan and Christian funerary banquets, according to Augustine, were "equally lavish." When Augustine tried to get his flock to sing psalms instead of feast, the North Africans argued with him. Why pick on us? How about the Romans, who in the basilica of St. Peter engage in "daily wine-drinking"?

---

88. Ibid., 26.

89. MacMullen, *Second Church*, 76–89, for a reconstruction of these funerary meals/observances.

90. Augustine, *Ep* 29, to Alypius.

Augustine's response was lame: the Romans include "many carnal-minded people," especially pilgrims, who violently cling to their abuses; and further, in Rome, St. Peter's was on the other side of the city, a long way (five kilometers!) from the bishop's seat at St John Lateran, and therefore much too far for him to give it personal attention. This struggle—so illuminating, so messy—went on well into the fifth century.[91] Why do I mention it? Because Leithart contends that "the very *form* of Christian church buildings" communicated something crucial about the church's identity (122; italics mine). Correct, but the "form" that these buildings communicated was more populist, less orthodox, and less controlled from the top than Leithart imagines. The "form" of these buildings tells us that where emperors and other powerful people exert pressure, top-down, to secure the conversion of people, the results will inevitably be messy. Instead of a baptism of Rome we get a process of inculturation involving the "assimilation" into Christianity of pagan practices.[92]

The Baptism of the Aristocracy

"The baptism of the aristocracy." Here we come to Leithart's other Roman baptism (227). Leithart devotes less attention to Constantine's approach to aristocrats than to buildings, but he observes that when Constantine appointed men to high office he preferred Christians. His favor to bishops, which he showed by giving them financial benefits and assigning them judicial responsibilities, was a part of his policy of "creating a Christian governing class." And by the end of Constantine's century, bishops such as Ambrose were the dominant figures in their cities, visible embodiments of the baptism of the aristocracy (226–227).

Once again, Leithart's rhetoric—and "baptism" makes for wonderful rhetoric—is undercut by reality. There is good evidence that Christianity made progress in "the urban middle class"—the *curiales*—from the late third century and throughout the fourth century.[93] And a growing number of curials were found not only in the imperial civil service but also among the church's bishops. But the empire's 2,000 senators were slow to be baptized as Christians. Michele Salzman's research indicates that "aristocrats from Rome and Italy were predominantly pagan well into the

---

91. MacMullen, *Second Church*, 62.
92. MacMullen, *Christianity and Paganism in the Fourth to Eighth Centuries*, ch. 4.
93. Rapp, *Holy Bishops in Late Antiquity*, 183–84.

last decades of the fourth century."[94] No wonder Constantine hesitated to challenge the Roman senators who wanted to keep Christian buildings out of the *pomerium*, the enclosed pagan space at the heart of Rome.[95]

And yet gradually changes were taking place in the aristocracy. Rita Lizzi Testa chronicles the privileges that Constantine granted to bishops—financial subventions, free travel by imperial post, exemptions from public civic duties—and shows that these, by the end of the fourth century, had led some senatorial aristocrats to convert to Christianity.[96] Also effective to this end was the increasingly harsh antipagan legislation of the second half of the century. The example of Christian emperors also was persuasive; many aristocrats looked upon Constantine's successors as "exemplars of how to be aristocratic and Christian at the same time."[97] Sermons by bishops such as Ambrose of Milan and Maximus of Turin persuaded aristocrats that areas they had worried about—including their wealth and their violence—were not issues they would need to address en route to Christian conversion. According to Maximus, conversion did not require an aristocrat to simplify his lifestyle—it was enough if he engaged in almsgiving, which he could, of course, repeat when necessary.[98]

For many aristocrats, violence was as much of an impediment to conversion as wealth.[99] One such as Volusian, who in 411–412 was engaged in conversations with Augustine. This pagan aristocrat, Augustine discovered, was deterred from conversion because the church's teachings about violence were "not adaptable to the customs of the state." In a succession of letters, Augustine corrected Volusian, telling him that Christians were to be governed, not by spineless love, but "by a sort of kindly harshness" for the benefit of others.[100] Sermons and dialogues such as these produced what Salzman calls "respectable, aristocratic Christianity." It was not necessary to be resocialized to become a Christian; indeed, "for the majority of fourth-century aristocrats Christianity did not entail a radical

---

94. Salzman, *Making of a Christian Aristocracy*, 77. See also Rapp, "Bishops in Late Antiquity," 155.

95. Krautheimer, *Rome, Profile of a City*, 31.

96. Lizzi Testa, "Late Antique Bishop," 531. She notes, "That did not always mean an authentic and deep conversion."

97. Salzman, *Making of a Christian Aristocracy*, 199.

98. Lizzi Testa, "Late Antique Bishop," 532; Salzman, *Making of a Christian Aristocracy*, 208.

99. See Kreider, "Mission and Violence."

100. Augustine, *Epp* 135–37.

reorientation from their previous way of life."[101] So, by the century's end, senators began to join curials as candidates for baptism. Some pagans who doubted the wisdom of becoming Christian were pushed over the brink by the severity of Theodosius I's antipagan laws.[102] By the mid-fifth century, the aristocrats who remained pagan were few and beleaguered. What Leithart calls the "baptism of the aristocracy" had taken place, but not until long after Constantine's death and at considerable cost. And the question remains: to what extent did the Christianization of the aristocrats result in an "aristocratization" of Christianity?[103]

Fourth-Century Baptismal Practice

So we have the baptism of an emperor, the "baptism of Rome," and the "baptism of the aristocracy." Now we turn to baptism itself. Constantine spent twenty-five years avoiding this rite and the journey of resocialization that preceded it; and Leithart is equally loathe to deal with it. Why? As we have noted, Leithart is happy to talk about baptism in grand, rhetorical terms—baptism not in relation to the experience of individuals and communities but of grand collectivities. For him, these baptisms represent breakthroughs that establish new trajectories. Of course, they were incomplete: "all baptisms," he asserts, "are infant baptisms" (341).

But how does this relate to what was happening on the ground, in the experience of individuals and communities? In an article in 2003, Leithart shows that he knows far more about the practices of the ancient Greco-Roman Christians than he indicates in *Defending Constantine*. In the article he asserts that pedobaptism was the practice of the apostolic church. But he recognizes that, across the early Christian centuries, all baptisms were not infant baptisms; indeed he concedes that "adult baptism very early became the model for Christian initiation."[104] Although there were areas in which children and infants were baptized, the third- and fourth-century churches primarily baptized adults. Further, Leithart notes that the practice of believer's baptism was reflected in the baptismal liturgies extending into the early Middle Ages. These liturgies at times allowed for the baptism of children who were too young to speak for themselves, but

---

101. Salzman, *Making of a Christian Aristocracy*, 202.
102. Ibid., 79–80.
103. Ibid., 201.
104. Leithart, "Infant Baptism in History," 251.

they were clearly "designed with adults in mind."[105] According to Leithart, this regrettable reality happened when the Christians succumbed to the "alien influences" of Stoicism and the mystery religions.[106]

So what was going on? Earlier, when we looked at the background to Constantine's baptism, we saw that baptism customarily happened as a result of choice—the choice of a candidate to apply for catechesis in a church, and the choice of the teachers to admit the candidate to the catechumenate. Throughout the catechumenate these choices were reaffirmed—daily as the candidate decided to follow "the example of living [that] is given to us in Christ"[107] as taught by the community, and at nodal points when the community's leaders decided whether the candidate should be baptized. The purpose of the catechetical process was profound: "to re-form pagan people, to resocialize them, to deconstruct their old world, and reconstruct a new one, so they would emerge as Christian people who would be at home in communities of freedom."[108] The process culminated in the ritual watershed of baptism, in which the new Christian emerges as a reborn human, a person "of choice and of knowledge."[109]

Choice and knowledge—these emphases continued for centuries after Constantine. They were present even at exceptional third-century baptisms that were not adult baptisms: in the baptism of newborn infants (more common in certain Christian communities than others); and also in the baptism of sickly children who were about to die.[110] Even in these cases, parents were choosing, without constraint by law or social convention, to have their children baptized. In the fourth century, thanks to the emperor's legalization and promotion of Christianity, the number of baptismal candidates increased markedly. As a result, fourth-century churchmen made adjustments to the classical pattern. Increasingly they admitted newborn infants to the status of catechumens.[111] In order to motivate the catechumens to choose to enroll as *illuminands* (serious candidates for baptism) they invented a new genre of evangelistic sermons, "exhortations

105. Ibid., 253.

106. Ibid., 250, 255–56.

107. Cyprian, *Ad Quirinum* 3.39, which Simone Deléani claims is at the heart of Cyrian's catechesis: Deléani, *Christum sequi*, 13–15; Kreider, *Change of Conversion*, 32.

108. Kreider, *Worship and Evangelism in Pre-Christendom*, 23.

109. Justin, 1 *Apol* 61, cited by Leithart, "Infant Baptism in History," 258.

110. Johnson, *Rites of Christian Initiation*, 91–92; Ferguson, *Baptism in the Early Church*, 370–79.

111. Ferguson, *Baptism in the Early Church*, 628; the most famous infant catechumen is Augustine of Hippo (*Confessions* 1.11).

to baptism," that enticed and terrified the ditherers.[112] Catechists no longer used the scrutinies to weed out unsuitable candidates; instead they made the scrutinies into exorcisms and ethically "lowered the hurdles," welcoming people who came with mixed motives.[113] Formation now had to do less with the apprenticeship of candidates who were learning how to live as Christians than with doctrinal instruction.[114] To impress the candidates with the seriousness of baptism, churchmen heightened the emotional temperature of the initiatory rites by drawing on the mystery religions. They hoped that this inculturation would make the baptismal ceremonies "awe-inspiring," terrifying the candidates into life-transforming conversion.[115] The baptism of children (many of them ill, just before their deaths) and of infants continued to occur, as they had in the first three centuries, but believer's baptism remained the norm.[116]

In the early fifth century the baptismal norms began to change in the West. Augustine of Hippo, embroiled in controversy with Pelagius, highlighted the radical nature of original sin that in his view made infant baptism imperative for infant salvation. This led to what David Wright has called a "baptismal revolution"[117] in the West. As Augustine's views spread, loving parents felt the pressing need to baptize their infants *quam primum*, as soon as possible. A parallel movement towards infant baptism was taking place in the East, though without the sense of fevered immediacy.

Whatever the theology, the change occurred gradually; the baptism of adults, in the West as well as in the East, continued to be common into the sixth century. In a law of AD 529 establishing Christian religious uniformity, Justinian I ordered all pagans within the empire to be baptized, including specifically "children of young age."[118] In a society in which the law required everyone to be baptized, infant baptism made sense. In Christendom, though not before, every baptism was an infant baptism.

---

112. Ferguson, "Exhortations to Baptism in the Cappadocians," 59–60.

113. Cyril of Jerusalem, *Cat* 1.5; Bradshaw, "Effects of the Coming of Christendom on Early Christian Worship," 276.

114. Johnson, *Rites of Christian Initiation*, 98.

115. Bradshaw, "Effects of the Coming of Christendom on Early Christian Worship," 277; Yarnold, "Baptism and the Pagan Mysteries in the Fourth Century," 247–67.

116. Ferguson, *Baptism in the Early Church*, 626–33, 379.

117. Wright, "Augustine and the Transformation of Baptism," 306–8; Wright, *What Has Infant Baptism Done to Baptism?*, 9.

118. *Codex Iustianianus* 1.11.10. The baptism of infants *quam primum* (as soon as possible) did not become normal practice, in the West and in the East, until the sixth century. Cramer, *Baptism and Change in the Early Middle Ages, c.200–c.1150*, 138.

In recent years scholars of many traditions have charted these developments. According to Anglican liturgical historian Paul Bradshaw, in the fourth and fifth centuries there was a shift "From Adult to Infant Baptism"; Roman Catholic scholar Alfons Fürst called this "a fundamental change in initiation . . . from adult baptism to infant baptism. . . ."[119] David Wright, a professor of patristic and reformed theology at the University of Edinburgh, called these changes "a massive baptismal reductionism."[120] When infant baptism was universalized many things were lost: the trust in God's patient love, so parents did not need to be frantic to have their newborn children baptized; the initiatory journey culminating in the rich baptismal liturgies in the paschal feast of Easter or in Pentecost; and above all, the connection of baptism with catechesis.

Leithart says grandly that "Rome had been baptized; now it needed to begin the slow work of Christian *paideia*" (204).[121] This is a sad sentence. Leithart shows no awareness that *paideia* was not Christian, but was a nonconfessional "neutral space" for the raising of young men from elite families.[122] He can cite no evidence that the post-Constantine church used the traditions of *paideia* for the training, pre- or post-baptismal, of Christians.[123] He does not recognize that as infant baptism was universalized, the *paideia* of the elite withered; so also, more important, did the catechesis that had formed all candidates to become Christians.[124] Baptism, which in early Christianity had been the ritually rich culmination of a process of resocialization, became in Christendom the ritually trivial sign of socialization—of compulsory belonging to a wider society whose deep cultural motifs, rooted in a millennium of development before Christianity's arrival, had immense, unmonitored power.[125]

So we return to the question of gestalts. A gestalt is the product of many constituent parts. We have looked at military service, and have argued that it was one of these constituent parts of the shift from the gestalt

---

119. Bradshaw, *Early Christian Worship*, 169.

120. Wright, "Augustine and the Transformation of Baptism," 310.

121. *Paideia* "implied a full and rounded educational process, the training of youth up to maturity physically, mentally and above all, morally." Young, "Paideia," 229.

122. Brown, *Power and Persuasion in Late Antiquity*, 125.

123. Historians discussing the *paideia* of early Christians deal almost entirely with fourth-century Christians who were baptized as adults. Young, "Paideia," 229–40; Cameron, "Education and Literary Culture," 665–73.

124. Brown, *Power and Persuasion*, 125, 131–32; Johnson, *Rites of Christian Initiation*, 119; Kreider, *Change of Conversion*, 71–79.

125. Russell, *Germanization of Early Medieval Christianity*.

of early Christianity to the gestalt of Christendom. Baptism was a second constituent part,[126] which established the connective tissue that held the gestalts together. But there were many other constituent parts in this gestalt shift, which together brought about "a fundamental reorientation in the relationship of church and world."[127] Each one of these constituent parts is worth careful study.[128] Of these, we shall look briefly at one—mission.

THE IMPERIALISATION OF MISSION

The shift of gestalts, and the role of Constantine in effecting these, becomes especially clear in the all-important area of mission. Leithart attacks Yoder for suggesting that the orthodox, Nicene Christians were less effective in mission than their heterodox rivals; and in general Leithart's arguments on this issue seem historically sound (e.g., 290). But as Leithart recognizes, the real issue is not about mission on the imperial frontiers but about mission within the imperial heartlands—"the conversion of the empire" (292). Leithart informs us that at the time of Constantine's accession to the throne 10 percent of the imperial populace was Christian. This percentage may inflate the number of Christians,[129] but it certainly indicates that since Pentecost the church had undergone spotty but remarkable numerical growth. What difference would Constantine make to the mission of Christians within the empire to their non-Christian neighbors?

As in other areas, in mission there was a gestalt-change. Prior to Constantine, Christianity was not a publicly acceptable *religio*; it was an extralegal *superstitio* that had to remain low-key and meet in private because it challenged commonly held convictions. The church grew, not because imperial campaigns promoted it, but despite the fact that imperial authorities opposed it. The church grew, not because Christianity was a way to prosperity or respectability, but because the Gospel made a practical difference to people's lives so that people espoused the message freely.

---

126. Yoder briefly discussed baptism's importance in the "shift" in his *Christian Attitudes to War, Peace, and Revolution*, 60.

127. Ibid., 57.

128. For a summary of "characteristics" that shape a distinctive Christendom gestalt, see Kreider, *Change of Conversion*, 91–98. Yoder gives eight "Social Axioms of Establishment" whose gestalt is different from the gestalt of the early centuries. "Primitivism in the Radical Reformation," 82–83.

129. MacMullen, in his *Second Church*, 98–104, suggests a downward revision of numbers commonly accepted; cf. Stark, *Rise of Christianity*, 4–13.

Constantine Revisited

As liberated and transformed people, the Christians were attractive.[130] Pagans were both irritated and intrigued when they heard Christians say that "they alone knew the right way to live."[131] A North African Christian asserted, "We do not preach great things; we live them."[132] As Lactantius put it, "religion cannot be imposed by force . . . we teach, we prove, we show."[133] The attraction of the Christians, who embodied an alternative way of living and were known to possess spiritual power, was sufficient to persuade large numbers of people to undergo the rigors of the Christian journey of catechesis leading to baptism. And the catechesis was rigorous because the Church's bottom-up missional approach depended on it to form attractively distinctive Christians.

With Constantine the Church's missional approach began to change—from bottom-up to top-down, from attraction to advantage.[134] As emperor, Constantine, even though unbaptized, identified himself with the church, and others came to identify the church with him. The number of Christians continued to grow, but for a new reason: because Christianity was the religion that the emperor promoted. Ambitious people saw that identifying with Christianity was a prudent career choice.[135] The jewel- and mosaic-encrusted basilicas that Constantine constructed conjured an ambience of energy and imperial favor.[136] The privileges, tax exemptions, and gifts that Constantine showered on clergy were designed to make Christianity attractive to ambitious people. An edict of 320 granting tax exemption to clergy stated the strategy: "that the church's assemblies may be crowded with a vast concourse of peoples."[137] According to Eusebius, the specifying of Sunday as a work-free day of prayer had the same function: "by encouraging this he [Constantine] might gently bring all men to piety."[138] Leithart recognizes this strategy and claims that it worked: "Under Constantine's power of concord, the church was flooded with new

---

130. Kreider, "'They alone know the right way to live,'" 169–86.

131. Origen, *Contra Celsum* 3.55.

132. Minucius Felix, *Octavius* 38.5.

133. Lactantius, *Div Inst* 5.20.

134. By the reign of Theodosius I at the end of the century the Church's missional approach had moved from advantage to compulsion, whose seeds had already been evident in Constantine's reign.

135. Salzman, *Making of a Christian Aristocracy*, 199.

136. Janes, *God and Gold in Late Antiquity*, 113.

137. *CT* 16.2.10.

138. *VC* 4.18.2.

converts, not through coercion but by force of imperial example and patronage" (145).

But Leithart does not state that under Constantine the missional strategy changed, nor does he weigh its costs as well as its benefits. Of course, Christians did not cease to be attractive overnight; but with the top-down approach to mission Christians no longer needed to be attractive. Fourth-century catecheses shifted focus from equipping catechumens to live in a countercultural way rooted in the "rules of faith" to protecting the catechumens against all forms of heterodoxy without preparing them for distinctive Christian living.[139] So when the catechumens were baptized they were no longer people who had been formed to live a distinctively Christian life. Contemporaries soon observed that some converts were hypocrites; already in the late 330s Eusebius noticed "an unspeakable deceit on the part of those who slipped into the Church and adopted the false façade of the Christian name."[140] In North Africa Augustine referred to "those who call themselves Christians"; he observed that pagans simply called them "bad Christians."[141] When the emperors' support of the church was strong, these "interested conversions" were tolerable.[142]

The new missional strategy required the adherence of society's natural leaders. Constantine wooed these leaders, especially the elites who were becoming the church's bishops, and this led to a change in episcopal lifestyle. In the 240s the high-flying Carthaginian rhetorician Cyprian was attracted to the church because he felt imprisoned by his opulent lifestyle; unlike the Christians that he knew, he was "glittering in gold and purple, and has been celebrated for his costly attire." Cyprian viewed this luxury as slavery, which held him in bonds. Through catechesis and baptism, Cyprian was set free to wear "ordinary and simple clothing."[143] In 258, when Cyprian as bishop of Carthage was beheaded, he was wearing a simple cloak and dalmatic—but no purple.[144] Fifty-four years later, when the newly victorious Constantine invited bishops to dinner in his Roman palace he discovered that they were living in the tradition of Cyprian—their

---

139. Ferguson, "Catechesis and Initiation," 229–68.

140. *VC* 4.54.

141. Augustine, *Sermon* 198 (Dolbeau) 9, 10.

142. Ando, "Pagan Apologetics and Christian Intolerance in the Ages of Themistius and Augustine," 201.

143. Cyprian, *Ep* 1, *Ad Donatum* 3–4.

144. *Acts of St Cyprian* 5.3; Musurillo, *Acts of the Christian Martyrs*, 174–75.

"appearance was modest as to style of dress."[145] In 326 a bevy of bishops were summoned to a banquet in Constantine's palace in Nicomedia to celebrate the twentieth anniversary of his accession. According to Eusebius, "Guards and soldiers ringed the entrance to the palace, guarding it with drawn swords, and between these the men of God passed fearlessly, and entered the innermost royal courts. Some of them reclined with [Constantine], others relaxed nearby on couches on either side."[146] Eusebius does not tell us what clothing they were wearing, but we may speculate that it was no longer "modest." Were they, the *Apostolic Tradition* (chap. 16) to the contrary, wearing purple? In the 380s the pagan Ammianus Marcellinus noted that the Roman bishops' lifestyle had escalated, "wearing clothing chosen with care, and serving banquets so lavish that their entertainments outdo the tables of kings."[147] By 430 the bishops' dress had become so opulent that a countermovement began; clerical clothing originated as an attempt to recover the clergy's earlier simplicity.[148] Romanizing the bishops and Christianizing the aristocracy—these processes, which began under Constantine, resocialized the bishops; and their thought as well as their clothing and comportment were those of an aristocracy that benefited from imperial approval. Were the poor still in church? No doubt some were. But it is notable that the clergy's sermons were primarily directed toward the concerns of other members of the elite, and they paid little attention to the faceless poor.[149] Constantine, by shifting the missional focus to wooing the aristocracy, has moved us far from the liberated simplicity and downward mobility of the aristocratic convert Cyprian.

What about the conversion of the masses in the empire, who were still committed to various forms of paganism? Leithart is helpful in dealing with the complexities of Constantine's approach: providing "limited freedom for paganism while simultaneously pressuring pagans" (140). He gives suitable emphasis to Constantine's "Letter to the Eastern Provincials" in which Constantine, following Lactantius, repudiated coercion of non-Christians while espousing the goal of "concord" in whose unity pagans would someday be included (110; *VC* 2.56). Constantine's vision was

145. *VC* 1.42.1.
146. *VC* 3.15.
147. *Res Gestae* 27.3.14–15
148. Cristiani, "Essai sur les origines du costume ecclésiastique," 69–79.
149. Ramsey, "Almsgiving in the Latin Church," 252–54. See also Hill, "Translator's Note," 165: "it's quite clear, again and again, that [Augustine] is in fact addressing himself to the men of the congregation . . . [indeed] to the upper class men in the congregation." Also MacMullen, *Second Church*, 14–15, 148.

magnanimous: "Let no one use what he has received by inner conviction as a means to harm his neighbor . . . It is one thing to take on willingly the contest for immortality, quite another to enforce it with sanctions."[150] It is not clear that Lactantius would have seen Constantine's plundering the pagan shrines for precious metals as consistent with this vision, or his prohibiting pagans from engaging in sacrifice. A policy of "tolerant concord" could be predatory, but vastly less so, Leithart points out, than the persecution of pagan emperors like Diocletian (152). And gradually, as the century progressed, many pagans enrolled their names for baptism and became Christian.

But what about the heretics? Leithart notes that "by 324 heresy had officially been declared illegal. . . . Heretics were exiled, and Arius's books were burned, just as the anti-Christian treatise of Porphyry was destroyed by imperial order. Constantine's religious policy created an 'atmosphere' of hostility to heresy as much as to paganism" (130). Leithart seems quite unshocked by these sentences. Using imperial power to enforce orthodox doctrine (of the moment) by exiling Christians who disagreed with it—should truth that was not to be imposed on pagans be imposed within the church, and by the emperor? The burning of the books of heretics as well non-Christians—to what conflagrations might Constantine's letter of 333 ordering the burning of "licentious treatises" lead?[151] Indeed, it seems clear that the "atmosphere" of hostility to heresy (130, 303) that Constantine fostered was far more emotionally charged than the "atmosphere" of hostility to paganism. Why? Possibly because Constantine knew that he would have to coexist with pagans, who in circles that counted—the aristocracy, the civil service, the army—were numerous and influential. So Constantine could not promote his overriding goal of *homonoia* (concord) by exiling pagan aristocrats. As he forbearingly stated his attitude to paganism, "It is one thing to take on willingly the contest for immortality, quite another to enforce it with sanctions."[152] But to Constantine the heretics were despicable; and any Lactantian rationale that emphasized the fruits of people's beliefs ("we teach, we prove, we show")[153] was incomprehensible to him. According to Stuart Hall, it is likely that since Constantine's accession the nonorthodox Christians were gaining in strength. So there was an urgency

---

150. *VC* 2.60.

151. Socrates, *HE* 1.9. Sarefield, "Bookburning in the Christian Roman Empire," 333.

152. *VC* 2.60.

153. *Div Inst* 5.20.

Constantine Revisited

in Constantine's letter after 330 to assorted heretical groups. The letter was an "imperial assault on voluntary Christianity."[154] Constantine berates the Novatians, Valentinians, Cataphrygians, and the rest: You gather, he writes, "not only in public but also in houses of individuals or any private places" to pursue "superstitious folly." "Everything about you is contrary to the truth." Despite "a pretext of godliness" you "wound innocent and pure consciences with deadly blows . . . Why should I go into detail? . . . Why should we endure such evils any longer?" Constantine saw himself in a prophylactic role—protecting healthy people from being "infected as with an epidemic disease," an image that heresy hunters would use throughout the Christendom centuries.[155]

So instead of inviting the heretics to engage in a "contest for immortality" with Catholics, Constantine waded in with sanctions. He did not exile the run-of-the-mill heretics; exiling was for big fish such as Arius and Athanasius. But he punished their "accursed and destructive divisiveness" by forbidding them to meet and by ordering their domestic meeting places confiscated for the use of the Catholic Church. The Christianity that Constantine promoted would be orthodox in belief and unitary in structure, and would meet not in houses but in duly sanctioned church buildings where there could be proper controls. Constantine's Christianity would be a *religio*, and he would suppress Christian groups that smelled of being a *superstitio*. Leithart comments that "domestic spaces could no longer house the crowds" (122). This may have been true in places, but it was not the point. Domestic spaces continued to provide attractive settings that housed voluntary Christian groups, and Constantine was determined to suppress this by confiscating the structures. Houses had been the matrix of early Christianity's growth. Christians had met in houses—in "inconspicuous community centers,"[156] in which the life of a nonrhetorical, interactive, mutually-supportive Christianity could be fostered. But Constantine, no doubt in agreement with many bishops, was repelled by a nonhomogeneous Christianity in which uncontrolled groups could grow because of their intrinsic attractiveness. Far better to have supervised Christians than free Christians! Far better to have pagans than sectarians! To be sure, as Leithart comments (130), it is not clear that Constantine's

---

154. *VC* 3.64–65. For comment, see. Hall, "The Sects Under Constantine," 5. Leithart dates Constantine's letter against the heretics at around 324.—Leithard, *Defending Constantine*, 129. I think that Hall (10) makes a credible case for dating it "after 330."

155. *VC* 3.64–65.

156. Krautheimer, *Rome, Profile of a City*, 33.

letter of the early 330s was enforced. And conventicles remained around for a long time, which I take to be a tribute to the viability of their medium, which was no doubt a part of their message.[157] They are the remnants of the missional methods of a previous gestalt—powerless Christians who attracted people precisely because they embodied Christian convictions that powerful, increasingly coercive Christians did not. Of course, as Leithart indicates, only at the end of Constantine's century, with Theodosius I, did the Diocletian-like Christians come into their own (145), beginning by attacking the heretics and then turning to the pagans.[158] But the die had been cast earlier. As Daniel Sarefield comments, "On many issues of religion, Constantine set precedents for later Christian emperors."[159] And at the century's end one could learn about the heretics, not by their books, which Christians had burned, but from a new genre of literature—short, distilled, antiheretical handbooks, written by the heretics' enemies—which

---

157. *CT* 16.2.23 (376); 16.5.6 (379); 16.5.48 (410); Sozomen, *Historia Ecclesiastica* 2.32.

158. Against the heretics, 380 (*CT* 16.1.2); against the pagans, 392 (*CT* 16.5.42). An edict of 382 provided for "inquisitors" who were to make sure that there were no "secret and hidden assemblies" of heretics (*CT* 16.5.9).

159. Sarefield, "Bookburning," 333. The precedents that Constantine established apply also to another hugely important issue—Christian approaches to Judaism. I can comment on this only briefly. Leithart is aware of Constantine's "violently prejudicial language" against the Jews, but does not quote it. He contends that Constantine's legislation "changed the lives of Jews very little," and concentrates his attention on Augustine of Hippo who "re-Judaized" Christianity by emphasizing the importance both of the Old Testament and the Jewish people in God's salvific purposes (131–36). Leithart is right to point to Augustine, but Augustine should not distract us from listening to Constantine. In his post-Nicaea letter on the celebration of Easter, Constantine calls the Jews "bloodstained men . . . [who] are as one might expect mentally blind"; they are a "detestable mob," a "nation of parricides and Lord-killers," whose traditions prevent people (including Quartodeciman Christians) from joining in what was most important to Constantine—a tidy, homogeneous, unified public religious culture in which "everyone everywhere" agrees and worships together—*VC* 3.18–19. In a letter of 329, Constantine calls the Jews a "feral" and "nefarious sect." (*CT* 16.8.1), though at least he did not call for them, like the heretical "sects," to be "eliminated like poison."—*VC* 3.61; (Eusebius's words)! Augustine's theological contributions state counterthemes, but they did not prevent Constantine's virulent anti-Jewish language and policies from having a portentous future. According to Guy Stroumsa, in the years after Constantine, "things began to change . . . [T]he Jews saw a series of grave infringements upon their rights and social status, limiting in drastic ways their integration into society. Judaism was now tolerated, at best, only because the Jews cherished the Old Testament. . . ."—Stroumsa, "Religious Dynamics Between Christians and Jews in Late Antiquity (312–640)," 151.

enabled one to categorize the heretics and to dismiss their errors without considering their arguments.[160]

Conclusion

Why devote so much attention to Leithart's *Defending Constantine*? Because of its intrinsic merits, but especially because it will be an important voice in today's debate about the use of history as a resource for Christian life and mission. The background to this debate is a widespread awareness in many societies that Christendom has waned and that Christianity is in crisis. Can the Christian past point a way forward? For centuries, while representatives of the Christendom churches have justified the established structures, thinkers in the nonconformist Christian traditions have called the Christian churches to rediscover the radical convictions of the early Christians. In the twentieth century something new happened: in response to the sense that Europe was a "mission field," Roman Catholic thinkers began a movement that had parallels with the primitivist impulses of the nonconformist Protestants. The French poet Charles Péguy gave it a name—*ressourcement*—and it became a movement that found in the patristic sources "a more profound tradition," one that would influence the second Vatican Council and alter the shape of Catholic worship and life.[161] In recent years Evangelical scholars have also discovered *ressourcement*, leading to the "deep church" movement in England and the Ancient/Future movement in North America.[162] Evangelicals and Catholics committed to *ressourcement* have varying emphases; but in general they believe that "the tradition of the early church"—encompassing both the pre-Constantinian and post-Constantinian periods—constitutes "an incomparable source for the contemporary renewal of the church."[163]

---

160. McClure, "Handbooks Against Heresy in the West, from the Late Fourth to the Late Sixth Centuries," 186–89; Shaw, "Bad Boys," 180, 196.

161. O'Malley, *What Happened at Vatican II*, 40.

162. In the United Kingdom, see Walker and Bretherton, *Remembering Our Future: Explorations in Deep Church*; in the U.S., see the many writings of the late Webber and, in particular, Baucum, *Evangelical Hospitality*.

163. Husbands, "Introduction," 11, 12. I am not convinced that it is useful to speak of "the tradition of the early church" of the first five centuries. To speak of a univocal early church tradition downplays regional as well as chronological variation; discounts the possibility of major changes in Christianity when it aligned itself with imperial power; and privileges the later "fathers" such as Augustine as summations of early Christianity. It rarely entertains the possibility that the later writers—at least in some

Yoder and Leithart represent perspectives on *ressourcement* that agree only in part with the Vatican II/Evangelical model. Yoder sees the pre-Constantinian church, far more than the post-Constantinian church, as a helpful source for contemporary Christian renewal. It was not that he idealized the church before Constantine; he devoted many pages to describe ways in which it was "beginning to drift."[164] Nevertheless, he saw the pre-Constantinian church as having a distinctive gestalt. It was voluntary, it was countercultural, and its approach to mission was bottom-up. The sacerdotal priesthood, infant baptism, and participation in the state's violence of later Christianity had their roots in the earlier centuries, but they were not characteristic of its gestalt. These changes were already compromising the early Christian vision; but it was Constantine who began a "fundamental reorientation in the relationship of church and world" that within several centuries of his reign had led to *Christianitas*—Christendom.[165] This reorientation, Yoder was convinced, represented a "fall" or "betrayal."[166] Christians today can of course learn from the texts and documents of the later early church—nascent Christendom. But the task of Christians in a post-Christendom world is especially to retrieve the Christianity of the marginal earlier Church under the Lordship of Jesus Christ. Yoder is far from alone in articulating this vision.[167] This is the *ressourcement* of uncompelled and uncompelling radical Christianity.

Leithart, by contrast, departs from the Vatican II/Evangelical model by showing little interest in the pre-Constantinian church. In *Defending Constantine* he dismisses any sense of loss or fall through Constantine's emergence on the Christian scene. If the church of the early centuries had an approach to baptism that was rooted in "choice and knowledge," it was captive to error, a product of "alien influences" from which Augustine rescued the Church.[168] If Christians in the early centuries, especially intellectuals, thought that Christians should be committed to nonviolent discipleship, this was a deviation that Augustine and Ambrose corrected

---

instances—may have deviated unhelpfully from earlier positions.

164. Yoder, *Christian Attitudes*, 48–56, quote at 49. I spend a lot of my scholarly energy documenting early Christianity's often less-than-ideal reality.

165. Yoder, *Christian Attitudes*, 57; Yoder, "Primitivism in the Radical Reformation," in *The Primitive Church in the Modern World*, 81, 83.

166. Ibid., 91–92.

167. For a statement of the priority of retrieving the emphases of the second and third centuries, see the Cuban-American church historian González, *The Changing Shape of Church History*, 37.

168. Leithart, "Infant Baptism in History," 250, 259.

Constantine Revisited

(276–277). But when Constantine "converted" and Christianity became top-down, Leithart gets animated. "Something had changed . . . Something new was being born. Rome had been baptized" (238). With the emergence of Constantine, a "revolution" occurs (248). With Constantine we get not a fall but a quickening, and the history of the church really begins. Of course what happened under Constantine was only a beginning—it was, after all, an "infant baptism"—but Christianity was now free to grow up as a distinctively Christian civilization. Leithart does not carefully analyze the development of this Christendom gestalt. Indeed, his language of "the baptism of the empire" renders superfluous careful thought. But it is not hard to discern what Leithart values: a Christianized social order in which the evangel is infused into the very structures of civil order; armies that have the cross on their shields; a "creedally-based empire," with a government that backs up the church's position with sanctions; a city in which the eucharistic blood of Jesus provides "a brake on bloodshed."[169] This is heroic rhetoric that begs for reality-testing.

The Christendom era was of course a mixture of good and bad. Like Menno Simons and John Howard Yoder I am grateful to live in a world shaped by the Nicene Creed and the biblical canon.[170] And I am profoundly shaped by theological, spiritual, and artistic fruits of the Spirit's work in Christendom. But today the Christendom system throughout the world is in various states of disintegration. Leithart is convinced that nihilistic politics, apparently brought in by the Enlightenment, led to a crumbling of the Christian city and an exclusion of Christian convictions from its public life (340). Western civilization has "apostatized" (341).[171] The only escape from this massive crisis is a *ressourcement*—going back to the political theology and Christianized polis of Christendom. To go back will require re-evangelization (evidently of the West), a revival of a purified Constantinianism, and the willing submission of modern civilization to be baptized. Leithart backs up this altar call with a warning: if this doesn't happen, "we are facing nothing short of apocalypse" (340–342). This is the *ressourcement* of the Christendom movement of the American Right, both Reformed and Catholic.

---

169. Leithart, *Defending Constantine* 232, 271, 292, 303, 340.

170. Cf. Weaver, "Missionary Christology," 411–40, and Finger, "Christus Victor and the Creeds: Some Historical Considerations," 31–51.

171. Leithart's critique of Yoder is not that Yoder finds an "apostasy" or "fall" in history; it is that Yoder finds the fall in the wrong place—in the fourth century instead of in some unspecified century in modern times. It would be helpful to understanding Leithart's argument if he were to describe the fall more precisely and at greater length.

Leithart's prescription makes me suspicious and uncomfortable. As a historian I am not convinced. Yoder was not working with the same degree of detail as is Leithart, but Leithart's repeated claim that "Yoder lost the historical argument" is unwarranted (333). Further, I am repelled by Leithart's Christendom gestalt, so confident, so untroubled by compulsion, so peremptorily benevolent—and so different from the gestalt of the early Christians. I fear that if a new Constantine gets to power, he (I imagine it will be a he) will silence pagans and heretics of every sort, to the loss of all Christians who seek to be orthodox, whose thought has repeatedly benefited from dialogue with people who disagree with them.[172] I thank God that Christendom is not retrievable. But, having learned from Yoder that vigorous conversation leads to truth, I find it salutary to listen carefully to Leithart, a brilliant controversialist, an uninhibited advocate of Christendom, and a writer with whose work I have found it stimulating to interact. As conversations with him continue, I believe it will be to our mutual benefit.

---

172. Wilken, *Christians as the Romans Saw Them*, 204. This point keeps recurring. Thus, R. P. C. Hanson writes, "Christianity needed its [pagan] critics and profited from them,"—"The Achievement of Orthodoxy in the Fourth Century A.D," 153; Edwards, *Catholicity and Heresy in the Early Church*, chap. 1. As we engage in dialogue, Yoder would remind us to keep in mind the categories of heresy and apostasy, for in our conversations faithful belief and faithful practice both matter.— *Radical Ecumenicity*, 193–221.

3

Against Christianity and For Constantine

One Heresy or Two?

Mark Thiessen Nation

Introduction: The Heresy of "Christianity"

Although this paper will focus on some specific critiques of Peter Leithart's thoughtful and well-researched book, *Defending Constantine*, I want to begin by naming striking similarities between Leithart's project and the primary target of his polemic, John Howard Yoder.[1] Leithart himself identifies some overlap between his position and Yoder's in *Defending Constantine*. However, these similarities are stated even more clearly and provocatively in Leithart's 2003 book, *Against Christianity*.[2]

The first 120 pages of *Against Christianity* are remarkably Yoderian. There is also a wonderfully provocative freshness of expression in the book that is rhetorically perhaps more akin to Stanley Hauerwas than to Yoder. In a phrase, the book was claiming, as Yoder had already in 1964, that the church is a *polis*.[3] The alternative to this understanding, Leithart says in various provocative ways, is what has become "Christianity." In

---

1. This essay originated as a lecture presented as a part of a panel discussion of the book, sponsored by the Christian Theological Research Fellowship, the American Academy of Religion meeting, November 20, 2011, San Francisco, California.

2. Leithart, *Against Christianity*. Emphases in any quotations from this book are Leithart's.

3. Yoder, *Christian Witness to the State*, 17–18.

fact, Leithart claims that standard-issue North American Christianity has become heretical.[4] How so? "Religion is private: This is the heresy of Christianity in a nutshell."[5]

Christianity, as a religion, argues Leithart, has reduced the Christian faith to a belief system—to merely "religious" beliefs and practices over against publically relevant convictions that animate political, secular and social practices. Thus, "Christianity is biblical religion disemboweled and emasculated by (voluntary) intellectualization and/or privatization."[6] Within this privatized understanding words like "salvation" are at most only tangentially related to the church; they are fundamentally words about one's private experience. But of course even if such theological vocabulary were more deeply connected to the church, the understanding of "church" itself has been domesticated. Church has been reduced to a merely religious entity, assuring us that it has nothing to do with a public social existence. To fill out his claims further, Leithart offers chapters on theology, sacraments and ethics, showing how the dominant language related to each of these terms—in the context of standard modern understandings—colludes in the privatization, the spiritualizing of religion, thereby rendering what goes by the name of "Christianity" innocuous.

So, what is the alternative according to Leithart? It is that the church is a *polis*. And what does this mean? It means, on the one hand, that salvation is inherently social; that is to say, "the Church is that social form of salvation."[7] Since salvation is inherently social this means that those who are members of the body of Christ embody a way of life peculiar to the salvation made available in Christ. Therefore, "to be a Christian means to be refashioned in all of one's desires, aims, attitudes, actions, from the shallowest to the deepest." "If one is a Christian at all, he or she is (however imperfectly) a Christian from head to toe, inside and out."[8] All of this implies, in terms of ethics, that "transformation of life is not an implication of the gospel but inherent in the gospel, because the good news is *about* transformation of life."[9]

---

4. "Standard-issue North American Christianity" is my attempt to add a bit of nuance to what I suppose Leithart might mean by "Christianity."

5. *Against Christianity*, 78.

6. Ibid., 17.

7. Ibid., 32.

8. Ibid., 15–16.

9. Ibid., 97.

Furthermore this entails that the church as a social body is also a public assembly—as should be apparent in the very word *ecclesia*. Thus the church is by definition secular, social and political. It is not some private "religious" club but rather an assembly of those whose lives are formed by the gospel of Jesus Christ. Therefore, to proclaim and live the gospel is to be political.[10]

With all of this understood, we will realize, insists Leithart, that the real "competitors" to the Church are not just other religions but nation-states, international bodies, Americanism, and any other ideology that embodies alternative beliefs and practices in the public realm.[11] Here is Leithart at the end of his first chapter:

> The gospel is the announcement that the wall is broken down and therefore the Gentiles are welcomed into the community of the new Israel on the same basis as the Jews; thus the gospel *is* sociology and international relations. The gospel is the announcement that God has organized a new Israel, a new *polis*, the Body of Christ, and that the King has been installed in heaven, at the right hand of the Father; thus the gospel *is* politics. The gospel is about the formation of one body in Christ, a body in which each member uses his gifts for the benefit of all, in which each member is prepared to sacrifice his own for the sake of others; thus the gospel announces the formation of a Christian *economy* in the Church.
>
> The gospel announces a new creation.
>
> The gospel brings nothing less than a new world.
>
> If we are going to stand for *this* gospel, we must stand against Christianity.[12]

John Howard Yoder could easily have written these words, as well as many of the other paragraphs in the first 120 pages of this book. So, what happens between these first four chapters and the last one, which is entitled "For Constantine"—a chapter which is, as it were, a précis for *Defending Constantine*?

Clues that help to answer this question can be found in the opening paragraphs of Leithart's response to the critics of his book, *Defending Constantine* in the October 2011 issue of *The Mennonite Quarterly Review*.[13] Leithart began by arguing that the central issue dividing his critics

10. Ibid., 35–36.
11. Ibid., 34.
12. Ibid., 40.
13. Leithart, "Defending *Defending Constantine*," 643–44.

NATION—*Against Christianity and For Constantine*

and himself was a disagreement about the gospel. Two paragraphs later he modified that claim by saying that the disagreement was not so much about the gospel itself but its trajectory. Some comments from Yoder will help us to see that it is *both* and that ecclesiology is crucial for understanding the link between the two.

A Second Heresy of "Christianity"?

In his seminal essay, "The Otherness of the Church" Yoder said: "*The most pertinent fact about the new state of things after Constantine and Augustine is not that Christians were no longer persecuted and began to be privileged, nor that emperors built churches and presided over ecumenical deliberations about the Trinity; what matters is that the two visible realities, church and world, were fused.*"[14] If Yoder spoke with the same rhetorical flare as Leithart does, perhaps Yoder would have described this as a second heresy. That is to say, when one conflates, and thereby confuses, church and world, the worldly powers are largely left to define the "public" realm for everyone, including Christians. And thus the public, social dimensions of the "gospel" will likely lose their moorings in the gospel of Jesus Christ (at least in certain important ways). And public vocations, such as those of (now "Christian") emperors, will be shaped not by the gospel of Jesus Christ but rather by the previous worldly definitions of such vocations. As a consequence, religion is, eventually at least, consigned to a chaplaincy function within a society that is (again, in important respects) defined by something other than the gospel. And thus the Christian theological and moral understandings that conflict with the dominant understandings are eventually rendered as private "values."

Is it possible that Leithart has committed this second heresy, which is perhaps a variation of the first? For what is at stake here is the gospel—which as Leithart's formal commitments would have made clear, is inherently social. Thus, what is also at stake is ecclesiology. What seems clear is that Leithart does not really believe that Israel, and later, the Church—in the context of "the [pagan] nations" that surround them—truly is a *polis*.[15] Or to be a bit more specific, perhaps he believes that Israel—once it has become like the other nations—fits the bill, but not the church. Or, at least not the church in its infancy, and thus in the New Testament and in

14. Yoder, "The Otherness of the Church," in *Royal Priesthood*, 57, emphases mine.

15. I was reminded that this claim in Scripture is really clear by reading the relevant chapters recently in Scobie, *Ways of Our God*, 469–612.

Constantine Revisited

its pre-Constantinian state. It appears that the church is not, for Leithart, really a *polis* until and unless it has aligned itself with those who—on worldly non-Christian terms—are already in positions of truly "public" power. Why else would it be plausible for him to see Constantine and the beginnings of Christendom as the logical flowering of what he argued in the first 120 pages of *Against Christianity*?

So perhaps what Leithart really meant in the first 120 pages of his book, *Against Christianity*, is that the New Testament erected expectations that would only be realized with Constantine, who is after all, according to Leithart, "a model for Christian political practice."[16] For, as Leithart sees it, it really took a "Constantine" who could wield power in the "normal way" *and* "is one of us" to realize the vision named in the New Testament—and thus truly to make the church a *polis* that mattered.

When Yoder, on the other hand, said formally similar things regarding the New Testament, what he meant was that a "politics of Jesus" was being articulated as a way of life for the Christian community from Matthew to Revelation, with the expectation that this politics would be, albeit imperfectly, embodied by the followers of Jesus from the outset. Moreover, Yoder began a project of naming the specific theological and moral contours of this politics. He was specific enough, following the lead of the various strands of New Testament literature, that one could thus see the trajectory of what would be faithful to "the politics of Jesus."[17] Therefore, with the specifics in mind, one could discern what trajectories—in theology, ethics and ecclesiology—are, in an ongoing way, faithful to the gospel of Jesus Christ. And fortunately for us, Yoder's project has been amplified and the details spelled out by many who have been influenced by him or simply saw the same things he saw.

The central challenge I would lay before Leithart is to go through the New Testament at least as thoroughly as Yoder and help us to see the specific theological and ethical contours of the gospel politics named there so that we can discern with him how this trajectory leads to the claim that Constantine is "a model for Christian political practice." So far as I know Leithart has not yet done anything like this.[18]

---

16. Leithart, *Defending Constantine*, 11.

17. See Yoder, *Politics of Jesus*. Of course one could also reference various other writings by Yoder.

18. As I write this I am aware that Leithart has written over two dozen books, several of them on the New Testament. It does not appear that any of them do what I am asking for. But I have only read three of his books.

To understand what Leithart *has* done in *Defending Constantine* we need to first briefly describe the nature of Yoder's central essay on Constantinianism, namely "The Constantinian Sources of Western Social Ethics."[19] This polemical essay was a creative attempt to introduce a paradigm shift within the field of Christian social ethics.[20] That the essay and its influence are largely responsible for Leithart writing this book shows that it has been quite successful. Yoder was trained in historical theology. Although he had read more than the average amateur in the field of early church studies as they related to this set of issues, he was, nonetheless, an amateur. Almost thirty years ago when I asked Yoder what church historian might confirm his claims, he pointed me to Alan Kreider. Since then Kreider has written numerous essays and a small book that confirm the basic contours of Yoder's argument, while nuancing and even challenging some details of the claims.[21] All of this is to say that I do not turn to Yoder for detailed historical confirmation of his arguments. I would look instead to professional historians specializing in the relevant historical periods.[22]

But what can be said briefly about the historical claims made in *Defending Constantine*? Here, I will limit my comments to Leithart's chapter "Pacifist Church?," his overall portrait of Constantine, and his appreciation of Augustine.

---

19. The central essay in question is Yoder, "Constantinian Sources of Western Social Ethics," 135–47, 209–12. Now one should also consult Yoder, *Christian Attitudes to War, Peace, and Revolution*, 42–74 and Yoder, "War as a Moral Problem in the Early Church," 90–110. And of course there are many other scattered references.

20. In his response to Kreider's critique of his book in the October 2011 issue of *Mennonite Quarterly Review*, Leithart, in addition to rallying alternative evidence, mentions that certain omissions or framing of arguments served a polemical purpose. If such rationales can be justifiably used in relation to a 370-page book, how much more in relation to a brief essay?

21. See, e.g., Kreider, "'Converted' but Not Baptized: Peter Leithart's Constantine Project" (included in the present book). Also see Kreider, *Change of Conversion and the Origin of Christendom*, as well as a number of essays on the early church and violence.

22. I say "periods," plural, because Yoder's claim is about a trajectory across time, with many variations. Certainly the realities in the medieval period vary significantly from the period of the Renaissance and Reformation, which vary from the modern period since the sixteenth century. And there are variations from place to place, etc.

Constantine Revisited

The Pacifist Church

First it must be noted that *some* of Leithart's rhetoric makes the task of Yoder or any who would follow him impossible.[23] Yoder's argument, says Leithart, depends on a "primitive pacific paradise" within the pre-Constantinian church. If this "uniformly pacifist" church does not exist "then the other stages of the argument collapse." On the other hand Leithart only has to establish that there was "diversity or ambiguity."[24] This, however, is a distorting way of framing the issues. The rhetorical ploy, with the biases of most readers already against Yoder, is the verbal equivalent of a magician's attempt at misdirection. Hoping the readers will not pay careful attention to the facts, the rhetorical move attempts to shift the burden of proof from Leithart to Yoder.

But for those who are truly attentive the ploy will not work. Indeed, the burden of proof remains clearly with Leithart. Attempting to transform the cameo roles of Roman soldiers in the gospels into starring and defining roles simply will not do.[25] We know next to nothing about these characters who are given bit parts. They are likely present in order to show that a Jewish rabbi is interacting, strangely, in a very positive way with enemy soldiers. And they provide an opportunity to display, even with Gentiles, the healing power of the truly central character, Jesus. Given the purpose of these narratives we do not, in these cases, need to know whether these soldiers renounced the typical idolatry of the Roman army or any other non-Christian practices.[26] The narratives are fundamentally about Jesus, not Roman soldiers. Contrary to Leithart's implicit claims, Jesus' interactions with these soldiers model precisely what he taught about loving our neighbors as ourselves and loving even our enemies. In fact, as Yoder and many others since him have shown, this teaching about being peacemakers and loving enemies is a consistent trajectory across the New

---

23. I specifically said "some of the rhetoric." Some of his rhetoric is a bit more nuanced. For instance, one place Leithart says that "Yoder is correct only if he can prove a high degree of early Christian consensus in favor of pacifism" (259). However, the sort of rhetoric I've quoted in the text certainly biases the discussion—establishing an unreachable threshold for Yoder (and those who in the main agree with him).

24. Quotes from Leithart, *Defending Constantine*, 258–59.

25. *Defending Constantine*, 260. For more detailed discussion of the Roman soldiers in the gospels than I will offer, see Alexis-Baker, "What about the Centurion's Great Faith?," 170–83.

26. For a discussion of Roman army religion and some of the ways in which it would conflict with Christian teachings and practices, see Helgeland, "Roman Army Religion," 1470–1505.

Testament.[27] And negatively, as Richard Hays has noted, "Nowhere in the New Testament is there an instance of any writer appealing to a principle such as love or justice to justify actions of violence."[28] In terms of biblical scholarship, the burden of proof seems clearly on Leithart's side.[29]

Establishing the trajectory of biblical teaching and implied practice is important. Then we know what to look for in the post-biblical teaching, with an expectation of faithful practices. For as the rule of faith developed in the early church, it was the apostolic witness that mattered. As it happens, the post-biblical teaching regarding peacemaking and love of enemies from those who came to be respected as the early Church Fathers has a remarkable consistency with what is taught in the New Testament. And like the New Testament, the emphases are different in different contexts. Sometimes the teachings are general, sometimes they are very specific, prohibiting various types of killing because of love of enemies.[30]

Leithart again attempts to shift the burden of proof by playing up the claim to ambiguity, highlighting those, such as Tertullian, who implicitly acknowledge that some unnamed individuals taught and practiced things that were contrary to the teaching of the Church. Thus, as with the New Testament, Leithart is attempting to grant marginal unnamed figures defining teaching and practitioner roles. Along with this, Leithart claims that

---

27. John Nugent has also very helpfully shown the roots for "the politics of Jesus" in the Old Testament. See Nugent, *Politics of Yahweh*.

28. Richard Hays, "Violence in Defense of Justice," 317–46, here 339. Also see Hays' debate with Nigel Biggar around this chapter.—Biggar, "Specify and Distinguish," 164–84; Hays, "Narrate and Embody," 185–98; Biggar, "New Testament and Violence," 73–80; and Hays, "Thorny Task of Reconciliation," 81–86.

29. To name just a little of the literature that would make this clear, besides *Politics of Jesus*, see Hays, "Victory Over Violence," 142–58, 313; Lohfink, *Jesus and Community*; Gorman, "While We Were Enemies," 129–60; and Swartley, *Covenant of Peace*.

30. A little over twenty years ago I wrote a paper for which I read everything published by John Helgeland, one of the few historians of the early church who argues that the early church fathers did not, by and large, teach pacifism. I looked up all of his references to the writings of the early church fathers. I then categorized them according to general teachings regarding loving enemies, relatively positive statements about governing authorities, negative statements about governing authorities, generally critical statements against war, general statements against killing, specific statements against Christians going to war and killing as soldiers, and finally reflections on Christians in the military. It was clear to me that Helgeland's work was not very careful. Some of his general claims were simply irresponsible. I came away from this research convinced that, despite his claims to the contrary, Helgeland's work is at least as biased as the detailed earlier work of C. J. Cadoux or Jean-Michel Hornus, not to mention the very careful, recent work of Alan Kreider.

even when the teachings are clear from Church Fathers we cannot know what was actually practiced. But this is clearly special pleading. It goes without saying that our knowledge of specific behaviors in the ancient world is spotty. However, it is hard, for example, to read Everett Ferguson's survey of "Love of Enemies and Nonretaliation in the Second Century" without realizing both that the early Church Fathers of the second century were consistent with the trajectory traced by Yoder throughout the New Testament *and* that these Fathers implied either that they themselves and others were, or certainly *should* be, living this way.[31] Between the New Testament and the time of Constantine there is indeed some ambiguity. But the ambiguity in all of its textured richness looks much more like the New Testament trajectory traced by Yoder than a trajectory that would realize its full flowering in Constantine.[32]

This relative consistency, however, should not lead us to be surprised that unnamed Christians long before Constantine either were serving as soldiers or justifying killing. This sort of thing was true as well in New Testament times when, in Corinth, for example, Paul corrected teachings and practices he considered to be wrong. However, it distorts the apparent realities to invoke the word "ambiguity" so as to suggest that the centuries before Constantine and after are more or less the same. Alan Kreider helpfully names how the ambiguities are *not* the same and how, in fact, a significant shift occurred between Tertullian and Augustine:

> The arguments that Augustine used were in part a recent addition to Christian ethics (the just war ideas), but in part they were old, having been aired in North Africa over two centuries earlier. So there was continuity. But who was it that used the arguments? In 210 it was Christian laity, probably soldiers, who appealed to Joshua, the centurions, and Luke 3:14, while the leading theologian in the province, Tertullian, articulated the position of the church to correct them. In 419 it was the leading theologian in the province, Augustine, who appealed to the same biblical passages to justify military service in a church that was rapidly becoming society-encompassing. . . . So Augustine was in continuity, not with the deep Christian moral tradition, but with the argument of the laity in the legions. This represents

---

31. Ferguson, "Love of Enemies and Nonretaliation in the Second Century," 81–93.

32. I refer to Constantine as the "full flowering" because of Leithart's own claims. But of course it is at least a century before further dimensions of Christendom are realized.

a shift—a shift from the gestalt of early Christianity to another gestalt—Christendom.³³

Constantine

Similar concerns arise around Leithart's interpretation of the central character in his book, Constantine. It appears that he has at times unfairly given the benefit of the doubt to sources biased toward Constantine, clearly wanting to provide an account of him that was as positive as possible. Having said that, much of what Leithart said about Constantine and his rule as Emperor is impressive. Leithart, for instance, helps readers appreciate some of what Constantine accomplished that benefitted many of his subjects. I was also impressed by his willingness at points to name honestly the moral failings of Constantine in his conduct as Emperor. So, for instance, after saying that under Constantine "there were some ameliorations of punishment," he also admits that "many of [Constantine's] decrees suggest a horror show." This "horror show" would include having criminals' hands cut off, tongues ripped out and other miscellaneous "exquisite tortures."³⁴ Leithart's final composite portrait of Constantine is a remarkable summary.³⁵

Admitting that I am not qualified to enter into debate about his detailed and nuanced account of Constantine, nevertheless I am unwilling to concede that it is only biased interpreters like pacifists who cannot see what Leithart sees. For instance, it is interesting to read some summary remarks from Michael Grant, a British historian who has written more than fifty books on ancient Greece and Rome, in the concluding chapter of his 1993 biography of Constantine:

> [Constantine] was a Christian of a very peculiar type, a type that would hardly be recognized as Christian at all today. For the God he believed in was a God of power, who had given him victory, and he would have had little sympathy with the idea that Christianity meant love, or charity, or humility, of which his 'middle-brow' view of religion did not have the slightest comprehension. Furthermore, he was utterly confident that he himself was the man of God, God's servant and representative who was constantly in touch with him and was told by him what

33. Kreider, "'Converted' but Not Baptized," 575–617, here 590.
34. *Defending Constantine*, 199.
35. Ibid., 301–5.

> to do—and how, by doing accordingly, he could avoid divine anger. This made Constantine a difficult man for other mere human beings to deal with, being on a direct line with God, he must always be right. . . .
>
> So, Constantine had a lot to answer for. An effort has been made, in this book, to assess his character, and it contained evil as well as good. Evil, it can be argued, is indispensible in a successful chief, and Constantine, despite his defects, enjoyed a great deal of success, both as a military commander and as a leader in civil life.
>
> But he was also murderous, and the many whom he murdered, or executed, included not only his rival Licinius (to whom he had promised survival) but also his own eldest son and his own second wife Fausta. There is no excusing those deaths, at any time or in any society. Certainly, it can be explained, as was suggested above, that powerful people are hardly ever nice, and that autocrats can do as they like, and if they want to commit murder, at the bidding of circumstances that seem to them to demand such action, then that is what they do. But this is no excuse. . . .
>
> It is a mocking travesty of justice to call such a murderer Constantine the Great. Or perhaps not: for what does Greatness mean? Constantine was, as we have seen, a superlative military commander, and a first-rate organizer. He was also an utterly ruthless man, whose ruthlessness extended to the execution of his nearest kin, and who believed that he had God behind him in everything he did. That surely, it must be repeated, is the stuff of which the most successful leaders are made.[36]

Grant is certainly aware of the ambiguities of a life like Constantine's. In fact, these are the summary comments of a specialist who has written numerous biographies of other leaders in the ancient Greco-Roman world. In light of this, Grant is saying that Constantine—considering all of the particulars of his biography—is more or less like the typical effective ruler of his time, except, perhaps, for the confidence that "God" was on his side. Yet it is not at all clear how this equals that Constantine is "a model for Christian political practice," especially if one has claimed that "to be a Christian means to be refashioned in all of one's desires, aims, attitudes,

---

36. Grant, *Constantine the Great*, 221–22, 226–27. Mark W. Chavalas, a professor of ancient history at The University of Wisconsin-La Crosse, in his review of *Defending Constantine*, points to Grant's biography as a careful work critically engaging primary sources (over against Leithart's less than careful work). Chavalas, "Review of *Defending Constantine*," 117–18.

actions, from the shallowest to the deepest"? But of course Leithart has never told us the particulars of what this "refashioning" means. Conveniently, the claim that he was a model is much easier to sustain if one has basically eliminated peacemaking and love of enemies—as well as humility, kindness, patience and other fruits of the Spirit that make substantive peacemaking possible—from the trajectory that runs throughout the New Testament and continues throughout the pre-Constantinian church.

Augustine

Leithart's interpretation of Augustine also bears closer scrutiny. Even though I believe modern Christians have much to learn from Augustine, I am also convinced that he is partially responsible for both heresies that have been named in this paper. Thus, it is puzzling that Leithart is not more critical of at least the one stream of Augustine's influence.

Fifty years ago Krister Stendahl wrote an intriguing and paradigm shifting essay, "The Apostle Paul and the Introspective Conscience of the West."[37] In the essay, Stendahl, a Lutheran professor of New Testament, claimed that Luther and, before him, Augustine, were largely responsible for the privatization of our faith—which is exactly what Leithart has called "the heresy of Christianity." Much more recently Phillip Carey has provided the evidence to substantiate Stendahl's claim regarding Augustine. According to Carey, Augustine, in his book, *Confessions*, is, among other things, attempting to solve a problem. Augustine, by the time he wrote *Confessions* is a committed Platonist as well as a Christian. As both, he feels compelled to solve the problem of how we see—or "know"—God, who is inherently nonphysical. He uses the first six chapters of the book to set up the problem. It is chapter seven in which he resolves the problem. This then sets the agenda not only for the rest of the book but, according to Carey, "for the rest of Augustine's life."[38] What is this solution that is so revolutionary and determinative for Augustine? It is that to "see" God is to turn from everything external, all flesh and blood. To see God is to

---

37. Stendahl, "Apostle Paul and the Introspective Conscience of the West," 78–96. The original version of this essay was presented as an essay in 1961. I say paradigm shifting because this is one of the earlier essays that eventually gives rise to what emerges in the late 1970s as "the new perspective on Paul," which is still very influential today.

38. Carey, "Book Seven," 107–26, 240–44, here 107. For his fuller argument, see Cary, *Augustine's Invention of the Inner Self*.

turn inward, to our innermost being; that is where God is to be assuringly found. As Carey puts it:

> Augustine does not associate the vision of God with the human face of Christ (like Paul), or with the light of the deified flesh of Christ on the mount of transfiguration (like Eastern Orthodoxy). His aim is ultimately to direct our attention inward to a vision of incorporeal Truth. Christ himself, he argues, intends this, for he ran his earthly race in a hurry, calling us to return to him and then departing from our bodily sight, "that we might return to our heart and there find Him" (4.12.19). Christ in the heart is not Christ in the flesh, but the eternal Wisdom who is our inner Teacher, revealing Truth that must be seen with the eye of the mind, not the eye of the body. The power of Augustine's distinctive brand of Christian Platonism is that it is the only form of orthodox theology after Nicaea that offers a powerful alternative to finding the glory of God in the flesh of Jesus Christ. For Augustine the humanity of Christ is indispensible, but it is only the road, not the destination. The destination is defined in Platonist terms, and it is the destination that is the point of the road, not the other way round.[39]

This destination, of course, is to find God within.

Given the huge influence of Augustine within Western Christianity, his focus on the turn inward to see God has shaped much of our understanding about knowing God, spirituality, etc. This influence was deepened and transposed into a new key when the Augustinian monk, Martin Luther, also turned inward to find a gracious God—igniting the firestorm that became the Reformation. Under Luther's influence, many Christians have been convinced that truly knowing God, i.e. salvation, is solely about an inward transformation.[40]

Augustine's Platonism also helps legitimate his turning from the teaching of pacifism to his own distinct way of appropriating the justifiable war tradition from Plato and Cicero. As Frederick Russell has shown, Augustine introduced the distinction between "the inward disposition of the heart and outward acts." "Central to his attitude was the conviction that war was both a consequence of sin and remedy for it. The *real*

---

39. Carey, "Book Seven," 122–23.

40. Though I do believe Luther, and Augustine before him, are somewhat responsible for the privatization of the Christian faith, I would also look for narrations regarding various forces in modernity that have led us too often to embrace the privatization of our faith. See, e.g., Cavanaugh, "Invention of Religion," 57–122.

NATION—*Against Christianity and For Constantine*

evils in war were not war itself but the love of violence and cruelty, greed and the . . . lust for rule that so often accompanied it."[41] It should be said that Augustine is not cavalier in his approach to war. On the one hand he says "'peace should be the object of your desire.'" More specifically, "'it is a higher glory still to stay war itself with a word, than to slay men with the sword, and to procure or maintain peace by peace, not by war.'"[42] These comments, of course, are merely hints of a full theory regarding the use of violence derived from Augustine. One can argue that Augustine's views, when taken seriously, offer substantial guidance for careful discernment regarding the employment of violence.[43] One can even go so far as to say that, taken with utmost seriousness, Augustine's most careful reflections entail what amounts to a practical pacifism.[44] These serious appropriations of Augustine are better than the alternatives. However, in light of the history of Western Christendom and violence, I would like to suggest an alternative stream of the appropriation of Augustine on violence. Augustine, in saying that war (or killing) is not in itself wrong but rather what is wrong is the inward attitude of, say, the love of cruelty, has effectively reversed teachings of the New Testament. It's as if Jesus had said: "You have heard that it was said to those of ancient times, 'You shall not murder'; and 'whoever murders shall be liable to judgment.' But I say to you that *only* if you love murdering will you be liable to judgment."[45] Jesus is the one in the New Testament who quite specifically offers teachings, such as the one I just alluded to, that highlight internal attitudes. But he does so in order to deepen, to strengthen the teachings regarding evil acts—saying that inward attitudes *also* matter. I can think of no instance in which he makes the move Augustine the Platonist makes of *substituting* inward attitudes for actions, suggesting thereby that killing or committing adultery in themselves don't really matter, it is whether one *loves* cruelty or *inordinately loves* someone other than one's spouse.[46]

I would suggest that Augustine's Platonism assists with what Leithart has named as *the* heresy of Christianity, namely the privatization of the

---

41. Russell, *Just War in the Middle Ages*, 17. Emphasis mine.
42. Augustine, quoted by Mattox, *Saint Augustine and the Theory of Just War*, 60.
43. Mattox would be within this stream of interpretation.
44. See Schlabach, *For the Joy Set Before Us*, esp. 119–42.
45. This is, of course, a serious misquoting of Matt 5:21–22.
46. Augustine has helped us *importantly* to see that inward dispositions such as these do matter. However, with Jesus, we should see them as added dimensions of our lives and potential actions rather than, with Augustine, as substitutes.

Christian faith. He also helps solidify the second heresy I have named (borrowing from Yoder), namely the conflating of church and world. Or to put it differently, with a bit more nuance, Augustine will keep alive instincts for the wonders and challenges of the gospel of Jesus Christ—through, for instance, his very helpful, rich reflections on rightly ordered loves. However, under Augustine's influence, outward, public behaviors for Christians will increasingly be shaped by non-Christian forces (since it is inward attitudes that truly matter anyway).

Conclusion

As I have shown in the first several pages of this essay, I believe in some of his writings, such as *Against Christianity*, Peter Leithart has helped us see that a biblically rooted understanding of our faith is inherently social. In doing this Leithart has also provided us with some clues for our narration of the beginnings of the "Christianity" that he has told us that we should be against. However, in *Defending Constantine* Leithart has reminded me of the truth of the adage that the enemies of our enemies are not necessarily our friends. Or, to put it more positively, perhaps we will continue to be tactical allies, learning from one another as we see some of the same enemies. And perhaps in these mutual struggles we will, together, move toward greater clarity regarding what we are for. But for now, so it seems to me, if we are to read Augustine or Constantine discerningly—if we are to know what we should be defending as the genuine article—then we also need to know the substance, the particulars, of "the politics of Jesus" we are for. For that task I continue to believe we are well served to follow the leads offered to us by John Howard Yoder and many of those who have learned from him.

4   What Constantine Has to Teach Us

William T. Cavanaugh

I TEACH AN INTRODUCTORY undergraduate course entitled "Catholicism in World History: Jesus to 1500." Since we are on the quarter system, and only have ten weeks for those 1500 years, we cannot linger too long on any topic. We do pause at Constantine, however, both because the theological stakes are so high and because the story is such a rollicking good one. As Peter Leithart, John Howard Yoder, and everyone in between agree, something momentous did indeed happen when the Roman emperor embraced Christianity. After reading excerpts from the *Apostolic Tradition* of Hippolytus, *The Martyrdom of Perpetua and Felicitas*, Eusebius' church history, and Athanasius' *Life of Antony*, I pose a simple question: was the conversion of Constantine a net gain or loss for the church? The class tends to divide about evenly, and the conversation is wont to be the most animated of the quarter. I try to play devil's advocate. To those in favor I ask "Don't you think it's odd that the sign of the man who died rather than fight is now being used by the Roman army to conquer others?" To those opposed I pick a student and say "Okay, you're the pope in Constantine's time. Pope Britney, are you going to tell Constantine he can't become a Christian unless he finds a new job? Will you insist we get a new emperor who will continue the persecution?" I feel I have succeeded if everyone leaves the classroom less sure of his or her own position.

I am not trying to feign objectivity or neutrality; I am a theologian with a definite stake in the debate, and I generally don't mind if the students in a class end up thinking like me. However, teaching beginning students to think about the theological importance of church history is

83

not, in the first place, getting them to endorse a particular theological position, but rather asking them to put themselves in the place of the figures from church history that we read. Sound theological judgments can only take place of we can get beyond the assumption that we are in a position to judge those who lived in circumstances that barely resemble our own. Entering into a tradition means first of all submitting to it.

I come to the debate over Constantine as a Catholic who has been attracted to the thought of John Howard Yoder, largely through Stanley Hauerwas, my dissertation director. As a Catholic, I have always been reluctant to accept at face value any Anabaptist-influenced reading of history that posits small groups of *cathari* who have maintained the true faith amid the overwhelming apostasy of the church as a whole. For this reason I find Peter Leithart's challenge to the "fall" narrative of the church important and necessary. At the same time, however, I am deeply grateful to Yoder for the way in which he tirelessly insisted that the cross of Jesus Christ is the key to the theological interpretation of history.

In engaging with Leithart's book and his polemic against Yoder, then, I want first to address their ways of reading history. Here I acknowledge that Leithart's book provides some important correctives to Yoder, though I want to steer both away from moral readings of history that too quickly separate sheep from goats. Second, I will address the theology underlying Leithart's reading of history and argue that only a theology of the cross can do justice to what it means to proclaim that Jesus is Lord. I will argue that Leithart is right to read church history pedagogically, as a movement toward greater maturity in Christ. Unfortunately, however, he is wrong to think that maturity means a greater ability to wield the sword.

The Long Pedagogy

Peter Leithart has written a book that needed to be written. We need to have a debate over the status of Constantine and Constantinianism in order to get past lazy assumptions and slogans on both sides of a polarizing topic in political theology. Beyond praising Leithart for his timely provocation, he should also be commended because he has done much well. Leithart successfully debunks the Enlightenment prejudice that saw the Romans as tolerant rulers who were only forced into repression by the intolerance of Christian monotheism (26–27).[1] He clearly evokes the

---

1. Leithart, *Defending Constantine*, 26–27. Henceforth all references to Leithart's book will be made with page numbers in parentheses in the text of the article.

savagery of the persecution and thus the deep sense of relief and gratitude that Christians surely must have felt to Constantine for ending it (28-29). Leithart presents sufficient evidence to show that Constantine's policies favored Christianity but did not impose it on all subjects of the empire. In a brilliant polemic against Locke, Leithart argues that Constantine tolerated paganism in a way that was at least more honest than modern conceits of toleration which feign neutrality but in fact marginalize Christianity and other faiths while leaving public space to the domination of state and market (141–145). In so doing, Leithart refuses the religion/politics and private/public distinctions that leave Christianity toothless in the face of injustice. Leithart makes a convincing case that Constantine did not rule the church autocratically, though in matters of ecclesiastical controversy he was rather easily talked into supporting the opinion of whomever he spoke to last (164–175). Leithart rightly takes Yoder and others to task for painting history with an overly broad brush. In the medieval period, for example, it is wildly inaccurate to say, as Yoder does, that "church government was in the hands of the civil government" (178).[2] In fact the relationship of ecclesiastical to civil government was hotly contested and went through many different permutations in what is lumped together as "Christendom," including a long period following the investiture controversy in the eleventh century in which popes like Innocent III freely intervened in the affairs of civil government. Leithart easily dispatches Yoder's assimilation of Augustine to Constantine (85-86, 284–85). Most importantly, Leithart rejects the idea of a "fall" of the church from some pristine early purity to a state of wholesale unfaithfulness to the Gospel by those who call themselves Christians (315–17).

There are a number of reasons why I think it is important to resist such fall narratives. First, they tend to be associated with anti-Catholic bias. The typical construction is that of Harnack, who posited an original Christianity that was subsequently tainted by Greek culture; the corrupted development of dogma was only corrected by the Reformation's return to a purer form of faith. Anabaptist histories place the fall later than liberal Protestant histories—with Constantine—but the implication is also that the development of Catholicism in the centuries between the fourth and the sixteenth is, on the whole, a tale of corruption and decline. Second, fall narratives make it difficult to construct a coherent pneumatology. While it is true that the Holy Spirit blows where she will, and the church can never rest content with a guarantee of the Spirit's presence, the burden of proof

---

2. The quote is from Yoder, *Christian Attitudes to War, Peace, and Revolution*, 60.

is on any account of the Spirit's historical occultation. Third, fall narratives fail to deal with the simultaneous holiness and sinfulness of the church. Paul's recognition of the very body of Christ in the church at Corinth comes in the midst of his berating the church for its manifest sinfulness: jealousy, quarrelling, sexual immorality, dragging each other before civil courts of law, ignoring the poor, and so on. The holiness and sinfulness in and of the church should not be neatly divided between visibility and invisibility, the pure and the apostate. As I have argued elsewhere, what we see when we look at the church is not the pure Christ but the Christ who "became sin" for our sakes (2 Cor 5:21).[3]

I wonder then if we can take a theological approach to church history that resists the impulse to judge immediately every episode in terms of faithfulness or apostasy. I wonder if we can read the church's reaction to Constantine's conversion not as either the faithful recognition of God's long-awaited triumph over the Romans or the selling out of the church to power, but as the church muddling through a wholly unanticipated set of circumstances and learning some lessons in the process. Perhaps God's history of salvation is more full of surprises than either Leithart or Yoder allows; perhaps neither Davidic monarchy nor diaspora was as firmly established as the definitive social form of God's people as Leithart or Yoder would have us believe. I am not at all suggesting an atheological reading of history as pure contingency—one damn thing after another. I am rather suggesting that Constantine's conversion be read as part of the long pedagogy of God's people that did not end with the advent of Jesus Christ, even though Christ showed us the definitive shape of the story's end.

The pedagogical reading of salvation history has long been the way that the church has dealt with difficult passages in the Old Testament, and is in fact the way that Yoder himself deals with the Old Testament narrative. In *The Politics of Jesus*, for example, Yoder considers the juxtaposition of a Christian opposition to war with the wars in the Old Testament that reportedly issue from the will of God. Those who offer this objection, Yoder thinks, are adopting a legalistic attitude, and the way they put the question makes over-generalizations.

> This approach hides from us the realization that for the believing Israelite the Scriptures would not have been read with this kind of question in mind. Rather than reading with the modern question in mind, whether it confirms certain moral generalizations or not, the Israelite read it as his story, as the account

3. Cavanaugh, *Migrations of the Holy*, 141–69.

of his own past. A story may include a moral implication, or presuppose moral judgments, but it does not necessarily begin at that point.[4]

Yoder's approach here strikes me as a salutary way to begin the reading of church history. It is *our* story, like it or not. Constantine's church is not someone else's church—the church of the impure, the church of those who abandoned what *we* know is the true gospel. Our first reading of church history is furthermore not a moral reading, not the attempt to separate the faithful from the unfaithful, but rather the attempt to discern how God is acting in and through this body of saints and sinners.

According to Yoder, what would have struck the Israelite reading her or his story in the scriptures is not any generalization about the morality of war but rather the way that God acts in history, specifically the way that God saves God's people without their needing to act. "When we seek to test a modern moral statement, we are struck by the parts of the story that do not fit our modern pattern; but the Israelite reading the story was more likely struck by the other cases, where Israel was saved by the mighty deeds of God on her behalf."[5] Yoder then proceeds to narrate a number of the latter types of cases, where the victories of the Israelites in war were not the result of superior weaponry and military preparedness but the miraculous intervention of God, overcoming the weakness of God's people. For Yoder, Jews in Jesus' time would have found it normal, or at least possible, to expect that the revolutionary messianic community that Jesus announced would not rely on military technique and violence but on God's miraculous deliverance. "If, with the cultural empathy that is the elementary requisite for honestly understanding any ancient documents, we measure Jesus' meaning not by what *we* can possibly conceive of as happening but by what his listeners can have understood," wrote Yoder, "then we are forbidden to filter his message through our modern sense of reality, of the uniformity of nature and the inconceivability of the extraordinary."[6]

Leithart points out that Yoder's preference for cases in which direct divine intervention saved the Israelites selectively ignores other cases in which weapons and preparations for war were decisive. The latter cases, says Leithart, are "part of our story, preserved 'for our instruction'" (336). Yoder's deeper point, however, is that there is a way of reading the Old Testament in which moral questions are suspended in favor of a more

4. Yoder, *Politics of Jesus*, 78.
5. Ibid., 78–79.
6. Ibid., 89.

profound theological message. Joshua, in other words, is neither to be read as giving license for Christian use of violence (as Leithart would use him) nor is he simply to be condemned as unfaithful for his treatment of the Canaanites. We are rather to read the Old Testament as the story of God's deliverance of God's people in spite of themselves, a story which will have its culmination in that of Jesus, who in his renunciation of violence, in the Sermon on the Mount, and in his cross and resurrection, showed that the ultimate shape of Christian witness to God's salvation does not involve weapons and bloodshed. Joshua is to be read as a precursor, a representative of an incomplete stage in the long pedagogy of the people of God. My suggestion is that we read Constantine in roughly the same way.

Oliver O'Donovan's distinction between historical authority and moral authority is helpful here. The coming of Christ has historical authority because it confers a unique meaning on all historical events, both before and after the mission of Jesus on earth. This means that even apparently contradictory events can be drawn together into one narrative, and moral judgment superseded. "Historical authority can reconcile, where moral authority can only judge."[7] When reading about the conquest of Canaan and the ban, O'Donovan, like Yoder, wants to "suspend the moral question."

> The moral question has pushed itself forward, either in indignant protest or (worse) in sophistic justification. Like the elder brother of the prodigal son, Christians reading the book of Joshua need to learn how to ask other questions before the moral ones: the history of divine revelation, like the waiting father in the parable, is not concerned only with justifying the good and condemning the bad. This Old Testament history is concerned only to reveal the impact of the divine reality upon the human in election and judgment.[8]

Greater than the scandal of moral contradiction between the Old and New Testaments is the scandal of the very historicity of God's self-revelation, that God reveals Godself in history in such a way that such contradictions can be embraced.

> In God's self-disclosure something had to come *before* the vindication of the moral order: the transcendent fire of election and judgment had to be shown in all its nakedness, in all its possible hostility to the world, if we were to learn what it meant that in

---

7. O'Donovan, *Resurrection and Moral Order*, 157.
8. Ibid., 158.

> Christ the Word of God became flesh and took the cause of the world as his own cause . . . Before we could learn of God as vindicator of the moral order we had to learn something even more basic.[9]

This "had to," O'Donovan makes clear, is not because God is bound by any necessity, but because of human weakness in understanding the full import of what O'Donovan calls "moral order."

This pedagogical approach is much like that which we find in Irenaeus. Against his Gnostic opponents, Irenaeus argues that the differences between the Old and New Testaments are not due to the existence of two separate gods, but to the patience of the one God with human development. Just as a mother gives milk and not "strong meat" to her baby, so God has nourished us through our infancy until we were ready to receive the full revelation of God in Christ. Even at Christ's advent, Irenaeus describes humans as still in their infancy.

> And for this cause our Lord in these last times, when He had summed up all things into Himself, came to us, not as He might have come, but as we were capable of beholding Him. He might easily have come to us in His immortal glory, but in that case we could never have endured the greatness of the glory; and therefore it was that He, who was the perfect bread of the Father, offered Himself to us as milk, [because we were] as infants. He did this when He appeared as a man, that we, being nourished, as it were, from the breast of His flesh, and having, by such a course of milk nourishment, become accustomed to eat and drink the Word of God, may be able also to contain in ourselves the Bread of immortality, which is the Spirit of the Father.[10]

The Old Testament is not the climax of the story, but neither is it discontinuous with the New. According to Irenaeus, even the sins of the Israelites were committed to writing "that we might derive instruction thereby, and not be filled with pride."[11] As this indicates, in reading the Old Testament theologically, moral questions are temporarily suspended but not forgotten. As O'Donovan says, "We are not mistaken to think that Joshua was morally unworthy of Gethsemane, any more than the elder brother was mistaken to think that the prodigal was unworthy of his

---

9. Ibid.
10. Irenaeus, *Against Heresies*, IV.38.
11. Ibid., IV.27.

father's compassion."[12] Christ is a moral challenge to all ages, but Christ's historical authority means that faith in Christ is able to take up the "fragmentary utterances of God's voice" in warlike conquests and ritual purity laws and put them into a coherent story culminating in the Gospel.[13]

Given that Yoder is already committed to reading the Old Testament story in this way, could we not read church history in an analogous way? Granted that church history is not scripture—there is no one canonical text from which to read—as a Catholic I am inclined to see scripture and church history as telling one continuous story of God's people, in many different subplots and with many highlights and lowlights. There is not an absolute divide between scripture and the continuation of the story in church tradition; as the Vatican II document *Dei Verbum* attests, "there exists a close connection and communication between sacred tradition and Sacred Scripture. For both of them, flowing from the same divine wellspring, in a certain way merge into a unity and tend toward the same end."[14] "Tradition" in this sense is of course a narrower term than the history of the church; tradition is the teaching that has been handed down from the apostles and the growth in understanding of that teaching as the church moves through history.[15] But the essential idea is that "God, who spoke of old, uninterruptedly converses with the bride of His beloved Son";[16] the story that God begins telling in the scriptural narrative of the people of God does not end when the canon is closed but continues to be told in the story of the Body of Christ as it moves through history. We ought not to have two completely different hermeneutics for reading the Old Testament and church history, "cultural empathy" in the former case, suspicion and the resulting narratives of corruption and decline in the latter. In both cases sin permeates in abundance and variety; how could it be otherwise when telling a history that is human? In both cases, however, it makes a difference if we do not give priority to the moral reading, but rather see the story as telling how God is acting now to lead humanity to salvation from itself.

Although the story comes to an unsurpassable climax in the events of Jesus' life, death, and resurrection, it might take a while for humanity to come to grips with those events. If the Irenaean reading of history is

12. O'Donovan, *Resurrection and Moral Order*, 158.
13. Ibid., 159.
14. Pope Paul VI, *Dogmatic Constitution on Divine Revelation (Dei Verbum)*, §9.
15. See ibid., §8.
16. Ibid.

correct, there is no reason to expect the early church always to "get it" in ways that the later church would not. Proximity to Jesus is no guarantee of faithfulness, as the crucifixion ought to make plain. Indeed, we might expect just the opposite to be the case; sometimes it takes a lot of maturity through hard experience for the church to get it right. Arriving at the doctrine of the Trinity took several centuries of argument. The ban on slavery and the embrace of religious liberty took far longer. The Christian critique of war that has gathered so much momentum and authority since the second half of the 20th century might not be—as some politically conservative commentators fear—the selling out of the church's "just war" tradition to a wooly liberalism but rather a new stage in the fruition of the Gospel. Whatever the case, the pedagogical model need not be strictly linear and progressive, as every parent and teacher knows. The Christian understanding is subject to reversals and detours, though in the long run it may be that something is learned in the process.

Is it possible, then, to read the "Constantinian shift" as something that "had to" happen, in O'Donovan's sense of "had to," in order for the church to learn something it otherwise would not? In this case, the learning would not simply be the way one learns from a mistake; there is something more positive to be learned as well. Perhaps what was learned is that God does not want the church to be a persecuted minority. The minority status of the early church is *not* normative; it is *not* the way that God wants it to be. God wants the whole world to be evangelized. Leithart presents a fairly convincing and "culturally empathetic" reading of the relief and joy of the church in Constantine's time who saw being fulfilled what they always expected: that God's control of history would be made manifest in God's deliverance of the church from torture and the evangelization of the known world. In that respect the Christians in Constantine's wake were little different from the Israelites who Yoder says were similarly struck by God's providential deliverance of the people of God from their foes in their reading of the Old Testament.

Nevertheless, the church was suddenly confronted by a new set of circumstances that they could not have foreseen and to which pre-existing models did not neatly conform. Neither Davidic monarchy nor synagogue-based diaspora models fit the new reality of a dual authority: the bishops on the one hand, and a Christian emperor on the other who claimed an ambiguous type of oversight (*epi-skopos*) with regard to the church. The church tried to muddle through this new situation as best it could. Throughout the middle ages the relationship of ecclesiastical to civil authority constantly changed. In the end I would argue that the church learned that God does not want the church to evangelize the world through the coercive apparatus of civil authority, for to do so is to try to wrest control of history from God's hands. Here I come down on Yoder's side. But if this reading of the overall sweep of church history is correct, then Leithart is right to reject the idea of a "Constantinian shift"; it is more like a "Constantinian moment," one more episode in the long pedagogy of God's people.

What the Church has Learned

If the pedagogical reading of history is right, the key question then becomes what the church has learned. Leithart concentrates much of his efforts on the question of violence as perhaps the key difference between his own account and Yoder's. The lesson that Leithart takes from the Old Testament is that the people of God are entrusted with greater access to the means of war as they mature. Constantine is then not a departure from Christian nonviolence but the fulfillment of what God has already been doing in history: preparing the followers of Christ for the assumption of the means of violence so that they may defend the church from its enemies, spread the gospel, and protect the vulnerable from injustice.

Leithart's portrayal of Constantine is not without discussion—brief though it is—of Constantine's occasional brutality (161, 228–30). What strikes Leithart most about Constantine, however, is his recognition that he is not a god, but stands in the service of the one true God. Leithart accepts Eusebius' contention that Constantine accepted the sacral trappings that surrounded the person of the emperor but "treated them lightly" (49). Crucial to Leithart's defense of Constantine is his portrayal of the emperor as a sincerely pious Christian believer. Most of the positive evidence of Constantine's character comes from Eusebius' *Church History* and Constantine's own writings. According to Leithart the Constantine we find there "expresses a soldierly faith in the powerful God of Christians, in the cross of Jesus as a victory over evil, and in the church as the unifier of the human race" (95). So great is Constantine's piety that he prays to the Christian God before battle and says of the Donatists "Those same persons who now stir up the people in a such a war as to bring it about that the supreme God is not worshipped with the veneration that is His due, I shall destroy and dash in pieces" (84). After military victory over his rival Licinius, Constantine installed a portrait of himself over the entrance to his palace that portrayed him, Christlike, trampling a serpent with a cross overhead. Leithart comments, "Constantine thought too highly of himself, but in thinking he could join Christ in crushing Satan, he was simply thinking like a Christian" (94).

There is certainly New Testament precedent for Christ's victory over Satan, but the identification of this victory with the Roman emperor's military victories is something quite new. In what way is the "powerful God of Christians" powerful? What theology of the cross underlies Constantine's idea of the cross as "victory"? Granted that Constantine saw himself not as a god but as dependent on the one God, it remains to be answered whether or not this God is really the God of Jesus Christ. These theological issues will need to be addressed theologically; it is unlikely that they will be answered by comparing the empirical church before and after Constantine. Leithart provides some evidence that the church was not as united on these questions before Constantine as any simple fall narrative will allow. But although Leithart provides some evidence of Christians serving in the military before Constantine (261–67), he does not provide evidence of Christian justification for serving in the military before Constantine. Indeed, most of the evidence of Christian participation in the military before Constantine comes from the condemnation of the practice by Tertullian and others. Leithart contends that all he need do to refute any fall narrative is show that there is diversity among Christians pre-Constantine on the question of violence. But Leithart clearly wants to do more than this; he wants to claim that those Christians who accepted the use of violence were more faithful readers of the tradition. What they had learned from both the Old Testament and New Testament—and what the church as a whole would learn after Constantine—is that God had prepared his people to accept the reins of history, using the means of violence when necessary.

Leithart's pedagogical reading takes Galatians 4 as its jumping-off point, where Paul describes the actions of Jesus and the Holy Spirit in history as rescuing both Jews and Gentiles from a "childhood" in which they were enslaved to the "elementary things of this world." Just as Jews were in bondage to dietary, sacrificial, and purity regulations of Torah, so the Gentiles occupied a world that revolved around animal sacrifice and the avoidance of contagion from unclean people and things (324–25). Roman society was held together by sacrifice: the gods were appeased by sacrifice, the entertainments of the Colosseum offered release for the bloodlust of the populace, and homage was paid through sacrifice to the Emperor, who was acknowledged as Lord and Savior. Constantine swept all of this out of Rome and replaced it with a bloodless sacrifice, a Eucharistic community that worships the one true God. Here sacrifice is, as Augustine claims, the compassion and mercy that unite Christians to God and to one another. The church did not fall under Constantine, but was recognized and honored as the true city that offers the true sacrifice (329–31).

Leithart's comments on sacrifice are to my mind one of the most compelling parts of his argument—Christ comes to replace bloody sacrifice with a bloodless sacrifice centered on the Eucharistic memorial of his death and resurrection. It would not be difficult here to link Leithart's comments on sacrifice with the work of René Girard, who likewise sees the sacrificial system of pagan Rome as maintaining social stability by deflecting intramural rivalry and conflict onto scapegoated victims. Jesus Christ, for Girard, is the undoing of violence precisely because he is the identification of God with the victims of sacrifice, and thus the revelation of the injustice of societal violence. According to Girard, the Old Testament anticipates Christ in its identification of God with the victims of violence. Girard contrasts, for example, the Oedipus story with that of Joseph, to argue that the Old Testament begins to undo the scapegoating mechanism of pagan myth by revealing the innocence, not the guilt, of the victim.[17]

It is precisely here that Leithart moves in the opposite direction from Girard, and from Yoder. According to Leithart "the Bible is from beginning to end a story of war" (333). Yahweh himself is a "man of war." "From the beginning, this Creator made men to participate in and prosecute his wars. His goal in history is to train hands to fight" (333). Furthermore, the modalities of that fight are not different from those of the world: "Eye for eye, tooth for tooth: so goes the pattern of biblical justice" (334). Given that humans under the old covenant were still in their childhood, however, God was reluctant to allow them full access to the means of violence. "Swords are sharp, and fire burns, and so long as human beings were in their minority, the Lord restricted access to dangerous implements" (334). Even so, God did give authority to some righteous men and women—Moses, Phinehas, Joshua, David, et al.—to carry out deadly acts of justice. But the fullness of our maturity would await the coming of Jesus Christ, the "warrior-savior" depicted in Revelation. Leithart acknowledges that the weapons of the Spirit that Jesus brings are "righteousness, truth, faith, salvation, the Word of God and the gospel of peace" (335). Nevertheless,

17. On Joseph and Oedipus, see Girard, *I See Satan Fall Like Lightning*, 103–20.

Leithart thinks a pacifist reading of the Bible is necessarily Marcionite (335–336). Here Leithart takes Yoder's point about Israel's reliance on Yahweh to fight for it in the Old Testament as support for his own position that our increasing maturity means increasing participation in the activity of God in ruling history. "When we were children, Yahweh our Father intervened to save us from bullies. Now that we have reached maturity in Jesus, we share more fully in those wars" (336). Leithart does not think this contradicts his earlier statement about the spiritual weapons that Christ gives to us. "Finally, we might make an argument from greater to lesser: if the Lord lets Christians wield the most powerful of spiritual weapons, does he not expect us to be able to handle lesser weapons? If he has handed us a broadsword, does he not assume we know how to use a penknife?" (336).

It strikes me as a severe abuse of analogy when "righteousness, truth, faith, salvation, the Word of God and the gospel of peace" are represented by "broadsword," while stealth bombers, drones, tanks, cruise missiles, white phosphorous, and nuclear warheads appear as "penknife." Leithart is attempting to place on a continuum of greater to lesser what are in fact two entirely different senses of "powerful" that do not belong on the same continuum at all. Yoder's work is marked by his emphasis on the way that the cross *redefines* power. Jesus oddly triumphs over the powers and principalities and makes a spectacle of them by dying rather than resisting with violence. Jesus does have a politics, but it is not politics defined in the same way that politics is usually defined. Leithart agrees with Yoder on the centrality of Jesus to politics: "If there is going to be a Christian politics, it is going to have to be an evangelical Christian politics, one that places Jesus, his cross and his resurrection at the center. It will not do to dismiss the Sermon on the Mount with a wave of the hand ('that's for personal life, not political life')" (332). Unfortunately, Leithart gives nothing like a politics that places Jesus at the center. He even acknowledges that "it seems I have left a blank at the center of the panorama: What of Jesus?" (336). He asks "Does he not go to the cross, like a lamb to slaughter, and just in this way win his great victory?" (337) and other similar questions, but he never really answers them. Leithart spends just two pages (338–39) outlining a "politics of Jesus," but he does not attempt to give anything like a theology of the cross.

In these two pages, Leithart does address the Sermon on the Mount in putting together a Christian ethic for rulers. He suggests that if rulers were instructed not to look at a woman lustfully, there would be fewer wars. He proposes that the Church insist that rulers tell the truth, and not give alms or pray or fast for public show. He recommends that rulers love their enemies, even when military force is used against them. He advises that the Church urge rulers not to lose sleep over budget shortfalls, but rather to store up treasures in heaven. All of these recommendations, if followed, would indeed alter the face of the nation's politics. But Leithart is evasive when dealing with the passages in the Sermon on the Mount that deal with violence. According to Leithart, "turn the other cheek" (Mt 5:38–42) is about honor and shame, not self-defense. He thinks that removing honor, insult, and retaliation from politics would reduce the instance of war, but he does not give any convincing reason why the reader should accept his assertion that this saying of Jesus is irrelevant to the question of self-defense. If it is irrelevant, why does Jesus pair it with "eye for eye and tooth for tooth"? Why does Jesus say "Do not resist an evildoer?" (5:39).

We need to look at the six antitheses (or, more accurately, hypertheses) in the Sermon on the Mount (Mt 5:21–48) to see what Jesus is saying about the maturity of which Paul writes in Galatians. In each of these, Jesus takes an aspect of the Mosaic law ("You have heard it said") and extends it ("But I say to you"). Now that the Messiah has come, we are capable of more than merely refraining from murder; we are now directed to remove anger from our hearts. Now that the Messiah has come, we are capable of more than merely abstaining from sleeping with another's spouse; we are now directed to overcome lust as well. The fifth and sixth (5:38–48) have directly to do with non-retaliation against enemies. Now that the Messiah has come, we are capable of more than merely limiting revenge to an eye for an eye or merely loving our neighbors; we are now instructed to renounce revenge entirely, and to love even our worst enemies and our persecutors. *Pace* Leithart, divine history does not seem to be moving in the direction of greater human access to the means of violence; quite to the contrary. The fulfillment, rather than abolition, of the law includes the movement toward the renunciation of violence. Thus we can reconcile what Jesus says about the law in the Sermon on the Mount—"Do not think that I have come to abolish the law or the prophets; I have come not to abolish but to fulfill" (Mt 5:17)—with what Paul says about the Law in Galatians—"Therefore the law was our disciplinarian until Christ came, so that we might be justified by faith. But now that faith has come, we are no longer subject to a disciplinarian" (Gal 3:24–25). The maturity of which Paul writes is not the mere abolition of sacrificial and dietary laws; it is also the completion of the moral law, such that the Decalogue is not ignored but extended. It is not that prohibitions on adultery and murder no longer apply in the adulthood of our faith. It is rather that now in our maturity we no longer need to be reminded to refrain from murder, just as we do not need to tell our friends not to steal anything when we invite them to our house. We have moved beyond the basics of the Ten Commandments. Now that the Messiah has come, we are capable of so much more, including renouncing revenge, loving our enemies, and putting up no violent resistance to evil.

Some such account seems necessary if the abolition of sacrifice is to accord with the movement of history that the Messiah brings to its decisive phase. In Leithart's account, increased access to the means of violence works at cross-purposes to the abolition of sacrifice; it would be odd for followers of Christ to mark the Messiah's reign by a decrease in the shedding of animal blood and an increase in the shedding of human blood.

Most significantly, Leithart never deals directly with the crucifixion of Jesus. The renunciation of revenge and the love of enemies that mark the fulfillment of the law are nothing less than what Jesus practices in his death on the cross. As Leithart himself acknowledges, "This is surely the most powerful pacifist line of argument" (337) and yet he never even attempts to refute it directly. This lack of a coherent theology of the cross leaves Leithart with an inadequate theology of martyrdom. According to Leithart, the martyrs shared Constantine's conviction that God would bless the friends of the church and frustrate its enemies, through military conquest when necessary. "It was an essential part of the theology of the martyr church, one of the bases for their utter confidence that someday their blood would be avenged" (83). Leithart makes clear his conviction that the martyrs expected this vengeance not only in heaven or on the last day but "on earth and in time" (309). But a theology of martyrdom that is based on vengeance rather than the renunciation of vengeance does not do justice to the fact that the martyrs chose to receive death rather than to deal it out. They did so as an act of *imitatio Christi*—not in the hopes that more blood would eventually be shed, but in the conviction that the triumph of Christ through his death and resurrection meant that the cycle of violence had been broken. Because of Christ's triumph, their deaths were robbed of their sting. Leithart's theology of martyrdom, on the other hand, is in danger of conforming to Nietzsche's caricature of Christianity as a resentful slave religion in which fantasies of revenge compensate for weakness.

Leithart is right to see the culmination of the pedagogy of the people of God in the abolition of blood sacrifice, but I am unconvinced that that abolition can be separated from the renunciation of the shedding of human blood that Christ's cross represents. At the end of his book, Leithart too acknowledges that animal sacrifice and human sacrifice are not easily separated. Despite his earlier contention that Constantine did away with sacrifice and "[t]o this extent, Constantine's polity has remained in place until the present" (328), Leithart sees that the modern state, in refusing to welcome the church as a model city, "reasserts its status as the restored sacrificial state. This means that there must be blood" (340). In medieval Christendom life could be brutish, "But believing that the Eucharistic blood of Jesus founded the true city provided a brake on bloodshed" (340). In modernity, as Leithart rightly sees, the state has been released from being disciplined by the church and has been resacralized. With no god to recognize, the state becomes god. Sacrifice has been reintroduced in the form of the "ultimate sacrifice" by soldiers on behalf of the state, the mortal god. Animal sacrifice is eliminated, "Yet there is blood, more blood than ever, more blood than any ancient tyranny would have thought possible, and *all of it human*" (341, italics in original).

This critique of the modern nation-state is exactly right, as is Leithart's intuition that the Eucharistic blood of Jesus founds a city that is essentially counter to violence. But Leithart's solution is not the Christian renunciation of violence. Instead, Leithart believes that violence is best held in check when Christians wield it. The problem is that "modern nations are post-Christian; they benefit from the new covenant privilege of handling the sword and the fire but refuse to listen to Jesus when he tells them how to avoid cutting or burning themselves" (341). But perhaps modern nation states "refuse to listen" because Jesus never tells them any such thing. Leithart provides no scriptural evidence of Jesus' instructions on how to use the sword and the fire because of course there is none. When one of his followers uses a sword, Jesus tells him to knock it off: "Put your sword back into its place; for all who take the sword will perish by the sword" (Mt 26:52; parallels at Lk 22:51 and Jn 18:11). This is hardly the drill sergeant Jesus that Leithart is looking for.

Leithart is right, I think, to present the medieval period sympathetically. It was not an era of wholesale apostasy, but fostered a series of often-serious attempts to apply the Gospel—the good news of Jesus' sacrifice and the embodiment of that sacrifice in the Eucharist—to the restraint of bloodshed. What we have learned from that experience is what is at issue.

If the trajectory of the story of the people of God is toward the peaceable kingdom of which Christ's cross is not the frustration but the first fruits, then we have learned that the church should not try to enforce the gospel through coercive power. To kill for Jesus is to move away from the new covenant; the same is true *a fortiori* of killing for the state. If on the other hand, as Leithart contends, the new covenant brings with it a privilege of handling the sword and the fire, then we must return to some version of Christendom, what he calls "Christianizing the state" (342). What we have learned is that the golden age has passed, and we must return. The long pedagogy of God's people has hit a dead end. The demise of Christendom has nothing to teach us except that, barring "the revival of a *purified* Constantinianism," "we are facing nothing short of apocalypse" (342). But Leithart says little about what this restored Constantinianism would look like. Should Christians support political candidates who will promise to shape a Christian social order? Should Christians attempt to Christianize the armed forces of the United States and other countries? It is hard to see what sword and fire Christians could wield except that of the nation-state. And if that is the case, the danger of blood sacrifice to the wrong god seems greater than ever.

Conclusion

Leithart's critique of the modern nation-state is devastating, though I fear that many readers will miss the seriousness of his emphasis on the transformation of the current order, and see his book as nothing more than an endorsement of Republican Party confusion of Christianity and patriotism. Leithart's rejection of a fall narrative for the church is a bracing challenge for Christians of a more radical stripe as well, primarily for the seriousness with which it takes our Christian forebears. Leithart will not allow us to cast stones from our postmodern enclaves without taking seriously the efforts of those Christians who were suddenly given the world and had to figure out how to act as though God really were King of it. Where Leithart's account fails to convince is in its conviction that the use of the sword was a central and permanent fixture of the new covenant. What the church continues to learn, I think, is that the King it serves still wears his crown of thorns.

5 Yoderian Constantinianism?

D. Stephen Long

PERHAPS THE MOST UNFORTUNATE sentences of Leithart's *Defending Constantine* are the opening lines: "Constantine has been a whipping boy for a long time, and still is today. In popular culture (Dan Brown's *Da Vinci Code*) among bestselling historians (James Carroll, *Constantine's Sword*) and among theologians (Stanley Hauerwas, John Howard Yoder and their followers), his name is identified with tyranny, anti-Semitism, hypocrisy, apostasy and heresy."[1] Although Leithart's argument becomes much more nuanced as it unfolds, this first sentence gives the impression that opposition to Constantine is primarily found among a secularizing novelist, a popularizing historian and a cadre of theologians following the lead of Hauerwas and Yoder.[2] This is unfortunate not only because Hauerwas and Yoder are associated with Brown and Carroll but also because neither Hauerwas nor Yoder invented anti-Constantinianism. Despite superficial portrayals of Constantine in popular culture, serious Christian scholars of all stripes have recognized the Constantinian shift as at best a tragic event. It undoubtedly brought benefits to the Church and humanity: ending persecution, de-divinizing the emperor and (perhaps) challenging Roman sacrifice. But with those benefits came liabilities that worked their way into the Church paralyzing its witness. Anti-Constantinianism traces the long-term effects of those liabilities. It is primarily a genealogical project discerning how we arrived at the present secular moment, which is not necessarily anti-Christian as much as it is superficially or instrumentally

---

1. Leithart, *Defending Constantine*, 9.
2. Much later in his work Leithart acknowledges the deeper sources of the anti-Constantinian critique, which he traces through St. Francis, Wycliffe, Hus, St. Bernard, Dante, the Waldensians, Troeltsch and Burckhardt. Ibid., 306–8.

Christian. For this reason, anti-Constantinianism is as much about the reception of the Constantinian legacy as it is Constantine himself, a reception Constantine made possible even if he was not its sole cause. There is a reason the forgery of a "donation" for unscrupulous political ends could take his name and not that of others.

If Leithart's purpose is merely to vindicate "Constantine" against "Constantinianism," his book would be one more in a long list of modern historical critical revisionists: Arius was not an Arian, Nestorius was not a Nestorian, Pelagius was not a Pelagian. All such works have their place; and this is in part Leithart's purpose. But his work is much more. It is also a genealogical project that defends not just Constantine but Constantinianism. He acknowledges his work has this polemical theological purpose. Like Yoder, Leithart also has a "fall" narrative, but it is not located in the fourth century; he locates it in modernity. His Constantinian retrieval seeks to persuade that we should be open to Constantinianism as a proper model for a political theology that can guide us after modernity.[3] For that reason historical information, as important as it is, will not adjudicate the differences between Leithart and Brown, Carroll, Hauerwas and Yoder. This is why the first sentence is so unfortunate. Leithart begins with a too easy rhetorical ploy placing Hauerwas and Yoder in the same league as Brown and Carroll. Brown and Carroll are not his true opponents. Hauerwas and particularly Yoder are. They are his opponents because they call the Church to accept its post-Christendom situation as a gift from God and not to engage in culture wars in some utopian desire to repristinate Christendom. Leithart offers a counter political theology. He fears theirs contributes to the "liberal Protestant metanarrative" even if they reject it. This is why he can begin by associating the darlings of that metanarrative, Carroll and Brown, with its avowed detractors Hauerwas and Yoder.

Anti-Constantinian political theology goes much deeper than the "liberal Protestant metanarrative" to which Leithart credits most anti-Constantinianism.[4] As he himself concedes much too late in the work, his real opponents are St. Francis, St. Bernard, Dante, Wycliffe, Hus and the Waldensians. Other names are omitted that should be added. John Wesley is neither a modern nor an Anabaptist. Yet he was a committed anti-Constantinian (and a Tory oddly enough). In his sermon, "The Mystery of Iniquity" Wesley admonished that sin is not obvious. Sometimes it

---

3. Ibid., 308.

4. Ibid.. After chalking up anti-Constantinianism to the "liberal Protestant metanarrative," Leithart does recognize Yoder's version of it does not fit. See ibid., 310.

lurks behind that which seems most noble. It often even appears good for us, a delight to behold and even able to make us wise. Such, he suggested, was the Constantinian shift. Wesley wrote:

> Persecution never did, never could give any lasting wound to genuine Christianity. But the greatest it ever received, the grand blow which was struck at the very root of that humble, gentle, patient love, which is the fulfilling of the Christian law, the whole essence of true religion, was struck in the fourth century by Constantine the Great, when he called himself a Christian, and poured in a flood of riches, honours, and powers upon the Christians, more especially upon the clergy.[5]

For Wesley the Constantinian shift troubled Christianity because it sacrificed its visible witness. True Christianity could no longer be identified.[6]

This opposition, of course, is not confined to Protestant holiness movements. Catholics also question the shift. The Catholic historian Hugo Rahner stated, "Constantine, and his successor's even more, still harboring the pagan idea of caesar-as-priest, attempted to fit the Church into their political program." Rahner finds this a constant threat to the Church's freedom even while acknowledging the good reasons fourth-century Christians had for embracing it. "All this added up to a great danger, but it was understandable that Christians, even bishops, in those first years of freedom and expansion, could see only the good side of imperial domination of the Church." Nonetheless, he concludes, it came at a cost. "The kingdom of God has never been established by bishops reclining in imperial dining rooms."[7]

In 1953 (and then revised and expanded in 1988) Hans Urs von Balthasar, seeking to help Catholics negotiate modernity, wrote and dedicated a book to "secular institutes" that drew on the poet and novelist

---

5. "The Mystery of Iniquity," in *Works of John Wesley*, 2:463, 465.

6. He wrote, "The few Christians that are upon the earth are only to be found where you never look for them."—Ibid.

7. Rahner, *Church and State in Early Christianity*, xvii and 46. Rahner finds Constantine preparing the way that leads to Justinian, who took it upon himself to act as bishop. Constantinianism and Caesaropapism are inextricably linked. Justinian sought to use his authority to overturn conciliar decisions. This is the charge Hugo Rahner brought against Eastern Christianity. The creation of an imperial Church led to the subordination of the Church to the Emperor rather than to the bishop of Rome. And without the "guiding role of the papacy," he suggests, the Church becomes vulnerable to the power of the state. "All the Churches who wish to withdraw from the unity of the Church dogmatically first of all seek refuge with the state but soon are absorbed by the state and fall with it." Ibid., xvi.

Reinhold Schneider. Schneider asked if when the Church "seeks power, she rejects the powerlessness of the Cross, is disobedient and promotes the work of Satan." Von Balthasar acknowledges that Schneider answered yes. "For him," wrote von Balthasar,

> there is no possibility of reconciliation between the worldly sword and the gospel that proclaims nonviolence and, if necessary the giving of testimony through suffering. This is why he sees the disaster that began with 'the arch-plotter Constantine' and continues in Charlemagne, whom he vigorously attacks, the entanglement of the Church in the nets of the secular power. . . .[8]

Von Balthasar's affirmation of secular institutes was his answer to Schneider's question.

Leithart's retrieval of a Constantinian political theology would be much more difficult had he acknowledged how deep and wide the anti-Constantinian analysis is among Catholic and Protestant, as well as Anabaptist, theologians. Critiques of Constantine were never limited to popular secular misreadings. They are found in the heart of traditional Christianity. This feature of the Anabaptists' witness never belonged to them alone. It has pervaded a broad spectrum of Christianity. Why? Because it helps us understand the secular triumph over Christianity. Critiques of Constantine were not some conspiracy from outside Christianity, but planted by faithful adherents from within.[9]

Despite its unfortunate beginning and unconvincing ending (more on that below), Leithart's retrieval points in positive directions. Had it been more nuanced and less polemical, he may have recognized that Yoder, more so than many in the anti-Constantinian camp, remained open to affirming a Constantinian political theology. In fact Yoder set up criteria to determine if such an affirmation had been made. Had Leithart taken up the text where Yoder discusses this, his argument would have been

---

8. I am indebted to Andy Alexis-Baker for pointing this out to me. Although von Balthasar originally published this in 1953 he revised and expanded it in 1988.—Urs von Balthasar, *Tragedy Under Grace*, 212.

9. Critiques of Constantine are, of course, never only about Constantine. Wesley critiqued Constantine to critique the Anglican clergy of his day whom he found willing to compromise the Gospel for political and economic status. Rahner's critique was also a subtle challenge to the "Imperial Church" of Orthodoxy. Schneider, and von Balthasars' interpretation of his work, were criticisms of Christian complicity with Nazism. In theology "Constantine" seldom represents a mere historical figure; instead, he stands for an ongoing trope. Leithart acknowledges this and nonetheless defends Constantine. Leithart, *Defending Constantine*, 317.

Constantine Revisited

more nuanced and thus, perhaps, more convincing. That work is *Christian Witness to the State*, in which Yoder's theopolitical framework assesses "Constantinianism" to see if it is a faithful and obedient expression of a Christian theopolitics. In what follows I will take up Yoder's criteria in order to ask if Leithart has produced such a Constantinian political theology.

Yoder's Theopolitical Framework

John Howard Yoder published *Christian Witness to the State* in 1964. The intended audience was Anabaptists and anyone else who was willing to listen.[10] The treatise had a negative and positive purpose. Yoder's negative purpose was to convince his audience to resist Reinhold Niebuhr's interpretation of Anabaptists as laudable, perhaps even a pure form of Christianity, but nonetheless politically irrelevant. Related to the negative purpose was the positive goal of demonstrating that Anabaptists had a constructive theological politics. Yoder began with a quote from his 1954 essay "Peace without Eschatology" where he set forth the state's function: "The Reign of Christ means for the state the obligation to serve God by encouraging the good and restraining evil, i.e. to serve peace, to preserve the social cohesion in which the leaven of the Gospel can build the church and also render the old aeon more tolerable."[11] Leithart and Yoder would agree, I believe, with this purpose. The state is obligated to "serve God." It does so through two means. First it restrains evil and encourages good, thereby promoting peace and cohesion. Second, it preserves sufficient order so the Gospel can do its work ecclesially. In so doing, it helps us endure the "old aeon" until Christ returns. Where Leithart and Yoder will disagree is the extent to which this function sets restrictions upon the role of the state in the divine economy. Leithart has a much more expansive (perhaps idealistic) view of the state, Yoder a much more limited (even realist) understanding.

Christian Witness to the State explains this theopolitical vision and what it should and should not require for discipleship. Yoder does not begin by reacting against Constantine, but by setting forth God's odd triumph in the cross and explaining what it means politically. Halfway through his explanation, he pauses to remind his readers that this means they cannot be dogmatically closed to Constantinianism. He writes, "Our minds should remain open to the possible rational or biblical arguments

---

10. Although Leithart draws widely on Yoder's work, this key text is not cited.
11. Yoder, *Christian Witness to the State*, 5.

of those who might claim that the attainment of a privileged social position by the church in the fourth century called for changes in morals, ecclesiology, and eschatology; thus far it must be admitted that clear and cogent arguments for this have not been brought."[12] Here Yoder distills his concerns about Constantinianism. Its defining feature is that the Church acquires a "privileged social position." If the "Constantinian shift" meant this, it would seem to be an undeniable historical fact. Clearly, the social position of the Church changed in the fourth century. Where Yoder and Leithart disagree is what this shift signaled. For Yoder it signaled ecclesiological decline; for Leithart it pointed to Christ's triumph over the principalities and powers. Rome gets "baptized."

The language we use to describe the constellation of events leading up to and arising from "Constantine" matter. Yoder, and Yoderians, sometime refer to these events as a "fall," sometimes as a "shift." The more maximalist "fall" interpreters find such a rupture between pre- and post-Constantine that nothing can be trusted after him—the Church's liturgy, creeds, ethics, theology and structures of authority are all so contaminated that they *must* be revised if not jettisoned. As Leithart rightly notes, this is also a common feature of the "liberal Protestant metanarrative." Everything from sexual ethics to orthodoxy was simply a power play by unscrupulous male bishops in the fourth century. The heretics were the true faithful remnant. On occasion, Yoder or Yoderians can be read to suggest as much as well.[13] In fact, we find Yoderians without ecclesiology, without doctrine and some without God.[14] If Leithart's work challenges this post-Yoder development, it does a great service. Of course, *abusus not tollit usum*, which is as true of the name "Yoder," as it is "Constantine."

Yoder primarily described these events as a "shift." It does not have the same sense of a thoroughgoing rupture, but of a change that produces new temptations. Yoder identifies those temptations and this does cast a suspicious posture toward creeds, liturgy, etc. They are not above revision, which is of course as true for Luther as it was Yoder.[15] This does not mean they must be revised, but they can be and can also be supplemented if we determine that they failed to maintain the fullness of the "original

12. Ibid., 56.

13. See Leithart, *Defending Constantine*, 180–81.

14. For example, two political philosophers who affirm Yoder's work and distance it from its distinctly Christian doctrinal standards are Romand Coles and Slavoj Zizek.

15. Gerald Schlabach has written an excellent critique of this "Protestant" posture. He shows how Yoder did embody it at times—not because he was anti-Constantinian or Anabaptist, but because he was Protestant. See Schlabach, *Unlearning Protestantism*.

revolution." Such possible revisions require a constant return to the sources. This is much less revisionist than the maximalist interpretations of the "fall" narrative.[16]

Leithart tends toward reading Yoder's position as the maximalist fall narrative. He does not distinguish between "fall" and "shift," and denies either term adequately describes fourth century Christianity. He prefers the term "moment" to describe the temptation the Church faced. He writes,

> If "Constantinian" is taken to mean a "merger" of church and empire in which Christians identify some nation or empire or ruler with the movement of God in history, there was a brief, ambiguous "Constantinian moment" in the early fourth century, and there have been many tragic "Constantinian moments" since. There was no permanent, epochal "Constantinian shift."[17]

So we find three terms: "fall," "shift" and "moment." Each acknowledges a failure, but in decreasing historical significance. In this sense, Leithart does not so much reject as restate and then diminish the importance of Yoder's anti-Constantinianism. His "moment" concedes that "Constantinianism" is a temptation to failure. The extent of that failure vastly differs from Yoder.

Yoder sees failure because he thinks this "shift" necessitated "changes in morals, ecclesiology and eschatology." Although these changes are not spelled out in *Christian Witness to the State*, he explains them elsewhere. Ethical convictions, for example, shift from taking Jesus as their reference point to something else, especially nature. A correlate of this is that his cross no longer defines God's power. Instead, God's power is defined as force, which can and should be used for the sake of the kingdom. For this reason, the dominant pacifist convictions of the early theologians shift to a more liberal permission of Christian participation in violence. Ecclesiology takes on the trappings of Roman power. Authority is limited to the few who ascend to positions of power. Eschatology gets flattened. No longer do Christians expect God to intervene on their behalf as with the "Yahweh

---

16. See Kreider's essay in this volume, "Converted but Not Baptized," for an interesting defense of this version of anti-Constantinianism. As Kreider notes, it is Leithart who must make exceptions to traditional liturgical practice because he can speak of "conversion" without baptism. Moreover, Kreider makes a compelling case that the kinds of revisions Yoder calls for fit more with what we find in the tradition of Catholic *ressourcement*.

17. Leithart, *Defending Constantine*, 287.

wars" of the Old Testament.[18] Instead, humans become increasingly responsible for ensuring that history comes out as they think it should, and the means for doing so are no longer consistent with how God triumphed in the cross, resurrection and ascension.

For the most part Leithart recognizes well Yoder's concerns.[19] He even agrees with his first point: Jesus must be the norm for Christian ethics and that this principle gets lost in nature-grace schemas. Leithart acknowledges this occurred but does not tell us how. Yoder finds it one of the consequences of the Constantinian leaven growing within the Church. Leithart denies Yoder's second and third point. Neither ecclesiology nor eschatology changed as a result of Constantine's conversion. God's mission was always to fit and literally train us to fight with him in wars against his enemies. This does not result from the fall, but was present in God's original creation. God fought for us when we were immature, but now

---

18. For the best discussion and defense of Yoder's reading of the "Yahweh wars" in the Old Testament, see John Nugent's *Politics of Yahweh*.

19. Leithart rightly notes the following nine points about the shifts in ethics, ecclesiology and eschatology Yoder finds in the Constantinian "shift":

1. Ecclesiology shifted so that one's manner of life was no longer expected to be a visible marker of what it means to be church. The church becomes invisible and thus we get a "double church" and with that comes a "double ethic" (311).

2. Ethics becomes marked by "natural standards," which simply affirm what already is internal to the institution (312).

3. The public political ethics gets separated from a private, putatively personal one (312).

4. Eschatology becomes too realized (312).

5. God's providence becomes identified with the success of the powerful (313).

6. Ethics becomes associated with the "universalizability principle" (313).

7. Ethics becomes associated with "seizing history," which is Satan's temptation to Jesus in the desert (313).

8. Efficiency replaces obedience (313).

9. Constantine produces a new epistemology and metaphysics. The latter becomes dualistic through Augustine. The former gets flattened out via the universalizability principle into a version of foundationalism (314).

Leithart agrees with much of this, especially how it shows family resemblances between nature-grace schemes and church-state ones. Leithart writes, "I abhor nature-grace schemes, I repudiate any effort to get to some deeper foundation for Christian life and practice than Jesus and his Word (though I differ with Yoder about what that Word teaches us. . . ." Leithart, *Defending Constantine*, 316.

we take on more responsibility for the task. "When we were children, Yahweh our Father intervened to save us from bullies. Now that we have reached maturity in Jesus, we share more fully in those wars. . . . We are being raised as kings to fight alongside our elder Brother in service to our Father."[20] For Leithart this is why Constantine does not represent a rupture and why we need a retrieval of Constantinian political theology. Because the pre-Constantinian church had an ambiguity and diversity in its ethics on violence, the Constantinian privileging of the church did not entail a change in eschatology or ecclesiological mission. It was its flowering. Although Leithart affirms Yoder's insistence that Jesus is the norm for Christian ethics, he disagrees as to what that means. Any discernment between Leithart's call for a Constantinian retrieval and Yoder's for lamentation must consider the relation between Jesus and ethics, ecclesiology and eschatology. Yoder provided nine "criteria of political judgment" to help us with that discernment.

YODER'S CRITERIA FOR A SUCCESSFUL DEFENSE OF CONSTANTINIANISM

Yoder stands open to a retrieval of a Constantinian political theology if it could be persuasively based on reason *and* Scripture—the "and" here matters. A rational argument for Yoder is not founded upon a doctrine of pure nature available to anyone. It explicates what Christians should expect of the state even if those in power do not know or honor the Christian faith. Reason and revelation, nature and grace are not divided into two separate compartments. They overlap. In *Christian Witness to the State*, Yoder offers his "criteria of political judgment;" each arises from his fundamental axiom as to the role of the state within God's economy noted above.[21]

1. The state exists for the sake of the church and not vice versa (*CWS*, 33).
2. Romans 13, 1 Tim 2 and 1 Peter 2 acknowledge that all persons, Christians and others, have a stake in social order and peace. Because order and peace are primarily internal to a social order, Scripture does not justify one government exercising it against another. "The use of force must be limited to the police function" (*CWS*, 36).

---

20. Ibid., 336. Could a clearer statement of the "liberal Protestant metanarrative" be uttered? Both Rauschenbusch and Niebuhr would rally around such a claim.

21. References to *Christian Witness to the State* are placed in parentheses (CWS).

3. The police function of the state must be kept limited. It can be so only when it is not used for "bringing into existence an ideal order." In other words, it never falls upon the state to bring in the Kingdom of God (*CWS*, 37).

4. Christians who critique the state must not do so through an unrealizable utopia or by advocating anarchy. When the order is under threat, Christians must offer practical counsel. "The Christian social critique will always speak in terms of available, or at least conceivable alternatives" (*CWS*, 38).

5. The state's limited role in the divine economy is to make the old aeon tolerable. For this reason it cannot be made a central actor in the divine economy. The "real meaning of history is on a level different from that of the function of the state." This prohibits a sacrificial economy where putative "personal values" are abandoned for the "establishment of a better order" (*CWS*, 40).

6. Christians are called most often to take the "unpopular side" within the state, that of the widow, orphan and stranger (*CWS*, 40–41).

7. Because the state cannot accept the Spirit, the Church should not accept any state-sponsored governmental violence. In other words, even if a police function is appropriate to the state, this does not mean that Christians could participate in it when it requires the use of violence—even if that violence brings about better results on a utilitarian calculus (*CWS*, 42).

8. Christians should not get caught up in questions as to which form of government is legitimate. "It is the powers that *be* to which we ought to be subjected under God for the sake of conscience." But "orderly succession" and "consent of the governed" are not thus "useless" (*CWS*, 43).

9. We do not have the foresight to calculate consequences and determine which course of action will bring about the expected results. For Yoder "results are not calculable." Instead "obedience" trumps "expected results." "The good action is measured by its conformity to the command of God and to the nature of God and not by its success in achieving specific results" (*CWS*, 44).

These are the criteria that a successful retrieval of a Constantinian political theology must meet on Yoderian grounds. Does Leithart meet these criteria? We will examine each in turn.

Constantine Revisited

1. The state exists for the church

Leithart's retrieval is at best mixed on this first criterion. On the one hand, his Constantinian political theology understands that the state's role is to serve the Church. Constantine created a cross shaped space found in architecture and politics.[22] But to what end? Here a theological judgment is required. Did Constantine fit the Church within Roman political space, or did he reconfigure Roman space within the Church? Yoder and Rahner suggest the former, Leithart the latter. Leithart provides ample evidence for his position, but he also concedes Yoder's argument. For instance, Constantine's theological convictions needed a "unified church" for the "health of the empire."[23] The Church is salutary because it promotes the "health of the empire." The latter is not necessarily opposed to Yoder's criteria, especially #2; but it is also a temptation because of criterion #3. Leithart concedes that Constantine resembled pagan emperors and the bishops were silent about it.[24] In 325 while contemplating invading Persia, Constantine "minted a medallion depicting him as Jupiter with an orb and phoenix, a symbol of eastern revival. The medallion also depicted Dionysus, a deity associated with Galerius and thus evoking the memory of that emperor's earlier triumph in Persia."[25] Does this not concede a shift where not only Rome gets shaped by the Church but the Church also takes the form of a pagan state? How could bishops remain silent in the face of such sin? Leithart critiques Constantine and the Church for this, but that seems to make Yoder's point. Both Leithart and Yoder would affirm this first criterion. Constantine's faithfulness to it is mixed at best.

---

22. "Fittingly, the cross also became the shape of sacred space. . . . The sheer fact of church buildings gave the church a fixed physical presence that it had never had before." Leithart, *Defending Constantine*, 124.

23. Ibid., 83.

24. "There is no evidence that any bishops criticized Constantine for his conquests and battles with family members, and the evidence that survives suggests that they warmly supported him. Perhaps they knew more than we, and knew that every last one of Constantine's actions was a justifiable act of self-defense. I find that unlikely. Constantine was less brutal than some emperors, but one does not have to be a pacifist to notice unpleasant resemblances between Christian Constantine's career and that of any of a dozen pagan emperors." Ibid., 237.

25. Ibid., 244.

2. Limiting violence to a police function in promoting order and peace

Leithart does not provide evidence for Christian participation in wars by one nation-state against another prior to or during the fourth century, but this is not very illuminating since nation states do not yet exist. He does, however, challenge Yoder's reading of Scripture that "earlier Christian participation in the military is defensible because it did not involve war but only 'police' responsibilities" (Leithart, 264). Yoder acknowledges such participation as part of God's economy to produce order and peace so that the Church can do its work. Leithart argues that a sharp distinction between war and police action cannot be sustained in the Roman military.

Leithart offers an intriguing discussion of a canon from the Council of Elvira that may support Yoder's position: "Concerning those who lay down their weapons in peacetime it is resolved that they be excluded from fellowship."[26] What does this mean? Did this mean it was permissible to maintain weapons during peacetime as a policing function, but Christians could lay them down in war, allowing for a kind of conscientious objection? If so, then Yoder's historical claim would have some merit. It assumes a distinction between the internal and external use of violence. Regardless of the merits of the historical argument, Leithart overlooks Yoder's theopolitical framework. He does not relate his criticism of Yoder to the reason why such "policing" might be permissible, which is Yoder's first criterion. It is a normative theological judgment and not a historical one—Christians have a stake in peace and order for the sake of the exercise of their faith. This limits how they can participate. It cannot conflict with the exercise of faith. A policing function internal to a social order may allow for that exercise; invading, conquering or determining the social order of another nation by one outside of it does not. To do so grants a universal mission to a nation or empire that it cannot possess. The state is not catholic. That is reserved for the Church.

3. Violence cannot bring into existence an ideal order, especially the Kingdom of God

Did Constantine use the military power of the empire to enforce orthodoxy or bring in the Kingdom of God? Constantine compelled the Donatists to reenter the Church through force, and Leithart recognizes this posed a

26. Ibid., 274.

Constantine Revisited

temptation: "Constantine could have, and ultimately did, stand back and stand down, but the murderous factionalism of the church had tempted him to dangerous precedents. Filled with both passion for Catholic unity and ambition for the empire, he did not always have the resources to resist those temptations when they appeared. They would appear again."[27] Is this not another significant concession to Yoder? Could this temptation have occurred prior to the fourth century? For the first time it is possible to use the violence of the empire in order to enforce orthodoxy and/or ecclesial unity, but these are matters that cannot be a function of compulsion. Even if Constantine's theological judgments were correct—the Son is homoousios with the Father—the means by which those judgments are preserved and promulgated matters. Leithart agrees: "I agree completely with critics to this extent: emperors have no right to define orthodoxy."[28] But he also questions if Constantine did this. "Constantine refused to take a place in the council until *invited*."[29] Does this concede too much? Can emperors make doctrine if they are invited to a council? Should they be, especially if they are unbaptized? That would seem to overthrow traditional liturgical precedent and suggest a profound shift in ecclesiological authority.[30]

4. Christians must offer practical counsel

Leithart acknowledges that the Church has, at times, been unfaithful and become the emperor's "whore" as depicted in the Revelation of St. John. He laments such unfaithful acts and responds, "All these were real, and often horrific, acts of unfaithfulness. But they do not imply a structural flaw. Once the emperor has kissed the Son, should he not honor the Son's Bride?" Here we find a new term introduced into Leithart's political theology—"structure." What is this "structure" that Leithart finds capable of faithlessness but not fundamentally flawed during the era of Constantine? What does it mean for the emperor to kiss the Son and honor his Bride? Leithart never spells this out with any precision in his political theology—a severe shortcoming that prevents us from a concrete determination whether his work satisfies Yoder's criteria. How the state "kisses the Son and honors his Bride" lacks sufficient concreteness to make an adequate theological judgment. Is it some kind of establishment Christianity that allows the

27. Ibid., 163.
28. Ibid., 151.
29. Ibid., 157.
30. See Kreider, "Converted but Not Baptized."

state to provide legal support of the Christian mission? If so, which kind of establishment? Imperial Christianity? Papal states? Territorial churches? Anglicanism? The "Three Self Movement" of the official Chinese church? America's civil religion? Proponents of each of these might very well say, "Yes. The state should kiss the Son and honor his Bride." But if so many different forms of political theologies could affirm Leithart's argument, many of which I think he would find faithless, the question must be raised as to whether his political theology is doing sufficient work to pass this criterion of practical counsel. Until he gives us more we can only reserve judgment whether his Constantinian retrieval sets forth a "conceivable alternative." This is especially important because Leithart locates the fall in modern politics and puts forth Constantinianism as a potential practical remedy for modernity.[31] But without a concrete proposal for what this looks like, it could only be utopian. Waiting for a universal emperor who uses his resources to honor and establish Christianity, or rebuild Jerusalem, would be an act of nostalgia or a romantic posture. Who expects this to happen in our post-Christendom situation? and who would think it could happen without such tremendous social dislocation that it would create more evil than good? Such a cultivated expectation would most likely tempt the Church from its true mission post modernity. We are, after all, waiting on such a universal King, but we already know his name. Yoder's work seems much more practical and concrete given our historical context. We are to wait for Jesus and no other, accepting our exilic situation until then.

Leithart agrees that Yoder's diasporic reading of Christianity has much to commend it. "I wrote above that Yoder's vision of Jewish mission in exile is invigorating, and I meant that. It is the key vision that should guide the twenty-first-century Christian response to empire in a world after Christendom." However, he thinks it lacks something: "But it does not address the question that Constantine's career raises: what does the church do if the emperor sees a vision and wants to help Christians start building a temple back in Jerusalem? Yoder does not think that is 'an available option.'"[32] I think Yoder is more politically savvy here. A world emperor who has a vision seeking to build a temple in Jerusalem (metaphorically or literally) does not seem to be something Christians should expect, or for which they should pray. Their prayer takes the form: "Christ has died. Christ is risen. Christ will come again."

---

31. "Modern politics is apostasy from the fourth century baptism." Leithart, *Defending Constantine*, 340.

32. Ibid., 297.

5. The state's limited role in the divine economy is to make the old aeon tolerable. For this reason it cannot be made a central actor in the divine Economy and create a sacrificial economy.

Leithart's most interesting contribution to the anti-Constantinian genealogy, and his important criticism of it, is his insistence that Constantine puts an end to sacrifice. No longer is politics defined by sacrifices that are rendered necessary for the stability of the political order. The Roman persecutions of Christians and others as well as the gladiator games and the spectacles "were not conflicts of church and state but conflicts between different visions of political theology, Roman versus Christian."[33] The former entailed sacrifices for the sake of the body politic. The latter could only acknowledge that Christ has made the perfect sacrifice and now the sacrificial economy has come to an end. Yoder argues something quite similar in his fifth criterion. It is why he denies a private/public split where Christian convictions are rendered private and thereby sacrificed for the public good. Yoder wrote,

> The Christian social critique will therefore distrust every proposal to sacrifice personal values in the present for future institutional benefits, especially if the making of the sacrifice and the later achievements of the good purpose are entrusted to the political authorities and envisaged as the establishment of a better order. A better order will come, if, when, and insofar as it can come on earth when the political apparatus is held in check and where the church is thereby most free to carry out her first task of evangelization and discipleship and her second task of witness to the social order. (*CWS*, 40)

Yoder and Leithart would seem to make common cause here. Christianity brings an end to sacrifice.

Nonetheless, they differ over how sacrifice works. For Yoder, sacrifice has an implicit as well as an explicit dimension. Sacrifice is not only the explicit offering to an idol such as Jupiter; it is also the implicit offering of life for the sake of political order whether it comes through economic systems, abortion, capital punishment or war. These are all sacrificial economies when they establish political order by sacrificing one life for the sake of the multitude. They challenge the sufficiency of Christ's sacrifice.

Leithart's "end of sacrifice" tends to stay on the level of explicit offerings to idols. He extols Constantine for putting an end to Roman pagan

33. Ibid., 28.

sacrifices. When Constantine defeated Maxentius and unified the empire, he refused to enter the Capitolium and offer a sacrifice to Jupiter. Leithart notes, "Diocletian's empire was built on sacrifice, his persecutions inspired by failed sacrifice. As soon as he defeated Maxentius, Constantine made it clear that a new political theology was coming to be, a political theology without sacrifice. It was a signal of the 'opposition to sacrifice' that he would hold to 'consistently for the rest of his life.'" But Constantine also enters Rome with Maxentius' head on a pike.[34] Is that an end to sacrifice? Maxentius' head gets lifted up on a pike for all to see. It is this act of violence that establishes Constantine's political order. It is yet another spectacle. This is not the political order by which Jesus creates the Church. As Origen put it,

> If a revolt had been the cause of the Christians existing as a separate group, the lawgiver of the Christians would not have forbidden entirely the taking of human life. He taught that it was never right for his disciples to go so far against a man, even if he should be very wicked; for he did not consider it compatible with his inspired legislation to allow the taking of human life in any form at all. Moreover, if Christians had originated from a revolt, they would not have submitted to laws that were so gentle which caused them to be killed as sheep and made then unable even to defend themselves against their persecutors.[35]

At most we can say that Constantine pointed in the direction to an end to sacrifice, but he did not yet recognize its full political significance.[36] Yoderians should be grateful for that and affirm a Constantinian shift that begins to let the leaven of the 'end of sacrifice' grow in human history. Leithart does us a service pointing it out and how Augustine should also be celebrated for affirming it. Nonetheless, the vision of Roman crowds passing by Maxentius' head raised high above them on a pike should create at least a moment of pause that Constantine truly put an end to sacrifice.

---

34. Ibid., 66.
35. Origin, *Contra Celsum*, 3.7.
36. Leithart notes Constantine recognized this. Constantine wrote, "This indeed is heavenly wisdom, to choose to be injured rather than to injure, and when it is necessary to suffer evil rather than to do it." Leithart, *Defending Constantine*, 93. But this was not the wisdom by which he unified the Roman empire.

6. Preferential option for the widow, orphan and stranger

Leithart's historical revision of Constantine makes a convincing case that his fascination with Christianity improved the lot of those on the margins of society. Constantine instituted laws and trials that improved the life of many. He proscribed spectacles and gladiators and sent criminals into the mines to avoid shedding their blood.[37] Not everything improved. His legislation on slavery, for example, was "mixed."[38] But the leaven of the Gospel had a salutary influence that would grow through the influence of laws that create the condition for peace and social cohesion that also tended to those on the margins. This is a Constantinian shift that should also be affirmed and strengthened. Yoder sets it forth as a criterion for evaluating any political theology. Leithart acknowledges it was an insufficient shift from paganism. Constantine still uses torture and violence against sexual and other crimes.[39] The execution of his wife Faustus and son Crispus, which occurred shortly after Nicaea, is indefensible. Does this suggest a "structural flaw" where emperors entrusted with power will inevitably be forced to use faithless means to maintain their power even if they use it for good causes? Perhaps not. Perhaps we can point to kings and rulers who lived more like monks than pagan warriors, but that is why Yoder acknowledges an openness to Constantinianism and asks for concrete, historical examples. Constantine's execution of his wife and child show he was not such an example. This is not what we should expect from saints. Indeed, unless we are moral relativists, it should be condemned as reprehensible.

7. The Church does not accept the state's inevitable use of violence

Yoder is not idealistic about what we should expect from the state. For him it has a limited role to insure social cohesion as best as possible so that the Church can fulfill its evangelistic mission in the times between the times. Christians should never ask the state to become the Church. They are different social orders with different missions. Yoder writes, "We do not ask of the government that it be nonresistant; we do, however, ask that it take the most just and the least violent action possible. For the state to take this least evil path would, in fact, in spite of what we have said above, call for a

---

37. Ibid., 196.
38. Ibid., 221.
39. Ibid., 199–200.

certain kind of faith" (*CWS*, 42). The state cannot receive the faith of the Church; it is not that kind of agent, but it can be called upon to trust that the God who speaks his definitive word in Jesus created a world where actions consistent with it work "with the grain of the universe." Thus the Church can, in faith, call upon the state to limit its use of violence and still expect it to produce social cohesion.

Did Constantine heed that call? Leithart makes a compelling case that within the violent context of his time he did somewhat. He acknowledges that Constantine's response to that call was ambiguous; yet Constantine diminished the violence of the empire. Leithart cannot understand why Yoder does not celebrate this more than he does. His seventh criterion explains why. That a government refuses to use violence to achieve its ends is to acknowledge, in the limited exercise of faith available to it, Christ's triumph. While that is an occasion for rejoicing, the response of praise and gratitude belongs to Christ. He puts an end to sacrifice. The bare minimum we should expect from a government is to acknowledge and respect Christ's triumph. The fact that so few do is a sign we still live in the time between the times.

8. Creating a legitimate government is not the Christian's primary occupation

Leithart offers a healthy corrective to Yoder given his eighth criterion. Leithart points out that although no particular form of government for Yoder is "legitimate," the most illegitimate is "Constantinian."[40] This can tempt Yoder to be reactive and find modern liberal democracies preferable because they are closer than Constantinianism to the freedom necessary for Christian witness. Despite his own criteria, Yoder (perhaps) has a preferential option for modernity. Leithart is much more critical of modern political institutions than Yoder. He finds them incapable of acknowledging any common good or truth that would place "brakes" on their use of violence. In turn, he suggests that Constantinianism could recognize limits to violence in a way that modern, democratic nations, based on the "consent of the governed," cannot. Yoder may very well overestimate the benefits of modernity and underestimate the benefits of Constantinian arrangements. Leithart may very well underestimate the benefits of modernity and overestimate Constantinianism. Nonetheless, Yoder's counsel is valid even if his practice did not always bear it out. The mission of the

40. Ibid., 317–19.

Church is not to legitimate governments or states. It should have a faithful indifference toward them for the sake of its own mission. It has much more important work to do.

9. Obedience rather than calculating success

This criterion should not be misrepresented. Yoder does not argue against prudential judgments; his fourth criterion acknowledges their importance. What he critiques is the assumption that we can know for certain the "unintended consequence" of our actions such that *disobedient* actions can be trusted to bring about more good than obedient ones. Within the context of obedience, prudential judgments can and must be made as his fourth criterion emphasizes. When we are encouraged to sacrifice faithfulness for effectiveness, then we must be suspicious for we are being told that Christ's sacrifice needs supplemented by our faithlessness for it to be effective.

Leithart's Constantinian retrieval acknowledges Yoder's point. He explicitly rejects those distinctions that would allow obedience to be trumped by a calculation of consequences. A Christian political theology must, as Yoder affirms, make obedience to Jesus its center. For Leithart this requires taking seriously Jesus' hard sayings. "It will not do to dismiss the Sermon on the Mount with a wave of the hand ('that's for personal life, not political life')."[41] Nor does Leithart pursue the normal escapes that render such hard sayings apolitical: a public-private distinction, a nature-grace schema, setting moral man against immoral society. He rejects all of these, refusing to draw upon any of them to defend Constantinianism.[42] Like Yoder he seeks a theopolitical vision grounded in obedience. Where they differ is the content of that obedience, which stems from their diverse readings of Scripture. This is the decisive difference. What is a faithful reading of Scripture for theopolitics?

Leithart finds Yoder to offer a "revisionist" reading of the early Church and its relationship to Judaism, which sets "'Constantinianism' at the center." There is some merit to this charge. Yoder's historical renderings could occasionally set a dynamic Judaism against a static Greek universalism. But Leithart overstates Yoder's putative "revision." In setting forth Yoder's revisionism he begins with this claim exegeting Yoder: "Jesus and Paul were thoroughly Jewish, and the earliest church operated within

41. Ibid., 332.
42. Ibid.

a Jewish conceptual and practical world."[43] But how is that revisionist? Jesus and Paul *were* "thoroughly Jewish." That is undeniable. The early church *did operate* in a "Jewish conceptual and practical world." That too is undeniable as long as we remember that there was no pure Palestinian Judaism immune from some supposedly corrupting Greek influence. Yoder's next putative revision has to do with the relation between the Gospel and Torah. Yoder claims that for the early church, "Jesus' commands were treated as commands, the Torah was not played off against the gospel, and the Christians patterned their communal life after the example of diaspora Judaism."[44] That Christianity shifted from the Gospel as a fulfillment of the Law to a Law-Gospel distinction seems undeniable and is correlated to the growing distance between church and synagogue in the second century.[45] Constantine may have inherited that divide. He did not create it. Yoder acknowledges this.[46] This tendency was exacerbated in much of the Christian tradition and had deleterious consequences.[47] The best New Testament scholarship has challenged this rigid law/gospel distinction. Yoder's position is not controversial.

Leithart does, however, have a point when he critiques Yoder for his next "revision"—that he primarily reads the Old Testament in terms of diaspora and does not have an adequate account of restoration. Revisions of Yoder along these lines will strengthen the direction of his biblical narrative.[48] Here Leithart makes a contribution to Yoder's biblical reading by calling us to read Jeremiah to the end and to take Ezra and Nehemiah more seriously. This could help in our reading of the New Testament, and actually support Yoder. The New Testament was born in an era of expectation for a return from exile. God will appear in Jerusalem and re-

43. Ibid., 133.

44. Ibid.

45. Leithart argues that there is some truth to Yoder's reading in the tradition of "adversus Iudaeos," but that contra Yoder it was Augustine who "stemmed the tide." "Crucially," he writes, Augustine "affirmed that the sacrifices and rites of the Old Testament were commanded by God and, moreover, that precisely by putting the law into bodily practice, the Jews became fitting types of the coming Lord." Ibid., 135. He also states, "I do not suggest any causal relation. I only note the fact: contrary to Yoder, Christian theology was *re-*Judaized in the century following Constantine." Ibid., 136. I think Leithart makes an important case for Augustine against Yoder.

46. Yoder, *Jewish-Christian Schism Revisited*, 37 n. 22.

47. John Wesley was an exception to this tradition. He claimed "there was no contradiction between the law and the gospel." See Long, *John Wesley's Moral Theology*, 125–70.

48. See Nugent, *Politics of Yahweh*, 158–62.

Constantine Revisited

establish the temple. In the New Testament, Jesus' body is God's return to Jerusalem. It is the "temple" where divinity and humanity unite as the first form of Christ's body. That body is then mediated to us through Word and Sacrament so that it creates the body that is his Church. Would this represent a critique of Yoder? I do not see how Yoder's work makes sense without these dogmatic claims. It is central to his theopolitical framework in *Christian Witness to the State*. What Jesus produced was a "new community," which is the Church that "has a task within history" (*CWS* 10). Yoder made bold, exclusive claims for it. The Church gives history its "meaning:" "The meaning of history—and therefore the significance of the state—lies in the creation and work of the church.... The function of the state in maintaining an ordered society is thereby a part of the divine plan for the evangelization of the world" (*CWS* 13). To be sure, there are Yoderians who develop his diasporic ecclesiology in an apocalyptic vein without any significant continuity for the Church. Perhaps those of us who read Yoder through Hauerwas find more of a place for the Church as an institution with continuity over time of doctrine, liturgy, authority and ethics than Yoderians of a stricter observance. If Yoder has no place for restoration, then their reading may be correct, but I remain to be convinced that this is the best reading of Yoder.

Leithart's biblical interpretation fails, however, when he seeks to demonstrate how his political theology is as Christological as Yoder's theopolitics. He promised to provide an ethics that refuses to discard the Sermon on the Mount, but makes only a brief allusion to it by setting the Sermon on the Mount within the honor-shame context of the first century. Instead of offering an extensive analysis of Christology he accuses Yoder of Marcionism and sets the Old and New Testaments within an overarching metanarrative of war.[49] He writes, "The Bible is from beginning to end a story of war.... From the beginning, this Creator made man to participate in and prosecute his wars. His goal in history is to train hands to fight."[50] Leithart cites no biblical evidence for this because there is none. Nowhere does God train Adam or Eve for war. He gives them no sword; he does not even provide implements for butchering animals. Yet Leithart reads Genesis 2:15 as a call to arms. Adam was supposed to keep the garden by guarding it with force. This is a thoroughly non-traditional reading of

---

49. The Marcionite accusation fails miserably. Yoder drew upon the Old Testament for his social ethics more so than most twentieth century Christian ethics. That Christ fulfills the law and resituates it is neither Marcionite nor supersessionist. It is the New Testament, which is itself a reading of the Old.

50. Leithart, *Defending Constantine*, 333.

Genesis 2:15: "The Lord God took the man and put him in the garden of Eden to till it and keep it." Tilling and keeping is not arming and killing. War and violence are not part of God's original good creation. For Leithart Adam failed when the serpent invaded the garden and he refused to kill it. "Instead of crushing the head of the serpent, he stood watching and doing nothing." But Genesis never presents the serpent as an intruder or the garden as a fortified camp protecting one part of God's creation from another. Leithart cites Genesis 3:8 for his peculiar interpretation: "They heard the sound of the LORD God walking in the garden at the time of the evening breeze, and the man and his wife hid themselves from the presence of the Lord God among the trees of the garden."[51] But this lends no support to his reading. There is no footnote that adds: "because they were pacifists who refused to use the violence God expected of them in maintaining the security of the garden." Leithart then reads the first biblical prophecy of Christ in Genesis 3:15 as evidence for God's original creation of humanity for war. He writes,

> This is famed as the first messianic prophecy of Scripture, but its content is too often ignored: it is a promise of a warrior-savior, a conqueror. That is nearly the last vision of Jesus we see in Scripture as well, the rider on a white horse who "judges and wages war" in righteousness, who is armed with a "sharp sword" that comes from his mount, who "smites the nations" and rules them with a rod of iron, whose eyes are flames of fire (Revelation 19:11–18).[52]

War and violence are not for Leithart, as they were for Yoder and traditional Christianity, consequences of the fall. They are intrinsic to being God's creatures, a form of participating in his rule.

In one sense, Yoder would agree that the story of the Bible is a story of "war." His final chapter in *The Politics of Jesus* is "The War of the Lamb." The Bible is a story of warfare—but not of a violence committed. It is of a violence endured. It has a "canonical-directional" movement that points to how Yahweh wars, culminating in the cross, resurrection and ascension of Christ.[53] Yoder reads the Bible Christocentrically. Leithart reads Jesus martially. The metanarratives by which they read Scripture differ. Yoder fits the Bible into a reading of God's address to us in the Word made flesh, the Lamb who was slain. Leithart fits the story of Jesus within the story

---

51. Ibid., 333.
52. Ibid., 334.
53. See Nugent, *Politics of Yahweh*, 11.

of war. This is why he finally cannot avoid reducing the Sermon on the Mount to individual exchanges of "honor and shame" that are, at most, indirectly related to politics.[54]

Conclusion

This may seem to be a harsh judgment against Leithart. I do not think it is a necessary consequence of his intriguing interpretation of Constantine, but it emerges from his unfortunate conclusion, "Teaching Hands to Fight," when he begins to spell out his Constantinian political theology. Is it faithful? Is it the obedient reading of Jesus' life that would require anti-Constantinians to rethink their position? Is it the kind of argument Yoder suggested might be forthcoming? I think not. Let us assume someone who did not know the Gospel read this concluding section on political theology. What would they learn? They might find it supporting the story of Sparta with its insistence on cultivating warriors and training hands for battle rather than Christianity. They might be tempted to venerate Thor more so than the Triune God. Such a reader would be surprised to discover that the "warrior" Christ rode into Jerusalem on a donkey, died on a cross, was risen and then ascended to the Father without marshaling an army and destroying the wicked rulers who committed such a heinous act against him. Yet Leithart's argument seems to suggest that Jesus' refusal to do so is a failure similar to Adam's. The second Adam, like the first, failed to stamp on the head of the snake. Would such a reader be surprised that when Jesus equipped his disciples for mission he breathed upon them the Holy Spirit rather than teaching them to use weapons? I think he would be. Moreover such a reader would not need to begin with the life of Jesus. Four pages into his argument, Leithart asks, "What of Jesus?" To which I want to respond—exactly! When you get to the end of your political theology and have to ask "What of Jesus" we have to acknowledge something has gone wrong.

Leithart's *Defending Constantine* offers an important historical revision that shows how "Yoderian" some of Constantine's shifts were. His reading meets, to some extent, Yoder's criteria 1, 5, 6, 8, and 9. It fails to meet 2 and 7. And it fails miserably at 3 and 4. Of course these are Yoder's, not Leithart's, criteria for assessing if we have a faithful defense of Constantine. Leithart's different understanding of obedience may very well qualify them. To be sure, on Yoder's own criteria, we still have much

54. Leithart, *Defending Constantine*, 338.

to learn from Leithart. Nonetheless, Leithart can envision a role for government authority to establish the faith in a way Yoder never could. He also has a profoundly different account of obedience than Yoder based on diametrically opposed reading of Scriptures. Both cannot be right.

I am left wondering what conclusion I should draw from Leithart's Constantinian retrieval. One conclusion is that Yoder's historiography of the fourth century is inaccurate. This is unfortunate because much of it would support his theopolitics. They are basically correct and Yoder failed to see the extent to which Constantine agrees with him. Constantine was a Yoderian. This does not fundamentally call Yoder's theopolitical framework into question.

A second conclusion is that Yoder is historically inaccurate and this renders his theopolitics incorrect as well. He has no place for the potential Constantinian retrieval that will produce the next global leader who will restore Jerusalem through training Christian hands to fight. I would like to think the first is the proper conclusion to Leithart's work. If it is the second, I am deeply troubled and need to see what this Constantinian retrieval asks of Christ's Church before rendering any final judgment. This will require a less polemical and more careful articulation of Leithart's political theology; something along the lines of what Yoder himself did in *Christian Witness to the State*.

6 *Defending Constantine* Taken Seriously

JONATHAN TRAN

I HAD A HARD time taking *Defending Constantine* seriously.[1] Perhaps this disqualifies from the start anything I have to say. That is for the reader to decide. Throughout, I saw the book's argument as empty because at a basic level it misperceived the Constantinian problematic in the work of John Howard Yoder.[2] *Defending Constantine* takes as its point of departure Constantinianism as a theological proposition derived from a specific reading of history. In turn, it seeks to overcome that proposition by showing how the reading comes up short. Demonstrating this and chronicling an alternative history occupies most of the book, which ultimately presses toward Liethart's own provocative theological proposal. Yet I am doubtful that Yoder thought he was doing anything like what *Defending Constantine* suggests—that is, contriving a theological proposition from a particular reading of history. Yoder understood the relationship between history, theology, and scripture to be infinitely complex, unfolding as interpenetrating temporalities (past, present, future) and subjectivities (reader, text, world). To suppose that he saw some kind of straight line from history to theology fails to understand scripture as Yoder saw it (under the influence of Karl Barth and Oscar Cullman), that is, apocalyptic history embodied in the church. If chrono-logical history is to be useful, Yoder thought, it

---

1. Leithart, *Defending Constantine*. Page references in parentheses refer to this text.

2. In this volume, John Nugent offers a different and fuller critique of Leithart's understanding of Constantinianism. Also see Leithart's penetrating defense in Leithart, "Defending *Defending Constantine*," 646–51.

must find its bearings within a hermeneutics of καιρός such that theology precedes and informs how Christians view history, or as he puts it, "historiography is theologically necessary."[3] Rejecting the straight forward account of history he associated with "the official churches," Yoder wrote, "The past must however be taken seriously in a very different way if one claims to critique the course of history using as criterion a point within history, namely the Incarnation, or the canon."[4] For Yoder, "Constantinian" is that which refuses to see history in this *priestly* manner, as annunciated and consummated in the reign of the Lamb, and so continues to imagine power in the terms of the old, now defunct, aeon.[5] Rather than backward looking—from a mythical fall to a corresponding lost golden age—Yoder's rejoinder to Constantinianism anticipates history moving forward from the "already, but not yet" consummated Christ; whatever history or power names, and whether it is good or bad, occurs here.[6]

Defending Constantine's misperception on this point renders its subsequent argument empty because even if it is correct historically (though I raise some questions about this below), it does not lead to the theological conclusions Leithart wants to propose. I also found the argument empty on another score, namely, whatever conclusion the argument advanced, it could not follow from the genre of work it purported to be—a "polemical" text that got lost in what it thought it was doing. Finally, I find it hard to believe that Leithart seriously wants to pursue a "purified Constantinianism." As a Christian, I struggled with Leithart's apparently unapologetic effort to affix imperial warrant to transcendent imperatives.[7]

These were my initial misgivings. Yet, slowly and reluctantly, I came to recognize that these reactions said as much about me as *Defending Constantine*. Eventually I came to understand the book's argument as making space for an important, and indeed serious, question—one that I, perhaps, did not want to confront. What if the problem is not Constantinianism, as Leithart understands it, but rather Constantine—a distinction that my rendition above could not imagine—and our willingness to come to terms with Constantine and his moral failings? And what if a renewed attempt to come to terms with Constantine—the Christian person not the theological

3. Yoder, *Priestly Kingdom*, 127. Emphasis added.
4. Ibid.
5. For further discussion, see Martens, *Heterodox Yoder*, 45–47.
6. See Yoder, "To Serve Our God and to Rule the World," in *Royal Priesthood*, 127–42.
7. Consider Agamben, *Kingdom and the Glory*.

Constantine Revisited

notion—forced certain questions about how we understand Christian faithfulness, or more precisely, Christian unfaithfulness? Leithart poses the question in the following way: Constantine was a faithful Christian; so why have we failed to acknowledge that? Accordingly, he goes about the task of historically demonstrating just how faithful Constantine's Christianity indeed was, and then holding up that faithfulness as a model for what Christian participation in politics could (should) look like. I am interested neither in revisionist attempts to dress Constantine up as more faithful than he was nor in exemplifying him as a model for Christian political participation. But what does strike me as interesting and important is the question of how we hold Constantine's failures as a Christian. One move could be to dismiss Constantine's Christianity altogether, to cast it as so much political smoke and mirrors. This is what Leithart accuses Yoder of doing. Reacting, Leithart goes the other way, propping up a version of Constantine's faith that cannot be dismissed (which, as I've said, proves less than serious). What if we refused both moves? What if we removed all of Leithart's embellishments and euphemisms while, at the same time, refused to dismiss Constantine? Then we would have to contend with a Constantine whose faith was genuine but deeply flawed. We would be left confronting faith at its most tragic, and honest. Are we able to come face to face with that Constantine? This is a serious question, making *Defending Constantine* a quite serious book, especially if we consider how many American Christians daily contend with it. Thus, in my own effort to take this enterprise seriously, I raise two questions that concern the rest of this essay—the first pertains to genre and the second to political theology.

The Question of Genre

What kind of book is *Defending Constantine*? My question here is not primarily about what Leithart says about imperial history (something I'm not qualified to judge) but what he thinks he is doing when he does history (something that has been a significant concern to me throughout my career).[8]

Beginning his bibliography, Leithart writes, "I have relied a great deal in this study on secondary literature" (342). The admission is forthcoming, and unnecessary since a quick survey of the footnotes reveals as much. The primary sources that Leithart relies on are Eusebius (used as one might expect), Tertullian (also used as one might expect), and Lactantius (used

---

8. See my *The Vietnam War and Theologies of Memory* and *Foucault and Theology*.

to explicate Constantine's political theology as interpreted by Leithart). Other than Yoder, these are the only primary sources Leithart attends to regularly. Leithart draws heavily upon one secondary source. And his use of this source furthers this question of genre. On numerous occasions, he references or engages H. A. Drake's *Constantine and the Bishops*. His use of Drake, however, is varied and perplexing. Sometimes he likes *Constantine and the Bishops*; sometimes he doesn't. The reasons he gives when disagreeing strike me as odd. When he follows Drake, he does so without comment (e.g., 64, 112, 218). However, when digressing from Drake (e.g., 106–107, 127), he does not supply the standard historiographical rationale, such as primary sources that dispute ensuing secondary conclusions. But how could he, since as he admits, he relies on secondary material "a great deal"? Another approach might be to hold up secondary source S1 against secondary source S2, explaining why one is better than the other (e.g., S1 better interprets the historical record than S2). However, Leithart's disagreements rarely follow such a course. Rather, he seems to cull from Drake selectively, and *thereafter* render judgments about its reliability. Along the way he gives us no key for his interpretive strategy. Is it that he thinks Drake cites the right (or enough) primary evidence but errs on his conclusions? If so, what would be the criteria from use to use for such judgments? He never lets us know.

Here is a specific example. In the chapter "Justice for All," Leithart cites *Constantine and the Bishops* and lifts from Drake a decree that supports his claim about judicial reform, even though Drake uses the decree to make a contrary point. Leithart then criticizes Drake for "miss[ing] the important religious thrust of the legislation." According to Leithart,

> [Drake] rightly notes that Constantine's concern was for "fair and speedy trials" (p. 327) and an effort to empower the poor (p. 339). He also recognizes that the emperor's solicitousness for the poor had little support in traditional Roman legal practice, where social privilege played an enormous role. Yet he doesn't put these two insights together to ask how Constantine came to be convinced of the need to use the power of the emperor to open avenues of redress for those who could not afford Roman courts. (216 n. 11)

Leithart's argument goes like this: Constantine did P, but P did not have precedent, so what (X) can explain P? Leithart solves for X: "The answer, it seems clear, is that Constantine was following Christian imperatives and impulses."[9]

9. Ibid.

Constantine Revisited

Two questions arise here, the second begging. First, what "imperatives and impulses" is Leithart talking about? He offers no indication, by way of either primary or secondary sources. Surely there is no definitive set of *Christian* "imperatives and impulses." Is he talking about specific scripture? or canonical church teachings? or even certain pre-creedal formulations? Is he referring to liturgical orders or rites—if so, which ones? Or is he banking on a common ecclesial practice that was abstracted toward a general concern for just legal procedures? I am not opposed in principle to any of these. In fact, I hope and imagine such sourcing exists. But Leithart specifies none. Perhaps "it seems clear" comes from logical deduction, deduction that in his eyes Drake's interpretation (i.e. efforts to secure divine favor) fumbles: the *only* thing (thus making *clear*) that could explain P would be these "Christian imperatives and impulses" (whatever they be). But that would be a non sequitur since any number of things could solve for X. Perhaps political expedience required it; perhaps Constantine sought favor with the bishops; maybe he had a grudge with specific judges and courts; possibly he had another one of those dreams or visions. Given the depictions Leithart proffers of Constantine's rather capricious connection to things Christian (imperatives, impulses, and otherwise), any one of these could work to explain what caused him to pursue these reforms. Intention is a notoriously difficult thing to pin down, only more so regarding acts that occurred nearly two millennia ago. The way historians have tried to get at intentions is by examination of the extant historical record. That would explain Drake's approach (and his copious primary bibliography), even if that makes Drake's Constantine far less likable than Leithart's.[10]

In place of Drake's approach, Leithart seems to presume a piety guiding Constantine, even though he never explicates the nature of that piety. In the end, Leithart may be right; I am in no position to dispute his claim. But there is good reason to query the logical fallacy at the heart of many of his "it seems clear" judgments. "The answer . . . is that Constantine was following Christian imperatives and impulses" begs the question to the extent that X (Christian imperatives and impulses) is legitimated by a presumption hidden in the problematic as he sets it up. Leithart does not prefer Drake's conclusion; but also does not supply any of the standard historiographical reasons. We do know, however, that Drake's conclusions disagree with those Leithart wants to make. Yet Leithart often invokes interpretive restraint in regard to conclusions he does not prefer, like the

---

10. See Drake, *Constantine and the Bishops*, 541–55.

various speculations surrounding the deaths of Fausta and Crispus. Here he cautions, "Many of the charges go far beyond the evidence that we have" (229). Why doesn't he exercise the same restraint toward the conclusions he prefers?

This is the most perplexing aspect of the book, one that was hard to get past as a reader. The most trying, however, is its disingenuous assertion of polemic as an obvious attempt to cover over the strange historiography just discussed. By "polemic" Leithart must mean something more than argument, for that is the genre of most academic work. I think "polemic" indicates something more than, as he suggests, looking for a fight. Positioning his book within the genre of polemic allows Leithart to skirt questions of historical accuracy. Leithart admits as much when in conceding a point to church historian Alan Kreider's review of *Defending Constantine*, Leithart says, "Such is one of the costs of writing a polemical book."[11] But this is merely a head fake. After all, the book wants to be taken seriously as a historical study. Leithart does not wish to be viewed (i.e., dismissed) as simply revisionist; the structure of his argument, the implication of his thesis, and what he is finally after (i.e., ecclesial entanglements with state power do not need to be accomodationist; let me give you the definitive example . . .), each require it. The double-faced use of the odd historiography combined with the visage of polemic allows him to have it both ways: against the theologian Yoder Leithart can say, "You got history wrong," while against the historian Kreider, he can say, "I'm just being polemical." As someone who is generally suspicious of "historical accuracy" I have no particular stake in arguments like those of Kreider or Drake; but Leithart must at least be clear about what he is doing.

The Question of Political Theology

Leithart's big argument—what drives the research, writing, and presentation of the book—is the very worthwhile project of theologically theorizing political space, the question of political theology. He is especially concerned with refuting one particular conception (Yoder's and Stanley Hauerwas' anathema of Constantinianism) and its causally related interpretation (Yoder's confidence in an historical Constantinian shift) by offering a rival conception through a rival interpretation. Leithart's assumption—that a different historical interpretation can yield a different political conception—will be ineffectual for some, mainly because they

---

11. Leithart, "Defending *Defending Constantine*," 652.

understand Yoder's argument as *tropic* in nature. That is, Yoder's concerns were rarely about the history, and indeed, the interpretation *should* be read backward from the conception.[12] Proving that Constantine was not so bad will not do much for those for whom the issue was never primarily about Constantine. To others, such an approach is self-defeating because history simply cannot be arranged for those sorts of arguments; for them, following Michel Foucault, "history" is itself a conception, a thing of this world.[13]

So let us treat Leithart on his own terms. Again, his argument is that a different interpretation of Constantine will yield a different conception of political theology. Even granting Leithart's historical interpretation, I still disagree with the political theology *Defending Constantine* endorses, one that materializes in Christians taking up arms to share in God's life as "we share more fully" in God's purposes (336). In other words, I do not prefer Leithart's Constantine either, and find the resulting political conception wanting. That reconfiguration—replete with Constantine's pious imperatives and impulses, desire for church unity, fine statuary, revamped sacrificial logic, great concern for the poor, regard for the abandoned, and favor toward Christian governors, and all this as "not the betrayal of the Gospel but, in some degree, its fulfillment"[14]—still fails as a proper political theology for the simple reason that its continuity with the world's sacramental ordering of power (its lack of something like Yoder's apocalyptic political vision) will leave the church wanting, even needing, the conversion of rulers as rulers—or, alternatively, writing revisionist histories about converted rulers.[15]

Yet this failure may be *Defending Constantine* at its most compelling, not for its political conception but for a series of philosophical questions it (unintentionally) raises. Leithart asks, "What does the church do

---

12. At its best, *Defending Constantine* can be read as a genealogical project along these lines. While Leithart refers to Alex Sider's use of "narrative trope," I am drawing "tropic" specifically from literary theorist White, *Tropics of Discourse*, as well as his *Metahistory*. White writes, "Tropic is the shadow from which all realistic discourse tries to flee. This flight, however, is futile; for tropics is the process by which all discourse constitutes the objects which it pretends only to describe realistically and to analyze objectively."—*Tropics of Discourse*, 2. See Leithart's reference to Sider in Leithart, *Defending Constantine*, 318. Elsewhere in this volume, Craig Hovey makes the interesting point that Yoder's ahistorical trope responds to prior ahistorical tropes in the cause of universal (i.e., ahistorical) moral orders.

13. Foucault, *Order of Things*, xxiii.

14. Leithart, "Defending *Defending Constantine*," 645.

15. An inability to distinguish between prophetic and apologetic speech is one of the dangers Yoder intends by Constantinianism. See his *Original Revolution*, 21.

if the emperor sees a vision and wants to help Christians start building a temple back in Jerusalem?" (297). What if our rulers converted? Not that we needed that to happen, not even that we wanted or thought to pray for it. But what if while American churches subscribed to Yoder's anti-Constantinian vision, American rulers converted? What then would we do? We could not, as Leithart rightly admonishes, be opposed to such conversions since we have to presume conversions of any type always a possibility. What would we do with their offices? Assuming faithfulness would not require resignation, what would faithfulness require (assuming one could ascend to office with Christianity intact, as fraught as that may be)?

That Rome might be baptized was always a hope. From Israel through the church, the covenant of promise ensues as God's blessing that we might bless the nations. The church is charged to "seek the salvation of the culture to which God has sent you" as Leithart reminds us. However, as his Constantine shows us, faithfulness is much thornier than conversion. After *Defending Constantine*, can anyone doubt that Constantine was a kind of Christian? Far trickier is nailing down the meaning of that Christianity. At every baptism, a child.

At the heart of *Defending Constantine* is this common and unsettling difference between our lives and our legacies (Constantine the Christian and Constantine the icon), the question of whether any of us can live up to our conversions such that baptism indicates, rather than simply symbolizes, rebirth. Sustaining this difference causes Leithart to balk against Yoder's invectives. If Yoder's anti-Constantinianism was meant to assuage these tensions by way of its "comparatively simple paradigm," to remove this difficulty—a difficulty none other than the persons we are—then Leithart is right to reinvigorate the question, to keep it "open" as Yoder at his most trenchant was so good at doing (316). It would be easier for us if Constantine were not Christian, but instead a sometimes virtuous pagan. (Imagine if Michel Foucault were not just a *secular* saint.[16]) It is harder to bear the reality that, in fact, Constantine was Christian and yet so wrong so often.

Near the end of *The Claim of Reason*, Stanley Cavell challenges the popular notion that slaveholders viewed slaves as less than human, and so treated them accordingly. What is closer to the truth, but harder to bear, is the reality that the slaveholders did in fact see them as human, and

---

16. By "secular saint," I am referring to an oftmade portrayal of Michel Foucault as saint-like given his political writings and activity. See Halperin, *Saint Foucault*.

still treated them as they did.[17] It seems to me that *Defending Constantine* stumbles into provoking something similar about Christianity: it is easier for us, like Yoder and the anti-Constantinians, to view Constantine as not Christian, so that we can disregard his faith and whatever unsavory Christianity that took place in the Empire he created; what is closer to the truth and therefore harder to bear, is the reality that Constantine was in fact a Christian, and likewise the Empire, and yet so amazingly flawed. In this way Constantine does come to exemplify Christianity and reminds us that Christianity is unwieldy in these ways. Similarly unwieldy are the associations we would rather not think about and so take off the table (call our ill-feelings about these associations "neo-anti-Constantinianisms"): residual church income from market economies; the ordinary aid of technology; the moral goods of secular humanism; the solidity of methodology; the availability of the desperate; the ear of a pious president; etc. We should not claim to need any of these (just as Yoderians would not claim to need Constantine's conversion), but few of us can deny benefiting from them (just as Yoderians cannot deny benefiting from neo-Constantinian arrangements). Too much political theology presumes choice, and an infinite space in which to operate. Rather, the church's politics names marriage—that the church is in, even if she is not of, the world.[18] In the world is where *Defending Constantine* leaves us, a very serious book indeed.

---

17. Cavell, *Claim of Reason*, 375–78.

18. The view of politics as marriage comes from Cavell's reconstrual of Rawlsian political liberalism in *Conditions Handsome and Unhandsome*.

7   The Emperor's New Clothes[1]

BRANSON PARLER

THE FAMOUS HANS CHRISTIAN Anderson tale of the Emperor's new clothes turns on the question of how to see the Emperor: is he clothed in garments befitting someone of his noble station or is he parading in nothing more than his birthday suit, exposed as vain and conceited? Likewise, Peter Leithart's *Defending Constantine* turns on the question of how to see the Emperor Constantine: is he the best thing to happen to Christianity since Christ or a problematic figure who begins a pattern of collusion between church and empire that has shaped the church up to the present day? Given the title, it is no surprise that Leithart advocates more for the former than the latter.

Leithart gives three stated purposes that shape his work. First, he draws on numerous scholarly works to provide an account of Constantine that answers basic historical questions: Who was he? What exactly did he accomplish? Did he truly convert to Christianity? How did Constantine himself think about the faith and its relation to his role as emperor? The historical survey serves Leithart's second purpose, that of undermining John Howard Yoder's critique of Constantinianism. Third, Leithart believes that Constantine can potentially serve as a model for contemporary Christian political theory and practice, especially in the Global South. While this third purpose is left largely to the reader's imagination, the first two purposes are addressed at length. Since Leithart's historical work serves his more polemical theological intentions, I will survey the former before proceeding to the latter.

1. Portions of this essay were first published as "The Emperor's New Clothes: A Review of *Defending Constantine*," *The Other Journal* 19 (2011) [http://theotherjournal.com/2011/09/06/the-emperors-new-clothes-a-review-of-defending-constantine/] and appear here with permission from *The Other Journal*.

Constantine Revisited

Leithart's Constantine

Was Constantine genuinely converted to Christianity? Leithart answers yes, although that answer must take into account what it would look like for a fourth-century Roman soldier-turned-emperor to convert. Like Roman emperors before him, religion and politics were not two separate worlds but one integrated whole. Constantine was no Machiavelli or Karl Rove, cleverly and cynically working Christian rhetoric in order to maintain and preserve power. Instead, like the pagan Diocletian before him, Constantine genuinely believed that worship of the correct god would ensure the peace and prosperity of Rome (152). Thus, Constantine was also no James Madison; his empire was not religiously neutral, but one in which Christianity was favored (112). In general, Constantine allowed a certain measure of freedom to non-Christians, but he also occasionally persecuted those considered heretics, schismatics, and non-Christians.

The most significant and persistent aspect of Constantine's reign, for Leithart, is the end he brought to sacrifice. As Augustine would point out nearly a century later, the earthly city functions by sacrificing to false gods in an attempt to ground its existence. This was certainly true of pagan Rome. Consequently, by refusing to offer sacrifices to pagan gods, Constantine undermined the foundation of Roman civic life and pointed to the church as the true *polis* in contrast to the pagan parodies. This was the beginning of something new, for Christianity was a "religion without sacrifice," a communal but not a civic religion (40). Given Christianity's rejection of sacrifice, it cannot be easily assimilated to Roman political theology without "cracking the system wide open" (40). A new *polis* is thus being forged in the midst of the old.

Although neither baptized nor an official member of the church, Constantine called church councils, most notably Nicea, and played a large role in theological disputes and church politics from 312 onward (149). When it is convenient for Leithart to critique Yoder, he downplays Constantine's involvement, but in his more quasi-Eusebian moments, Leithart trumpets Constantine's role in bringing orthodoxy and unity to the church. So on the one hand, Leithart criticizes Yoder and others who suggest (based on Eusebius' reports) that Constantine overstepped his bounds in the various councils and controversies of his day (180). On the other hand, Leithart labels Constantine a "common bishop" (149) and argues that without his political skill and strength of personality, the bishops would probably not have come to a conclusion. As a result, "we should not underestimate Constantine's achievement" at Nicea (170).

Constantine not only oversaw key theological developments but also initiated legal and civic changes that were significant in their intent, if not always in their application. The changes Constantine brought are nothing less than "Rome's baptism," a metaphor that Leithart employs throughout the book to signify the way that Rome's army, empire, worship, cityscapes, law, and society all were being transformed under Constantine (238). Whereas some might see the interweaving of the gospel and civic law as a prime example of the misguidance of Constantinianism, Leithart sees it as the reign of Christ being made concrete with respect to the functioning of the civil order.

Constantine appears troublesome to modern liberal Protestants because they buy into a Lockean division between the interior and exterior, the religious and public. This strict dualism, as Leithart convincingly argues, is untenable (Leithart also recognizes that he and Yoder are companions on this point). For Leithart, the proto-Milbankian Constantine allows for more true freedom than does Locke, who's "doctrine of religious toleration deconstructs in practice into tyranny over religion" (144). Although Constantine was involved in destruction of pagan temples, the exile of heretics, and the persecution of schismatics, he recognized what Locke did not, namely, that there is no such thing as a naked public square (139–45). The emperor must wear the clothes of some god, whether that is the Christian God, a pagan god, or the god of society itself (191). Although he does not turn a blind eye to Constantine's faults and abuses, Leithart argues that the modern myth of religious neutrality has cast out one demon only to welcome seven more, for sacrifice has returned with a vengeance in the modern secular state, which has no god to sacrifice to but itself. So it is not Constantine's age but the modern era that has produced the flow of human blood in unprecedented levels (340–341).

Although Leithart's criticisms of Yoder surface occasionally, his final chapters focus on providing an alternative narrative to Yoder's account of Constantinianism. This difference is not merely about Constantine, but also entails a different understanding of Jesus, violence, and the church's relationship with earthly power. Since Yoder claims that the church's movement to accepting imperial violence and power entails a shift, Leithart sets about to prove that the church was never pacifist. As Leithart sees it, if he can prove diversity or ambiguity on the point of military involvement, he has falsified Yoder's account of a Constantinian shift (259). At the same time, Leithart recognizes that Yoder acknowledged diversity and ambiguity in the second and third centuries (265). For Leithart, army service and justified violence are not wrong; rather, it is the idolatry inherent in the Roman army. So when the imperial liturgies were purged from the army, there was nothing intrinsically wrong about Christian participation (271). Given these factors, Leithart argues that the church did not "fall" into Constantinianism; Constantine purified the army and made possible Rome's baptism.

This acceptance of war and violence fits with Leithart's telling of the biblical narrative. Humanity was created, Leithart holds, to fight: "from the beginning, this Creator made men to participate in and prosecute his war. His goal in history is to train hands to fight" (333). The Old Testament is filled with the wars of Yahweh, Jesus is a David-like conqueror, and the church is commanded to take up the armor of God. So Leithart asks: "if the Lord lets Christians wield the most powerful of spiritual weapons, does he not expect us to be able to handle lesser weapons? If he has handed us a broadsword, does he not assume we know how to use a penknife?" (336) Leithart answers yes and then outlines how the politics of Jesus (as he sees them) would instruct rulers: it would teach them to prosecute wars justly, tell the truth, do good without hypocrisy, seek the common good rather than the good of one party or demographic, store up treasure in heaven rather than lose sleep over budgets or stock markets, and be willing to be the first to die in combat rather than sit safely at home. The real target of criticism is thus not Constantine but the modern state which refuses to acknowledge the true *polis* of God and thereby absolutizes itself. The only remedy for this, Leithart argues, is for modern civilization to humble itself and come forward to be baptized (or re-baptized?).

Furthering the Conversation

Leithart openly admits that he is not trying to be even-handed but is painting Constantine in the most positive light possible, emphasizing the good and downplaying the bad in order to redress the generally negative view of Constantine (318). The most glaring weakness of Leithart's work, then, is that he bases a polemical argument and constructive theology upon an admittedly-biased historical portrait of Constantine. Consequently, Leithart's suspect historiographical method places a large question mark next to the theological conclusions he might draw—the very sin of which he accuses Yoder.

Although Leithart's historical portrait can be challenged, my primary concern is to defend the church's status as a trans-territorial body politic that rejects participation in the violence of earthly powers precisely because Christ—not Constantine—has brought about the end of sacrifice in Christ. To be a community that truly affirms the end of sacrifice is to embrace not only Jesus but the active shalom-seeking and commitment to nonviolence that comes with him.

Since Leithart takes Yoder to be the prime representative of this position, I highlight three areas where Yoder's position differs from Leithart's portrayal. All three areas indicate that the real point of difference is not the fourth century but the first century.

Who Was Constantine?

For Yoder, Constantine is a key historical figure, but he is also a type. Yoder provides a succinct and clear summary of what he means by Constantine and the Constantinian shift:

> It is also a mistake to focus our interpretation of the change, as legend has done, on the man Constantine, as if he were the only major actor. Constantine was in fact a larger-than-life figure; the orders he gave did in fact reverse the course of history with regard to the place of Christianity in the empire. Yet his coming to be seen as a savior figure, as an inaugurator of the millennium, was not his work alone. He was decisively abetted by the mythmaking capacities both of popular culture and of Eusebius of Caesarea. Some of the systematic changes that Constantine as a mythic figure symbolizes for the historian (such as Christians' believing that God favored the empire against its enemies) had begun before he came along, and some (like the legal prohibition of the pagan cult or the persecution of Christian dissent) took a century after him to be worked through. So when his name is used as a mythic cipher it would be a mistake to concentrate on his biography.[2]

This quote helpfully highlights several points. First, any historical account of Constantine must refuse a punctualistic view of how change happened. Numerous factors were in play before and after Constantine, so to attribute too much to just one man ignores how history actually transpires.[3] Second, Leithart's aim of undermining Yoder's theology by focusing on

---

2. Yoder, "Primitivism in the Radical Reformation," 81–82.

3. For Yoder's account of how this shift was underway well before Constantine, see Yoder, *Jewish-Christian Schism Revisited*.

Constantine Revisited

Constantine alone misunderstands how Yoder uses Constantine. Yoder states at several points that he uses Constantine as a type in Christian history.[4] One could just as easily insert Ernst Troeltsch's "Church type" or the term "Christendom" in most places where one reads "Constantinianism" in Yoder's work, and little would change. Thus, the crux of Yoder and Leithart's debate is not Constantine, but Jesus. Leithart spends only about ten pages on his potential differences with Yoder regarding biblical interpretation and he interacts with no other exegetes. He does not substantially engage Yoder's own biblical work or the biblical scholars on whom Yoder depends and interacts, many of whom were the foremost biblical scholars of Yoder's day. So while this is where the real heart of the debate lies, Leithart unfortunately does not engage it very carefully.

Finally, Leithart's Constantine may, in the end, not be that much different than Yoder's. Despite his positive spin, Leithart also acknowledges Constantine's many shortcomings: he executed his wife and son (72); pagan symbolism never disappears from Constantine's propaganda but merges with Christian symbols (76); Christ is often merged with the sun god Sol (78); he had an intense ambition for personal power, territory, and glory; and he was willing to use brute force to attain his goals (96, 236). The problem here is not that Constantine cynically used Christianity, but that he was a sincere Christian who believed that this imperial behavior was somehow compatible with Christianity. Indeed, Leithart focuses on the question of Constantine's sincerity in a way that misses the point. A President who believes truly and sincerely that there is no incongruity between Christian discipleship and the current duties of the Commander-in-Chief is actually *more* worrying than a President who simply uses religion as a tool to appeal to voters. Pointing out that Constantine was a capable syncretist, merging Christianity with pagan imperial propaganda, or a capable civil religionist, merging Christianity with imperial ambition, seems to lend itself to Yoder's analysis of Constantinianism, which focuses not on the subjective sincerity of the parties involved but on the objective alteration of the Gospel in a way that renders it "compatible" with the exercise of violence and carnal power.

"Fall of the Church" Historiography

How should we interpret church history? On the matter of historiography, Leithart charges Yoder with simplistically going along with an Anabaptist

4. For example, see Yoder, *Priestly Kingdom*, 201 n. 3, and 209 n. 3.

"fall of the church" narrative. According to Leithart, the sixteenth-century narrative about Constantine is "fixed and foundational" to everything that Yoder does (319). Yoder's interpretation, on Leithart's reading, seems to be that God abandoned the church due to its Constantinianism. Or, in the words of William Cavanaugh's blurb on the back of the book, "the Holy Spirit did not simply go on holiday." Thus, Yoder's narrative not only castigates Constantine, but also "freezes time" in the first century (316 n. 20).

This interpretation of Yoder reads him through a pre-established and ready-made critique that magisterial Protestants have often thrown at the Anabaptist wing of the Reformation. But it does so at the expense of listening to what Yoder himself says on the topic.[5] Although Yoder does refer to the "fall of the church," he almost always does so in scare quotes to indicate that he is referring to a motif that Christians (and not just Protestant Christians) have used to highlight unfaithful developments in church history.[6] Leithart himself notes that many Christians—including Francis of Assisi, John Wycliffe, Jan Hus, Bernard of Clairvaux, and Dante—have also employed a "fall of the church" narrative, which indicates that this is not just a peculiar Anabaptist malady (306–307). To treat Yoder as though he is a precritical biblicist or naïve restitutionist ignores his numerous and nuanced discussions regarding church history, where Yoder consistently emphasizes two things: fidelity is possible and translation of the Gospel is necessary. Does history and language shift and move? Yes.[7] Does the Gospel need to cross boundaries and cultures? Of course; the Bible itself is evidence that the Gospel is always already in translation.[8] The question is not whether we will translate the Gospel literally and metaphorically. The question is whether we test that translation to see if we have rendered it faithfully in a new context. If faithfulness means anything, then infidelity does too. For Yoder, the biblical narrative (not Constantine) is fixed and foundational, and it reaches its apex in Jesus' rejection of violence and

---

5. For example, see Yoder, "Anabaptism and History" in *Priestly Kingdom*, 123–34; "Biblicism and the Church," 67–101; "Is There Historical Development of Theological Thought," in *Radical Ecumenicity*, 223–35; "Primitivism in the Radical Reformation," 74–97; "The Restitution of the Church: An Alternative Perspective on Christian History," in *Jewish-Christian Schism Revisited*, 133–43; and "Thinking Theologically from a Free Church Perspective," in *Doing Theology in Today's World*, 251–65.

6. Leithart (316 n. 21) refers to places where Yoder mentions the "fall of the church" in *The Royal Priesthood* and *Priestly Kingdom*. Upon examination, both of these references use scare quotes to show that Yoder is not using this term in a simplistic way (likewise with almost all Yoder's references in *Jewish-Christian Schism Revisited*).

7. See Yoder, *Priestly Kingdom*, 200 n. 7.

8. E.g., see Yoder, "'But We Do See Jesus?" in *Priestly Kingdom*, 46–62.

his embrace of the cross and resurrection as the inauguration of God's kingdom. Constantine should then be read in light of that Archimedean point rather than vice versa.

So where does the *real* difference between Yoder and Leithart lie? Both would agree that the church is peccable and fallible (331). Both would agree that God's presence and blessing can be withdrawn from some communities of the universal church. Leithart acknowledges that Yoder sees good things happening in the time between Constantine and the Reformation, so the difference cannot be, contrary to Cavanaugh's quip, that Yoder simply thinks that the Holy Spirit took a 1,200-year break from involvement with the church (321–323). Leithart regards this as an inconsistency on Yoder's part because he presumes that Yoder projects an absolutely downward trajectory from Constantine to the Reformation. So Yoder either made a glaring mistake by accidentally acknowledging the "good middle ages" at several points, or else he does not have the simplistic narrative of church history that Leithart presumes he does. A reading of Yoder's corpus as a whole lends toward the latter as the most plausible reading of his historiography. Thus, the real difference between Yoder and Leithart is not over whether or not the church is automatically faithful (it isn't) or whether history has to move (it does). The real difference is whether what happened with Constantine was a faithful iteration of the Gospel or not.

The End of Sacrifice

For Leithart, the most crucial change enacted by Constantine was the end of sacrifice. Since sacrifice was at the center of life and politics in Rome, Constantine's acts to abolish these practices constituted the de-sacralizing of Rome. Leithart contends that "every polity has been a sacrificial polity. We are not, and we have Constantine to thank for that" (329). This overreaches a bit and seems to give to Caesar what belongs to God, namely, the credit for ending sacrifice.

The most surprising thing about Leithart's "end of sacrifice" language is that he seems to unwittingly employ a split between religion and politics that he criticizes elsewhere. That is, he seems to think of a purely "religious" sacrifice of animals or oblations offered in the imperial cult that is disconnected from the political theology and practice of the empire (making his own stance "Lockean" in the sense he earlier criticizes). Elsewhere, however, Leithart underscores the inherently religious nature of warfare:

"War was no exercise of sheer power, no secular Realpolitik. War involved bloodshed, and bloodshed was always hedged about with ritualized taboos. Diocletian's force constituted a 'sacred retinue,' and Constantine would have thought of his army in the same way. Armies won by divine intervention, and the victory of an army was the victory of the army's god" (74). In other words, there is no such thing as secular warfare or a secular army, in part because "the *sacrifice* of barbarians and rebels maintained Roman honor" (236). The sacrifice necessary to maintain the Empire is not merely a religio-political ritual offered to a god or the emperor; it is the religio-political sacrifice of the enemy and the outsider offered up in the name of honor, peace, liberty, and justice. Therefore, to argue that sacrifice ceases with Constantine seems to have a truncated view of what counts as sacrifice.

Where Leithart's account of sacrifice falls back into a Lockean split between religion and politics, Yoder's does not. Yoder argues that when God allows for the taking of human life in the Old Testament (in Gen 9 or the holy wars of Joshua), it is not under the rubric of "legal" or "political" punishment but under the cultic category of sacrifice. Leithart's book would have been much more interesting had he engaged Yoder's reading of sacrifice in the light of the entire biblical narrative. For Yoder, the Bible sees both animal and human blood as sacred (Gen 9). All bloodshed is therefore either a proper or improper sacrifice because God owns the lifeblood of all living things. This is why the blood of animals is not to be eaten and why murder is such a heinous sin. Murder undoes the cosmos, so to speak, because it strikes down God's image-bearer.[9] So in the Old Testament, "the killing of a killer is not a civil, nonreligious matter. It is a sacrificial act. . . . If there is killing, the offense is a cosmic, ritual, religious evil, demanding ceremonial compensation."[10] God thus limits the human tendency to violence and vengeance by claiming all human blood as his own.

Further, to think of killing as sacrifice is conceptually useful, especially when we remember Augustine's point that the earthly city operates by sacrificing to false gods. Yoder also saw clearly the human propensity to offer up other persons as sacrifices to various causes, ideas, forces, and nations. The result, according to Yoder, is that "general labels like 'freedom'

---

9. Yoder, "Against the Death Penalty," in *The End of Sacrifice*, 128. Readers interested in Yoder's understanding of capital punishment, atonement, and sacrifice will find much of interest in this book.

10. Ibid., 127.

or 'justice,' 'socialism' or 'capitalism,' 'order' or 'humanism' become positive or negative values in their own right, causes to combat for or to destroy. The modern word for this is 'ideology.' The biblical word that fits best is probably 'idol.'"[11]

Given this understanding of sacrifice, the atonement becomes central to Yoder's political theology of war and the earthly city. Sin requires expiation, and "it is the clear testimony of the New Testament, especially of the Epistle to the Hebrews, that the ceremonial requirements of the Old Covenant find their end—both in the sense of fulfillment and in the sense of termination—in the high-priestly sacrifice of Christ."[12] Thus, the "death of Christ is the end of expiation."[13] Once sacrifice has been understood not just in the narrow Lockean "religious" sense but in this broad biblical way, it is clear that Constantine did not in fact end sacrifice inasmuch as he continued to persecute and kill his enemies, both inside and outside the empire. What is worse, the sign by which he conquered should have been understood as the sign that the sacrifice of enemies is no longer needed. Sacrifice ended with the cross, and the trans-territorial body politic that is the church needs to sacrifice no one to ensure its survival. Indeed, Yoder is the more thorough-going Augustinian here, for all violence follows in the steps of Cain and Romulus, both of whom assume that the good must be seized from the brother by violence rather than shared. This is why Constantine is more dangerous than Diocletian: one must live either by Cain's myth of scarcity and brother-sacrifice or by the new Abel, whose blood cries out to God on behalf of his brothers.[14] Since judgment begins with the household of God, the main problem is not the earthly city that runs by sacrificing the blood of its enemies and children; Christians should expect that pagans will generally act like pagans. What we should not expect or tolerate is the perpetuation of sacrifice—of the enemy, of our soldiers, of our children—as somehow compatible with the Christ who declared, "It is finished."

New Clothes

In baptism, we are asked to discard our old clothes and put on Christ. To Leithart's credit, he recounts how Constantine waited until the end of his

11. Yoder, "The Spirit of God and the Politics of Men," in *For the Nations*, 232.
12. Yoder, "Against the Death Penalty," in *End of Sacrifice*, 128.
13. Ibid.
14. Yoder, *He Came Preaching Peace*, 68.

life to exchange his purple imperial robes for his white baptismal clothes, exchanging his imperial power for sole devotion to God. Even Constantine saw a "basic incompatibility between being an emperor and being a Christian, between court and church, warfare and prayer, the purple and white" (300). Whatever rose-colored glasses Leithart employs in reading Constantine, this stark admission stands out as a profound point: if Constantine baptized Rome, it was not as a minister of the Gospel but as a servant of the empire. While some of the content of his civil and imperial religion may have changed, the form was basically the same. How different from Jesus, who submitted to baptism at the beginning of his reign, rejected kingship like the nations, took up the purple robes only with a thorny crown on his head, exposed and disarmed royal presumption on the cross, and offered himself rather than his enemies as a living sacrifice. Jesus' ascension is not in spite of, but because of how he wore the purple. In light of this king, Constantine appears a naked emperor bereft of his baptismal garb.

8 History and Figural Reading

Another Response to Leithart[1]

TIMOTHY J. FURRY

THE THEOLOGICAL SENSE ONE makes of Constantine the Great reflects deeply on other theological commitments. Beyond the simplistic judgments that Constantine's reign was obviously a regrettable fall or that Constantine was truly great, anyone interested in questions of theology, politics, and violence must attend carefully to the sweeping changes that he wrought. We are all fortunate that Peter Leithart has so ably taken up the task of tackling these difficult theological questions through his theo-historical argument in *Defending Constantine*. While Leithart's most specific targets are John Howard Yoder, Stanley Hauerwas, and their "increasing tribe," his presentation of Constantine has broader implications for our current political milieu where separation of church and state are taken for granted as obvious goods. In short, Leithart challenges Yoder's critique of Constantinianism—that is, the attempt by Christians to make

---

1. This essay is a revised version of a review published in the *Journal of Lutheran Ethics* 11 (Sept. 2011) [http://www.elca.org/What-We-Believe/Social-Issues/Journal-of-Lutheran-Ethics/Issues/September-2011/Review-of-Peter-Leitharts-Defending-Constantine.aspx]. The majority of the subsequent revisions in this essay are a direct result of Leithart's generous reply to that review also published in the same issue. I have foregone the section of my initial review that summarizes Leithart in order to focus on more central theological issues that Leithart raises in his text as well as in response to my review. Thus, the relationship between theology and history orients my entire response but does not result in a single linear argument for or against *Defending Constantine*. Instead, I seek to probe deeper into the issues that Leithart and his conversation partners raise and to push the conversation forward.

history turn out "right" by grasping the reins of power and by using violence to achieve their goals. Such means, Yoder contends, contradict the life and witness of the crucified Lamb.

We are in Leithart's debt for his insightful historical survey and summary in *Defending Constantine*, especially his argument that Constantine thought of himself as having converted to Christianity. Thus, after such a rich historical summary and exposition, Leithart's critique of Yoder's theology is surprisingly disappointing. The final chapter—devoted exclusively to Yoder—is the weakest part of Leithart's argument and overall splendid book.

One imprecision in Leithart's argument is evident in his account of Yoder. Leithart rightly understands the essential eschatological impulse of Yoder's pacifism and theology. He also understands that Yoder's historical thesis regarding Constantine is theological in nature. But he fails to recognize, or to grant, the more radical theological point: theology logically precedes historical inquiry for Yoder. In short, Yoder—rightly, I think—understood that every historical narration implies a theology. Yoder is just more explicit about the normative theological claims that animate and structure his historical argument. I think Leithart actually understands this, yet ambiguity remains. This is not necessarily an error; ambiguity seems the most accurate description. More importantly, it does not affect Leithart's overall case against Yoder. Regardless of their claims about the relationship of theology to history, I think both Yoder and Leithart know they cannot and should not "fudge" history. Just because history rests on non-historical grounds does not mean that every historical claim is valid. However, when Leithart implies that we must get our history right before we do theology, I think he misreads Yoder, since Yoder learned from Barth that theology is first philosophy.[2] At the very least, Leithart should engage Yoder on this theological level instead of simply presuming Yoder's error. Again, in my estimation, this does not require Yoder, or anyone else, to be "fideist" or to dismiss rigorous historical inquiry; only that the task of history is to hold theology accountable even as theology structures it. I think Leithart has done an outstanding job of holding Yoder's theology accountable to historical inquiry. Therefore, and despite this theological imprecision, Leithart's main point that Yoder's theology comes under judgment when it fails to account for all the complexity of the Constantinian shift has serious merit.

---

2. See, e.g., Leithart, *Defending Constantine*, 267.

Constantine Revisited

In responding to my initial criticism about the relationship between theology and history, Leithart argued,

> Furry claims that for Yoder theology is "first philosophy" and therefore "logically precedes historical inquiry" (12). I wonder if that is accurate. For myself, I do not say that theology "logically precedes" history, since Christian theology centers on the Son of God incarnate *in history*. If every historical account implies a theology, it is equally true that every theological account implies a history. Theology is not a foundation for an account of history; it *is* that account. In my reading, Yoder, Barthian that he was, worked with similar assumptions about the mutual embedding of history and theology.[3]

I agree with Leithart that theology and history belong together, and I did not mean to imply that history is a kind of second tier addition to theology.[4] Drawing on contemporary philosophy of language (e.g., Quine), the historical theorist Frank Ankersmit has distinguished between two levels in historical writing: description (speaking) and representation (speaking about speaking). Description admits empirical verification while representation does not. For example, historians can speak of the U.S. war for independence as a revolution, but not all historians do so. Marxist historians, for example, do not think of this war as a revolution because it lacks the essential aspect of class conflict. Historians can argue about the revolutionary character of the war, but they cannot appeal to empirical data to do so because how one defines a revolution cannot be reduced to empirical events. To be sure, empirical events impinge on the definition (e.g., an obvious change in political authority), but the definition cannot be *reduced* to those events. Moreover, how one defines such an event logically precedes the description of the event. That is, the Marxist historian brings her understanding of what constitutes a revolution to the empirical events under investigation.[5]

Thus, when I say that theology logically precedes history, I mean to make the finer philosophical point about how conceptual—and, in this

---

3. Leithart, "Response to Timothy J. Furry."

4. In what follows, I am summarizing the argument in Ankersmit, *Historical Representation*, 39–48.

5. Note that I have not cast description and representation onto an object vs. subject grid. That is, I am not claiming the descriptive moment in history writing is objective and the subjective representation. For more on this, see Ankersmit, *Historical Representation*, 75–103. Here, Ankersmit uses the language of objective and subjective but subverts its usual modern connotations.

case, theological—claims form and shape how we understand certain historical events.[6] Of course, the conceptual and the historical are always bound together and are distinguished only through abstraction; but they can, and, in fact, must, be distinguished even though historians do not write or say, "Now I am describing and now I am representing." Both happen simultaneously. An example from Leithart illustrates why this point is significant. It also addresses his rebuttal to my concern, shared by others, with his use of the label "Marcionite."

Always the rhetorician, and usually in delightful ways, Leithart sometimes overly indulges himself. For example, after narrating his theological politics from Scripture's own development from the Old Testament to the New, Leithart avers "unless one follows an almost Marcionite contrast of Old and New, the Old Testament remains normative for Christians. Though it is normative in a new covenant context, it is impossible to escape the fact Yahweh carried out his wars through an Israel armed with swords, spears, and smooth stones.[7] Leithart certainly knows how to raise the stakes! Here he directly implies that Yoder's reading of the Old and New Testaments—or that of any pacifist—is Marcionite and therefore heretical. However, in so doing he glosses over the important theological question: What does the normativity of the "old" covenant mean in the context of the new covenant? This is where he and Yoder disagree—not on the authority of the Old Testament, but on the relationship between the two covenants. Unsurprisingly, Leithart musters no evidence that Yoder is seeking to deny the authority of the Old Testament. Yet he slants the rhetoric so severely in his disagreement with Yoder that he implies heresy. To be fair, Yoder does call Constantinianism a heresy, so in one sense Leithart is simply continuing the rhetorical flare of his interlocutor. But I think that Leithart reads Yoder unfairly here and that both authors assume an unnecessary and excessive rhetorical posture.

Leithart actually concedes this rhetorical point. "Furry is not alone in charging that I bandy about the 'Marcionite' charge so recklessly that I knock vases and delicate figurines off the mantelpiece. The critics have a point."[8] Still, Leithart's understanding of the relationship between the

---

6. I have done more extensive work on this in my dissertation, *From Past to Present and Beyond: The Venerable Bede, Figural Exegesis, and Historical Theory*. A revised version is forthcoming with Pickwick Publications, an imprint of Wipf and Stock Publishers.

7. Leithart, *Defending Constantine*, 335–36.

8. Leithart, "Response."

Old Testament and the New Testament, which is the background for the discussion of Marcion, merits further exploration.

In his response to John Nugent's critique, both of which appeared in a special issue of *The Mennonite Quarterly Review* devoted to the *Defending Constantine*, Leithart makes a case that Israel and her governance assumed increasing responsibility throughout the Old Testament. He ultimately reads Constantine as part of this trajectory of increasing responsibility that began in the Old Testament and is fulfilled in the gospel.[9] In the same essay, Leithart notes perceptively that the issue between him and others is less about Constantine and more about the gospel and its historical trajectory. I think that is an accurate observation. Indeed, I want to press both Leithart and his interlocutors further and say that there is not only disagreement about the gospel and its more precise political implications, but also on the place of history itself in their theological arguments. In other words, my main disagreement with Leithart—and that of others as well—is about the role of history.

This disagreement is only rarely about the descriptive aspect of history—that is, discerning what actually happened. After all, most of the arguments between Leithart and others are not about the putative historical facts. Instead, the disagreement about history resides in how descriptions hang together and *re-present* the historical argument and biblical events. Moreover, sometimes this difference is about what counts as historical or about what constitutes history. For example, as noted above, for Marxists the American war for independence mentioned cannot even *count* as a revolution. The same happens in the discipline of history.

Leithart wants to use the image of YHWH as a warrior to link the Old Testament and the New Testament.[10] In fact, Leithart provocatively states that God's "goal in history is to train hands to fight" (333). To be sure, Leithart sketches the biblical trajectory from "the iron sword and fire that Joshua used to the sword and fire of the Spirit and the Word that Jesus uses to overwhelm his enemies" and make them into allies (335). Hence, Leithart sees here a kind of spiritualization (i.e., an allegorizing of sorts, to put it in terms of early Christian exegesis). In short, God begins with a literal sword and fire and ends with the spoken word and baptism in the Spirit. I want to suggest that the ancient practice of figural/allegorical reading could benefit this debate since both parties share a desire to read

---

9. See Leithart, "Defending *Defending Constantine*," 645–48.
10. Leithart, *Defending Constantine*, 333–37.

Scripture theologically and since I have not yet seen Leithart or any of his interlocutors explicitly engage such biblical readings.

One of Origen's rules for biblical interpretation, later adopted by most subsequent Christian interpreters, is that Scripture cannot be read in such a way as to speak inappropriately about God, including anthropomorphisms and immorality. Origen was concerned that Christians would make the biblical God out to be like other barbarian gods and deities.[11] Moreover,

> Unless those physical wars bore the figure of spiritual wars, I do not think the books of Jewish history would ever have been handed down by the apostles to the disciples of Christ, who came to teach peace, so that they could be read in the churches. For what good was that description of wars to those to whom Jesus says, "My peace I give to you; my peace I leave to you." [...] And in order for us to have examples of these spiritual wars from deeds of old, he wanted those narratives of exploits to be recited to us in church, so that if we are spiritual—hearing that "the law is spiritual"—"we may compare spiritual things with spiritual" in the things we hear.[12]

Note here that Origen does not deny that these wars happened. His point is that their significance or meaning for Christians is spiritual—they are figures of the spiritual warfare in which Christians are constantly engaging. In other words, we should read Origen as saying that the events happened, but God's instructions (e.g., Deuteronomy 7:2–6; Joshua 6:17–21) or the Israelites' justification of their killing by appeal to God in the Scriptures (e.g., Joshua 10:40) are signals for Christian readers that more is going in this passage than meets the (literal) eye.

"Consequently," Origen says, "the Word of God has arranged for certain stumbling-blocks, as it were, and hindrances and impossibilities to be inserted in the midst of the law and the history.... Sometimes a few words are inserted which in the bodily sense are not true, and at other times a

---

11. Origen, *On First Principles*, 4.2.1. (All subsequent quotations from *On First Principles* will be from the Greek text). See also how Origen treats passages where commands appears to defend indiscriminate killing: Origen, *Homilies on Joshua*, 138–56 (homilies 15 and 16). For another example of this, see how Origen treats incest and other sexually illicit acts by Patriarchs in the Old Testament in *On First Principles*, 4.2.2. On the reception of Origen's approach to reading Scripture, see de Lubac, *Medieval Exegesis*, 143–224.

12. Origen, *Homilies on Joshua*, 138 (homily 15).

Constantine Revisited

great number."[13] Could God's instructions and authorial justifications that invoke the divine command be such stumbling-blocks and hindrances? Interestingly, both Yoder and Leithart want to read these passages literally.[14] That is, they refer to historical events and occurrences, and that this is *how* the passages should be read by Christians. But Origen clearly did not think these events should be read in this way and instead opted to read them as primarily as an allegory or figuration of the Christian's fight against sin and the devil.

Up to this point I have used the terms "literal" and "historical" interchangeably.[15] However, these must be distinguished. Origen believed that not all the Scriptures have a bodily sense or historical referent. His rationale for this—namely, that the Christological center around which all Scripture moves—dictated in advance such a reading.[16] Therefore, what counts as historical language, that is what describes or refers to an actual event, must be interpreted in light of this christological stance. These passages from Joshua may refer to spiritual matters literally, but not historically (that is, bodily, in Origen's terms). Their primary referent is not to a physical event or occurrence at all but to the life of those who follow Jesus.

To recall Ankersmit, the christological "hermeneutic" is the representational aspect of history writing or for interpreting the literal sense of the Scripture in Origen. Since Jesus comes to bring peace and condemns violence and death, these passages, in order to remain consistent and in unity with Jesus and trinitarian theology, must be referring to something other than God telling the Israelites to indiscriminately kill their enemies whom Jesus later says to love. However, as Ankersmit argues, this representational aspect is essential to the historical task and cannot

---

13. Origen, *On First Principles*, 4.2.9.

14. For a summary of Yoder's reading on this, see Nugent, "The Politics of YHWH," 78. I take it to be evident from Leithart's own narration of Israel's wars in *Defending Constantine*, which I mentioned above, that this is how he would read it as well.

15. These are some works I find useful regarding the literal sense in the Christian tradition: Ayers, *Nicea and Its Legacy*, 32–33; Rogers, "How the Virtues of an Interpreter Presuppose and Perfect Hermeneutics: The Case of Thomas Aquinas," 64–81; Frei, "The 'Literal' Reading of Biblical Narrative in the Christian Tradition," 36–77; and Tanner, "Theology and the Plain Sense," 59–78. Specifically on Aquinas, see Johnson, "Another Look at the Plurality of the Literal Sense," 117–41.

16. See e.g., *On First Principles*, 4.1.6: "Now the light which was contained within the law of Moses, but was hidden away under a veil, shone forth at the advent of Jesus . . ." I think Yoder, Leithart, and Nugent all seek christological readings of Scripture, but how this is accomplished, both theologically and philosophically, is what I am seeking to highlight.

be eliminated.[17] Thus, when Origen, Leithart, Yoder, and Nugent disagree about how Scripture should be read, they are not only disagreeing about theology and the gospel, as Leithart notes. They are also disagreeing about history, specifically about the significance of Jesus and his teachings in and for history.

I will not speculate as to what Leithart and Nugent might think of Origen's reading that I have presented here. In truth, I am not certain about it myself—that is, whether or not Origen is right, though I admit I am very sympathetic. My point is show that Origen has certain conceptions about history and Scripture that shape his readings.[18] These representational components allow Origen to read Joshua in quite different ways than Leithart, Yoder, and Nugent. My suspicion is that the differences lie in their conceptions of the historical and literal sense of Scripture—and perhaps even in their understanding of the gospel as Leithart notes. I do think a conversation that engages some of these ancient Christian readings and thinkers would prove illuminating for what is stake theologically and historically in the debate regarding violence, peace, and Jesus in the biblical narrative.

At the end of *Defending Constantine*, I am also left wondering: Who is this argument for? The influence of Yoder and Hauerwas on younger theologians clearly concerns Leithart.[19] Is this book simply for them? If so, I wonder if Leithart has granted these theologians more influence than they actually possess. Do non-liberal Christian pacifists—or any pacifist for that matter—really occupy a position of power in our culture or in churches? I doubt it. However, the way Leithart focuses his attention so narrowly on Yoder makes his argument appear to be more provincial than necessary. Leithart's case would be more effective if he attacked more explicitly those contemporary versions of liberal politics that are glaringly inattentive to the complex history he so articulately narrates. As mentioned above, Leithart does soundly criticize the liberalism that comes from Locke, but thematizing this more explicitly would prove a more theologically germane task than his focus on Yoder. Although I am no Yoderian, given the current ecclesial conditions in America, I would be

---

17. Ankersmit, *Historical Representation*, 30–103.

18. The best treatment of Origen on history and the relationship between the literal and figural senses in Scriptural reading is Dawson, *Figural Reading and the Fashioning of Identity*.

19. Interestingly, Hauerwas gets named on occasion, but his work is never substantively addressed.

Constantine Revisited

thrilled to have throngs of Yoder's (and Hauerwas's) followers filling the ranks of the church in the United States.

Leithart tentatively agrees with me on this point regarding liberalism. Interestingly, he suggests that Hauerwas and Yoder are still liberals, despite their protestations against it. He, once again, provocatively and helpfully cuts right to the chase. "The choice," Leithart insists, "is between secular liberalism and some version of Christendom."[20] I do not think such a stark choice is the only option before us.

In his recent book, *A Brutal Unity: The Spiritual Politics of the Church*, Ephraim Radner argues against Cavanaugh and other anti-liberal pacifists to show the tensions inherent in making sense of Christians and violence.[21] Based on his own ministry in Africa and knowledge of the church in Africa, Radner argues that there is such a thing as religious violence and that the liberal state is a *limited* good. Both Yoder and Nugent would agree with Radner here in so far as both recognize how God has made use of humanity's sin and the sword to attain his purposes.[22] However, Radner wants to counter arguments that the Church was not deeply involved with the violence that followed the Reformation and the rise of the modern nation-state. Radner does not seek to diminish the role of the rising modern nation-state in the 16th and 17th centuries; instead, he argues that the Church was not simply relegated to the sidelines during the wars and outbreaks of violence in Europe in these centuries. On the level of ecclesial involvement is where Cavanaugh and Rader mainly differ, not that political machinations and power struggles had nothing to do with these violent times. In Radner's own summary of Cavanaugh's historico-theological thesis, "It is [Cavanaugh's argument] a kind of theodicy of abandonment: evil does not penetrate the sanctuary, because its embodiment lies in a world where faith cannot be said to determine action in a primary fashion."[23]

Radner makes several points against Cavanaugh, and I will briefly summarize two of them. First, using the work of Peter Biller he argues that there were preceeding words that functioned like "religion" in its reifying aspects prior to the 15th century (e.g. *lex*—in the sense of way of believing, *fides*, and *sectum*).[24] He marshals evidence from the writings

---

20. Leithart, "Response to Timothy J. Furry."
21. Radner, *Brutal Unity: The Spiritual Politics of the Church*.
22. Nugent, "Politics of YHWH," 78.
23. Radner, *Brutal Unity*, from the introduction to chapter 1.
24. See Biller, "Words and the Medieval Notion of 'Religion,'" 351–69.

of Sebastian Castellio on this score as well to show that some thinkers named religious violence as scandalous and not simply as an opportunity for ideology and political advancement. Second, Radner uses the work of Timothy Longman on the genocide in Rwanda to argue that there can be ostensible and empirical content to the description "religious violence."[25] In other words, Radner attempts to show that religious violence can be empirically discerned and described, which is directed towards Cavanaugh's empirical challenge to find som*ething* that can be called "religious violence." In Radner's argument, these two points, offered only in cursory fashion here, challenge views that the developing liberal state is inherently and completely anti-religion or Christian.

Ultimately, from Radner's view, the liberal state does result from Christians wielding violence against each other, albeit this is not the *only* cause, and it exists *because* of Christian unfaithfulness and disunity. Consequently, the liberal state has providentially appeared on the modern scene to punish and teach Christians who engaged in such tragic and sinful behavior. To argue otherwise, as Cavanaugh does, is to disenchant the world in problematic ways that leave the church and God untouched by violence and sin. Radner, who is no friend of liberalism, offers a wonderfully complex and enriching account of the disintegration of the Middle Ages and the formation of the liberal state in *theological and even figural* terms.[26]

Leithart, of course, cannot be faulted for failing to engage a text yet to be published when his own book went to press, but I raise Radner's argument here to draw Leithart's attention to it and elicit a response. I also want to put forth these provocations to suggest that liberalism, while perhaps quite problematic in numerous ways—and, as I acknowledged in my original review, perhaps even the biggest cultural and political challenge Christians in America face—is not utterly godless. That is, ontologically speaking, there can be no secular even in the putatively secular world we inhabit. No matter how hard humans try, we cannot get God out of the world or create a space where God is not at work and present. I would be shocked if Leithart would disagree with this point (or Yoder or Hauerwas for that matter). However, it would be helpful if he would nuance this more specifically in regard to the liberal state we currently inhabit. After all, he

---

25. See Longman, *Christianity and Genocide in Rwanda*.

26. I want to thank Ephraim for sending me a few of the chapters prior to their publication, some of which he initially presented for a colloquium at the University of Dayton in September 2011.

does such a good job complicating the older, overly simplistic, narratives regarding Constantine and the putative fall of the church. Without such an account, I worry that Leithart (and others) unintentionally perpetuate such a extreme position, despite their protesting to the contrary, insofar as they describe the liberal state in such polemic terms without regard for its historical and theological origins. In other words, and to turn the question back on Leithart, who is the secular liberal? The one who argues that liberalism is godless, or the one who discerns God's providential work in its midst, despite all its problems and prejudices against "religion"?

As I stated in the beginning, how one makes theological sense of Constantine is deeply rooted in other theological commitments. As Leithart and other have noted, it also reveals historical commitments. To be sure, theology and history are not identical, but they are entangled in ways that frequently make it difficult to discern where one ends and one begins. Such fluid boundaries, I have tried to suggest through Ankersmit, however briefly, are not simply indicative of the truth of Christianity but inherent in the practice and writing of history itself. Consequently, figural readings of Scripture, that many in this debate read in strictly literal ways, could open up new and productive avenues in this debate both theologically and historically.

9   Leithart's *Defending Constantine*

A Review[1]

Charles M. Collier

In *Defending Constantine*—a book as polemical as it is enjoyable—Peter J. Leithart admits that Constantine the Great was capable of tremendous brutality: he was "responsible for the deaths of his father-in-law Maximian, his brother-in-law Maxentius, another brother-in-law Licinius along with his son, his wife Fausta and his son Crispus, and a few other relatives" (304). Moreover, "Many of his decrees suggest a horror show" (199); for example, "he threatened death to anyone who possessed a copy of Arius's writings and failed to burn them" (168).

Leithart also admits that the late Mennonite theologian John Howard Yoder presented a critique of Constantinianism with formidable strengths: it has the power to "explain a great deal about the history of the church and the West," to reveal "the bonds between foundational theological grids . . . , conceptions of church-state relations, theological method, and the social location of the church," and to challenge myriad aspects of Christianity that are "so familiar, and so wrong" (316).

That these admissions of the brutality of Constantine and the incisiveness of Yoder appear in a book *defending Constantine against Yoder* is a testimony to the honesty and seriousness of Peter Leithart; that the book manages largely to succeed in its aim is a testimony to the same's considerable genius. And Leithart is abundantly clear that this work is as much

---

1. An earlier version of this review was first published in the Spring 2013 issue of *Pro Ecclesia*, and is reprinted here by permission of the editors.

Constantine Revisited

about John Howard Yoder and the future of Christian political theology (see esp. 10–11 and 305–6) as it is about what actually happened in and through the life of the first Christian emperor. Leithart defends Constantine from Yoder's critique and from those who follow in Yoder's wake.

As one of those followers it is tempting to respond to Leithart in kind—by defending Yoder against Leithart. Reasons can be found for doing so. For example, Leithart opens the book with a tendentious and facile association of Yoder's (and Stanley Hauerwas's) theologically sophisticated critique of Constantinianism with the pop-cultural conspiracy theorizing of Dan Brown and the liberal-Catholic, baby-out-with-the-bathwater approach of historian James Carroll (9). Leithart surely knows that the works of Brown and Carroll are underwritten by the very Whig view of history—i.e., interpreting historical events as the steady march of progress from *their* darkened past into *our* enlightened present—that Yoder decisively rejected as itself a modern iteration of the Constantinian habit of reading history from the perspective of the victors.

Yet responding to Leithart in a defensive posture would be a mistake, for Leithart has not only read Yoder carefully and sympathetically (see esp. 175–76 and 309–16)—a rare achievement among Yoder's detractors—he has also subjected Yoder to the scrutiny of Yoder's own, avowedly non-Constantinian convictions about taking history seriously (see esp. 317–21). Leithart's critique is in key respects Yoderian, and for that reason alone *Defending Constantine* should be received as one of the most important tributes to Yoder to date. The book honors Yoder's deepest convictions by inviting his followers to let go of a major, problematic aspect of Yoder's historical narration. Furthermore, Leithart goes beyond critique to positively commend Yoder's critical contribution to contemporary theology and ethics (e.g., his importance for contemporary just war reflection [see n. 1 on 255] as well as his vision for a contemporary Christian diasporic engagement with "the powers that be" [295]).

Even Leithart's description of the critical task he sets for himself in *Defending Contantine* is reminiscent of Yoder, who in *The Politics of Jesus* claimed to be doing nothing more than bringing important revisionist implications from professional historical scholarship to the much-needed attention of theologians and ethicists. Leithart thus sets Yoder against Yoder, turning the tables by demonstrating that one "standard view" in need of toppling was propagated by Yoder himself. Indeed, the book culminates with Leithart harnessing the careful historical work of chapters 1 through 11 to denounce, in chapters 12–14, the Constantinianism (!) of Yoder's Anabaptist-inspired narrative of the fall of the church (see esp. 317–21).

It is Yoder's declension narrative that Leithart most skillfully attacks, and he does so with a dazzling array of primary and secondary sources. Leithart argues persuasively that Yoder's narrative of the fall of the church presupposes a purity and uniformity to early Christian history on the question of war and peace that cannot be substantiated: to the contrary, "the story of the church and war is ambiguity before Constantine, ambiguity after, ambiguity right to the present" (278). Yoder's "fall narrative" thus amounts to a simplification of history that, despite Yoder's own polemic against doing so, creates a "handle on history" by which Yoder attempted effectively to push contemporary Christians in his preferred ethical and ecclesial direction.

Yet Leithart begins not with Constantine but with the church's preceding experience of martyrdom at the hands of the emperor Diocletian, who, Leithart suggests, was troubled by the failure of traditional sacrifice to produce desired results (16). These two themes of martyrdom and sacrifice are crucial for the book, for Leithart wants readers to imagine the relief fourth-century Christians must have felt when Constantine put an end to persecution, and also to appreciate the contemporary political-theological significance of Constantine's "desacrificing" of Rome.

I have emphasized the book's engagement with Yoder for two reasons. First, it *is* the central aim of the work, and second, I'm less competent to judge the adequacy of the historical reenactments of the first eleven chapters. However, as that historical narration sets the stage for a critique of Yoder's failed historical narration, the judgments of historians will be important to receive. Leithart does not shy away from providing clear answers to what he calls "the traditional 'Constantinian questions'" (9). Constantine's Milvian bridge conversion was probably the result of two events, not one, and the vision probably had to do with a meteorological occurrence. Yet this really was a sign from the Christian God, and Constantine really did take on, if not baptism at first, the name and substance of Christian faith (ch. 4). Indeed, Constantine was a missional (88) and "Lactantian" Christian (110) whose public building campaigns baptized public space without directly outlawing paganism (125). His alleged dominating role in the Council of Nicea is a myth that covers over his genuine achievement in skillfully assisting the reaching of near unanimity on Trinitarian orthodoxy by a large and unruly group of bishops (168–70). He reformed Roman law "in a Christian direction" (201 and esp. 212–32), helped undermine some sexist and elitist elements in Roman family life (204–7), and worked to protect both the weak and animals from senseless,

Constantine Revisited

if traditional, predation (208–9). All things considered, Constantine showed us what good Christian government looks like (201).

Returning to the theme of sacrifice, Leithart's claim that Constantine desacrificed Rome is among the most interesting in the book, and we can only hope Leithart will develop it in subsequent works. Yet there are strains in the argument. For example, we are told that the desacrificial polity enacted by Constantine "has remained in place to the present" (328). Yet not twenty pages later, Leithart claims that modern states have become "resacrificialized." A charitable interpretation, keeping in view Leithart's treatment of Rome's baptism by Constantine (see ch. 14), would see this resacrificialization not as a contradiction but as the adult backsliding from the once-and-for-all baptism of the infant Christendom. Modern apostate nations are being invited by Leithart to rejoin the fold, to renew their baptismal vows.

But the metaphor of "backsliding" suggests its own declension narrative, and one that Leithart himself might have to rethink. The desacrificing that Constantine allegedly effected with the baptism of Rome manifestly did not extend to a refusal to shed human blood in wars and judicial punishment, and, aware of this, Leithart also rejects Yoder's nonviolence—a position Leithart tacitly acknowledges is distinct from Yoder's fall-of-the-church narrative. Yet Leithart's reflections about the desacrificing of Rome are suggestive for followers of Yoder because they open up a line of convergence with Yoder's interpretation of the person and work of Christ. In Yoder's writings, and even more in Stanley Hauerwas's recent work, to speak of Christian "nonviolence" just is to speak of the end of sacrifice, for the crucifixion of Jesus was the blood sacrifice to end all blood sacrifice. If Yoder and Hauerwas are right about this, Constantine's effort to desacrifice Rome was inadequate from the start.

Leithart is aware of the importance of Yoder's christology. One has to wait for the recognition until the end of the book, but Leithart finally makes it clear that the most important question is not, "Did Yoder get Constantine right?" but rather, "Did he get Jesus right?" Defeating Yoder's fall-of-the-church narrative might win for Leithart a battle, but the larger war is lost if Yoder is right about Jesus (333), for whom "kenosis is the very form of his lordship" (315).

And yet here is where Leithart mounts an uncharacteristically weak response. He offers up several pages about the centrality of war to the entire biblical narrative (333–36)—as if this constitutes any sort of lesson or corrective to the author of "God Will Fight for Us" and "The War of the

Lamb."[2] Moreover, in response to Yoder's insistence that the cross and not the sword is the way in which Christians participate in the Lamb's militant victory, Leithart offers a disappointing appeal to Augustine. He reminds us that Augustine believed that violent war is waged for the sake of peace, not the other way around. True enough, but Augustine, a eudaemonist, thought everything, even evil, was done for the sake of peace (see Augustine *City of God* 19.12–13). Lies are told for the sake of peace, Augustine would have conceded, and yet lying was strictly prohibited. Clearly, a eudaemonist framework doesn't itself yield the theological criterion by which acts are judged. The Word made flesh provides the decisive criterion, for Augustine as for Yoder; and Augustine sees that justifying the lie would make this criterion unreliable. Could God have lied to us in speaking the Word that became Jesus? In rejecting the lie, Augustine reinforces the very christological reliability that Yoder depends upon for his renunciation of violence. Nothing Leithart has to say in this book shows us why Yoder was wrong about his critique of violence in light of that criterion.

This is a real weakness in an otherwise compelling book. It's also a weakness that will likely generate additional interesting work. For anyone as honest, serious, and smart as Peter Leithart is is unlikely to rest on weak arguments for long. When it comes to celebrating the Lamb's nonviolent victory over the powers, the messianic community can use all the help it can get. The help of one formidable scholar, teacher, and preacher is, whatever else he might think, not that far away.

---

2. See Yoder, *Politics of Jesus*, chs. 4 and 12.

10   Is There a Christian Ethic for Emperors?

CRAIG HOVEY

PETER LEITHART LIKES A good fight. Jesus may have been meek and mild, but it seems that, for Leithart, that was just a passing phase. Jesus brings a sword, relentlessly attacking evil, bringing judgment, and overthrowing the prince of this world.[1] He reveals to us a God who is perfectly at ease deceiving his enemies, and does not hesitate to lead them into traps. "He is not a God who plays softball," writes Leithart. "He is a warrior who fights to win, and deception is part of his art of holy war."[2] The macho Jesus and the new breed of American muscular Christianity opposes any wimpy compromise with the modern spirit. Moreover, Leithart believes the church ought to follow God in this.[3] The theologian John Milbank (Leithart's doctoral supervisor) recently also defended tough-guy Jesus by appealing to Christ's many offices, observing that "in the end it is Christ's kingly role which is eternal, and not his mediating priestly role."[4]

In taking up themes like these, one quickly notices that Leithart's biography of Constantine is also a defense of larger theological positions.

---

1. Leithart, 1&2 Kings, 139.
2. Ibid., 163–64.
3. Recently, the home page of New Saint Andrews College where Leithart teaches displayed a slogan inviting secularism to a tussle in a back alley.
4. Milbank, "Power is Necessary for Peace." My reply is to point out that God was *always* to fulfill the Israelite office of king and, as long as he was faithfully confessed by the people as such, Israel had no need for other kings. Likewise, might not the power of Christ's kingship be an alternative to human sovereign power rather than its justification?

Indeed, Leithart admits that *Defending Constantine* is intentionally polemical. He is not just addressing the past, but also the present. He promises another book that will specifically tackle contemporary questions about the American empire and whether Christians can learn anything from the life of Constantine about a genuinely Christian response to the wars in Iraq and Afghanistan (11–12).[5] Constantine looms large in history for many reasons, but the painful questions that American Christians are asking in the present about their own nation are among the most interesting, both for Leithart and his supposed readership. Clearly, Leithart is not opposed to polemics—he just wants us to be honest in how we carry them out.

It is clear that Constantine does not have many contemporary defenders. Those who advocate separating church and state often find him to be the first and most noteworthy champion of uniting them; he is accused of abandoning the gospel of Jesus for the sake of political and military expediency; he is indicted for conflating what is good for the empire with what is good for the church; he is denounced for interfering heavy-handedly in church affairs and serious theological debates; and his personal devotion to the Christian faith is questioned as being either cynical or doubtful. Aware of the many ways that Constantine has been made into a whipping-boy for these ills and more, Leithart considers the immediate problem to be one of details—of giving an account of this man's life with sufficient care. "Without detailed attention to the details of history, political theology becomes perfectionistic. Relative judgments . . . give way to absolute, global, often ill-informed polemics against a Constantine who has become more an idea than a man" (29).

My question—Is there a Christian ethic for emperors?—is intended to get at the heart of one of the main concerns Leithart has with those whom he calls the "theological critics of Constantine" (28). A standard response, one that Leithart thinks is far too simple, is to say that if there is indeed a Christian ethic for emperors, it is only because there is a Christian ethic for everyone. Jesus does not give emperors any special passes or allowances. They are bound by the same ethic as any other Christian. The flip side of this argument, while possibly a challenge for those in power, is actually good news: even emperors can be disciples. Like Peter, I earned my doctorate from Cambridge. While living in England and taking part in the liturgies of the Church of England, I found myself repeatedly praying "God save the queen," something that feels a little odd as an American. But

---

5. Leithart, *Defending Constantine*. Page references will appear in the text.

even the queen needs to be saved—and she cannot save herself. If this is all that is entailed in saying that there is no separate ethic for emperors, then there is probably little to discuss.

But of course there is more to it. We cannot ignore the emperor's job description or the duties performed in the office of emperor by focusing only on the person. Here Leithart thinks there is plenty in Christian teaching that can and should guide those who hold political power. As much as any other Christian, a Christian ruler ought to seek justice and mercy, turn the other cheek, love his enemies, and lay down his life for others (338–339).

Leithart consistently reprimands John Howard Yoder for promulgating what he regards as overly simple and abstract characterizations of historical realities regarding the possibility of a Christian ethic for emperors. Yoder claims, for example, that post-Constantinian Christians had to reach back to Cicero to come up with an "ethic for officials and rulers, since Jesus offered little guidance on the subject (not expecting his followers to be in charge)." Yoder's pacifism, Leithart continues, "blinds him and keeps him from seeing that the whole of Jesus' teaching and activity is abundantly instructive to rulers. . . . [Rulers are taught] to rule like Jesus" (338). Leithart does not settle the historical question of exactly where these Christians found their ethic, but he clearly reads Constantine much more generously as a genuine Christian who contemplated the Gospel to help guide his rule.

All this gives rise to some interrelated questions that I explore here in brief. Is there a significant difference between saying there is no separate ethic for rulers and saying that rulers cannot learn anything from Jesus? Yoder assumes that a ruler who follows a Christian ethic will incur serious, even grave, losses as a ruler.[6] What would this say about power if it were true? What should Christians conclude, if anything, from the fact that Jesus died a victim of sovereign power? If the normal experience of Christians is to be like Jesus'—facing hostile sovereign power rather than exercising it—does this rule out more licit forms of power, such as good governments? Available space prevents me from doing full justice to any of these questions. But they do provoke some thoughts that are as often in line with Leithart's own as they are against them.

---

6. "It might happen that he would be killed: but most Caesars are killed anyway." Yoder, *Priestly Kingdom*, 146.

Power, Rule, and Violence

To begin with, what instruction should a ruler take from the Gospel about how to rule? This question is acute if, like Yoder, one concludes that the Gospel requires Christians to be nonviolent. A truly Christian emperor is welcome to try being nonviolent. But if that effort does not go well, should he reject the nonviolent Gospel ethic in favor of another one? This has very often been the response of Christian rulers who have found themselves in that kind of situation. For a twentieth-century ethicist like Yoder, the clear example of someone who thought this way was Reinhold Niebuhr. Closer to our own time are the responses of some Christian academics who wanted to retool just war theory's immunity for noncombatants after 9/11 when it appeared too restrictive of U.S. military interventions in the face of potential terrorists.[7]

Thus, Yoder writes:

> I am not arguing that the Christian must avoid being in a position of power, nor that there is nothing to say about how rulers behave. . . . What I reject is (a) considering the ruler as the primordial mover of history, and (b) modifying the content of moral obligation in order to approve of the ruler's doing things which would be wrong for others.[8]

Yoder's main complaint about the possibility of a Christian emperor has to do with the ways that ethics for emperors has set the agenda for public theology and social ethics generally, particularly when it uses the language of "realism." Here the emperor is, for Yoder, merely a cipher for gaps in Christian thinking about power and politics. But if Constantine, in Yoder's account, is merely (or mostly) a trope, as Leithart accuses, it is because Yoder is responding to a series of moves that are just as abstract and ahistorical. Ironically, the questions that Christian realism asks are not generally concrete or historically contingent. Instead, they tend to be normative hermeneutical questions about how, for example, Christians ought to understand Jesus' teaching about loving enemies—a teaching

---

7. So George Weigel insists that while just war is not obsolete, it must be updated: "What we must do, in this generation, is to retrieve and develop the just war tradition to take account of the new political and technological realities of the twenty-first century. September 11, what has followed, and what lies ahead, have demonstrated just how urgent that task is." Weigel, "Moral Clarity in a Time of War," 20–27.

8. Yoder, "Ethics and Eschatology," 127 n. 12.

Constantine Revisited

potentially so obviously at odds with the actions rulers will find necessary, that realists conclude there simply must be another interpretation.[9]

Relating this to a slightly different discourse, Yoder is concerned with what Noam Chomsky calls the *principle of universality*: if it is wrong for others to torture political dissidents or to support the overthrow of democratically elected leaders, then it is wrong for us (Americans) as well.[10] The transcendent aims of America, so routinely invoked throughout its history, function the same as the special calling emperors use to justify the exceptional nature of their ethical decisions. As a result, the perceived reality that "so much is at stake" trumps everything else. America, like any other empire—including banks, those neo-imperial strongholds—is given a pass because it is "too big to fail."

I think Leithart is right to show us that, in Constantine's case, we do not have a simple replacement of one normativity by another: for example, military might in the aid of transcendent purposes replacing the Gospel's inherent (or perhaps implicit) nonviolence. Nor was the early Christian refusal of military service identical with the pacifism of contemporary Christianity as we know it (a point Leithart argues at length). Instead, the question about the *separateness* of an ethic for emperors arises when an imperial self-perception collapses the fate of the church into something much more narrow—albeit more urgently and palpably felt—namely, the future security, prosperity, and survival of the nation.

It is true, as Leithart charges, that Augustine sought to separate what the latter thought never should have been joined in the first place. I suspect that when political theologians clumsily lump Augustine in with the "Constantinians" it is because, in reaching for a category to describe the church's increased invisibility, Augustine in his effort to rescue it for God's eternal city seems to be conceding to the very forces that made the church invisible. Almost always overlooked are the salutary effects the Gospel is having on the wider society, whether directly through top-down sovereign mechanisms or by a more general leavening.[11] Yoder calls attention to the

---

9. "Making the ruler the prototypic moral decider . . . is part of the Constantinian legacy to which our culture is heir." Yoder, "'Patience' as Method in Moral Reasoning," i, 37.

10. Chomsky, *Failed States*, 81–88.

11. To give just one example: while the many successes of nonviolent political movements are often cited as evidence of their inherent goodness, others have argued that they tend to work only when the enemy culture has within it a history of embracing notions like justice, compassion, and human rights. Gandhi succeeded against the British where the demonstrations at Tiananmen Square failed. Then again, as Yoder

way that the "progressive limitation of killing by the state (apart from the problem of war)," particularly related to capital punishment, is one way that Christianity has had an indirect influence.[12] Scores more could easily be enumerated.

If one possible response is to reach for a new normative ethic when the Gospel's nonviolence does not suit the emperor's calling as an emperor, another response is to conclude that there is something *inherently* mistaken about Christians trying to occupy certain offices that seem to require reaching for another ethic. In practice, there probably would be something wrong with this—the offices seem so overwhelmingly to justify themselves according to another ethic. But nothing *actually requires* a Christian emperor, when the pressure is on, to abandon the way of Jesus for the sake of the empire rather than vice versa. One of Leithart's examples of how this might happen, while not exactly nonviolent—he has us imagine an emperor charging first in battle—is still a way of the emperor sacrificing his "political future and his reputation, for the sake of righteousness" (339). Yet I wonder whether we would still conclude this if a ruler's commitment to loving enemies were more thoroughgoing. Could we imagine a government whose commitment to truth-telling surpassed its commitment to secrecy? At the very least, such a government would not produce WikiLeaks as its obvious inverse. And why should Christians gauge such things, as Milbank does, according to our own survival?

> [P]erhaps the most uncomfortable historical fact for contemporary Christians is the debt we owe to kings. Should Charles Martel in the face of the Muslims or Alfred of Wessex in the face of the pagans simply have laid down their swords? If one feels that that would have ensured their salvation then one has to add that it would also have apparently rendered impossible our own within the course of historical time.[13]

---

argues, Gandhi refused to call himself a Christian because to him it meant empire, something for which Yoder indicts Constantine.—Yoder, *The Royal Priesthood*, 260. If future Christians judge that Gandhi was nevertheless following Jesus (which Yoder thinks is a better question than whether he was a Christian), then we should not only ask with Yoder, "Which Jesus?" but also wonder what to say about a Christian reality that simultaneously, when present among the British, allowed Gandhi's movement to succeed while also making it difficult for Gandhi himself to recognize Christianity in his own nonviolence.

12. Yoder, *Christian and Capital Punishment*, 13.
13. Milbank, "Power is Necessary for Peace."

I find this a startling thing to suggest, particularly as it risks rendering impossible not only Christian martyrdom but also the cross. Or is Milbank saying that a Christian must weigh the relative worth of his own life—whether he is a king as opposed to a commoner—and its importance for the survival of others before deciding whether to fight or to die a martyr's death?

To be sure, power takes many forms. It is very difficult to make a stark contrast between "power" and "nonpower," and Leithart has done us a great service in complicating our temptation to think that there is a single and crystal clear thing as "power" or even "sovereign power." All sides have frequently fallen headlong into this temptation. On the one hand, there have been great prophets like Marx who warned us of the dangers of ideology and the abuses of all power; on the other are those who tout what is licit about some kinds of sovereignty over against others. Yet both can be seen as ideological mirror images of the other, subverted by Foucault and friends whose warning is much more severe and haunting: power is not obvious. And precisely when it seems obvious—as when an emperor marches into battle under the sign of the cross of Christ—we are most likely to be blind to the many other ways that power is being exercised in unexpected places.

Yoder was aware of this and, at his best, resisted defining things like "power" once and for all.[14] Once we have done that, we permit ourselves to stop looking for its new expressions. It is certain that the obvious forms of sovereign power are the low-hanging fruit for any critique of violence. But while they therefore ought to be addressed, it is crucial that we not stop with them.

One danger, especially pronounced with the most obvious forms of sovereignty, is how they can skew the ways Christians view the historic significance of events. For example, I like to invite students to think about how they imagine Jesus will return. Given Jesus' own warnings about being attentive to the signs of the times, it seems that we ought to be cultivating the kind of vision that looks for God's presence and activity in unexpected places. So I ask students to imagine Jesus returning in Tijuana. Would we

---

14. Instead, Yoder saw that power and violence are often bound up with epistemology, in which cases the antidote is not so much *peace* as the *patience* needed to await categories for debate that are not now available. Such patience is identical with what is needed when confronted with an "absolute" conception of anything, including power, peace, and violence. See Yoder, "'Patience' as Method in Moral Reasoning," esp. 24–35.

see it? Are we paying attention to Tijuana? To paraphrase Nathanael's guile from John's Gospel (1:46): "Can anything good come from Tijuana?"

The obvious forms of sovereignty play to our desire to be clearly on the winning side of things. Milbank's suggestion that we partially owe our salvation to the willingness of Christian kings to kill falls into this way of thinking. Some are actually privileged by being on the winning side, while others grasp for their share. Liberation and sovereign executive power, while by no means morally equivalent, at least share this.[15] Of course Christianity speaks of victories too, but the paradigm victory is the cross, which is manifestly a *defeat* just about any way you look at it. The fact that God vindicates Christ in the resurrection is either against all sovereign power, however conceived, or against historically contingent ones such as pagan Rome. What kinds of power must be relativized in order to see Jesus coming to Tijuana?[16] Christ has not defeated all power, obviously, since his victory is won with power. But what kind of principle for political theology will guide our discovering Jesus among the poor?[17]

We Are All Infants

One of Leithart's most memorable refrains is that every baptism is an infant baptism (324, 341). He means this as a metaphor, drawing attention to the many ways that a baptism marks setting out on a journey as much as it marks an arrival. It is as much a confession of one's inability to believe as it is a confident and certain declaration. In the same way, in Leithart's telling of the story, something serious and genuine happened when Rome under Constantine was made to turn away from being a political order dependent on sacrifice—away from bondage to the elemental spirits about which St. Paul talks. To claim that Constantine "merely" granted Christian approval to something abstract like the pagan celebration of military power is far more ideological than is warranted historically. But

---

15. This is what Yoder means by employing his typology of neo-forms of Constantinianism. See his "Christ, the Hope of the World," in *Royal Priesthood*, 192–218.

16. Yoder again: "Instead of asking, 'What is God doing in the world?' the church should ask, 'How can we distinguish, in the midst of all the things that are going on in the world, where and how God is at work?'" *Royal Priesthood*, 203. Could it be that an inherent aspect of sovereignty is the pressure it exerts against this kind of discernment?

17. At its best, this is precisely what liberation theology seeks to do. But there remains to my mind a question about the normativity of the *anawim* (the poor) existence for this discernment for disclosing something inherent in the Gospel itself or primarily for the sake of political change.

neither was the "baptism" of Rome (one way that Leithart describes the pro-Christian changes that Constantine brought to the empire) a mature believer's baptism. Leithart cautions against perfectionism since we always act in the middle of things and prior to all of those other things that we are not very good at anticipating. We never act out of mastery of the past because the past is never really done with us.[18] One value of history is that in studying it, we are reminded that we are also always in the middle of unfolding events. If we can make any sense of the past, then just as surely others will come after us and try to make sense of what we cannot. Leithart urges that being fair to Constantine at least involves recognizing those things of which he himself was in the middle, as well as acknowledging the desperation of Christians whose courage under persecution for the first time seemed to be vindicated.

Leithart may be right that Yoder has set the ethical bar so high that he has no patience for "the interim"—this "middle time" in which we fervently pray for forgiveness and grieve over the ways that the Kingdom is not yet a full reality—and so is only able to label Constantine apostate (341–342). But I think we might still uncover a profound agreement between Leithart and Yoder. If, as Leithart insists, every baptism is an infant baptism, this is because in undergoing it, we are opening ourselves to a future that is not finally ours to determine. When a Christian unites himself with the body of Christ in baptism, he is joining the history of the Son of God, whose future will be the Christian's own future. Baptism is not only a death, but a resurrection into what is, in many ways, unknown and mysterious. It is a promise to be something in the future that I cannot know based solely on my past. Leithart may therefore be right to suggest that a believers church ecclesiology is, in practice, vulnerable to contradicting its own counsel that Christians ought to restrain their obsession with managing the course of history. If my baptism is part of the history of Christ in the world then my baptismal confession may confess my ignorance as much as my sincere belief.

Even so, in opening myself to a future that is truly Christ's own, I become dependent on others—notably in the church, though not exclusively—to show me how this really is the case. One thinks of the sixteenth-century Anabaptist conviction that, through baptism, they became subject to fraternal correction. But much of this correction and sense-making will

---

18. Constantine's own deathbed baptism is ironically a problem for the precise reason that many find him to be a convenient stand-in for everything that is wrong about the church's accommodation to culture and the wedding of Christianity with secular and military power—or, anachronistically, with the sword.

need to happen in the distant future. After all, unlike my biological future, the future of the risen Christ is everlasting. This means that future generations may have things to say about the meaning of my life as they discern how it is bound up with Christ's. Now, it is also entirely possible that future generations may actually have nothing whatsoever to say about my life. The point is that all Christians, Constantine included, are indeed infants in a much larger story and therefore will not necessarily be the best interpreters of the meaning of their existence. It is certainly damning for future Christians to come along and say, "What you thought was faithful turned out to be a disaster for the West and its victims." Such judgments may be more or less true, more or less careful—but they should not be ruled out. The corollary of every Christian's infancy is the hope that the church will on occasion reach maturity on some things.

Maybe Constantine is not a heretic. But if he is, it is *because* he tried so hard to be a Christian emperor, not despite the fact.[19] By simply becoming a Christian he made himself vulnerable to the future judgments of the church. Before Constantine, no one knew what being a Christian emperor would entail. His was an infant political theology in some respects even while, as Leithart argues, it brought to a certain maturity the victory of Christ over the principalities and powers. And yet, had not Christians for a few centuries already been inhabiting this victory?

The End of Sacrifice

Leithart counts on pacifists being squeamish of the Bible's violence, particularly in the Old Testament (335–36). His challenge seems to be: prove that you are not a Marcionite by facing up to the military stories and images the Bible presents. He even makes the startling claim that "the Bible is from beginning to end a story of war" (333).

---

19. In one instance, Yoder describes the shift inaugurated by Constantine as "the confusion between the Good News and the establishment for which the son of Constantius Chlorus and a Serbian barmaid was partly the agent, partly the beneficiary, and mostly the symbol." Yoder, "Is There Such a Thing as Being Ready for Another Millennium?" 65. Yoder elsewhere emphasizes the symbolic character of "Constantine" for his theological purposes: "I here use the name of Constantine merely as a label for this transformation [the fusion of church and world], which began before A.D. 200 and took over 200 years; the use of his name does not mean an evaluation of his person or work." *Royal Priesthood*, 57. On his blog (leithart.com), Leithart argues against Craig Carter, an interpreter of Yoder who is deeply sympathetic, that Yoder in fact *does* try to make a historical case for Constantinianism.

Constantine Revisited

Let us grant for a moment that this claim is true, that the Bible really is a story of war.[20] How would one then go on to argue against Christian pacifism on this basis? One could do this if the idea were to derive some kind of normative teaching, attitude, or perspective about war from this broad summary of the Bible's plot. Is this a valid thing to do? Indeed, Leithart claims merely to be painting with "broad strokes" in his claims about violence in the Bible and the various hermeneutical options available for talking about it. While I sympathize with the limitations that probably make it necessary to paint broadly, there is an element of carelessness in Leithart's argument—for example, in his suggestion that anything less than embracing a normative ethic based on the Old Testament battles amounts to some form of Marcionism.[21]

Why not rather conclude that this story of war is one that leads progressively toward war's final overcoming? The war of the Lamb in Revelation is surely to be read as the end of war, much more than as merely another instance of it.[22] Leithart is right, and even profound, in portraying the extraordinary revolution that Constantine represented for Rome in bringing an end to imperial sacrifice. The "new political theology" that he attributes to Constantine is, in this respect, eminently Christian and a radical break with paganism. But why call it new? After all, Christians had *always* refused to sacrifice. With Constantine, the only thing that was new was that now an emperor agreed with them. What if the relativization of sovereignty affirmed by early Christians was simply an aspect of displacing imperial war-making? Maybe we do not go far enough in suggesting that even emperors may share in the cross of Christ by sacrificing themselves in the risks of battle. Maybe the cross is still a scandal, not having changed from what it was originally: a death at the hand of sovereign power and a tool of social control.

---

20. Yet surely we can think of better options: the Bible as the story of God, of redemption, of salvation, of Christ, of Israel, of covenant(s), of grace. All of these seem more prominent than war.

21. Elsewhere Leithart's concern is more generalized into a form of Christian squeamishness at any form of condemnation: "Marcion and his host of modern disciples teach that while condemnation is characteristic of the Old Testament, in the New Testament condemnation yields to affirmation and inclusion. The reality is very nearly the opposite." God's encounter with evil forces is no longer confined to Israel's borders but now plays out on the whole world where, according to Leithart, the church is "the aggressor." Leithart, 1 &2 *Kings*, 139.

22. Leithart allows for this in theory but stops short of embracing it for reasons that are opaque to me.

It is not the case, as Leithart claims, that the "spiritual weapons" of which the New Testament speaks are just the more advanced weaponry God has, with Christ, entrusted to the mature ones (336). Rather they are spiritual *alternatives* to material weapons. Of course a Marcionite can say that with little difficulty, but Marcionism is certainly not the only way to explain this.[23] After all, one can also say that animal sacrifice came to an end with Christ without rejecting the Old Testament.

If Constantine "Christianized" Rome by ending sacrifice for Rome's former gods of imperial well-being, are there yet further sacrifices that must also come to an end—for example, the sacrifices that war makes, also for imperial well-being? This, after all, is precisely what enabled the Christians to see their own deaths as a sacrifice.[24] They understood their deaths as the ultimate irony: for their refusal to sacrifice, they were themselves made into sacrifices to a God who needed no more sacrifices. Only then can the martyr deaths be both vindicated by God and freely given to their killers (for not being necessary).[25]

In conclusion, Leithart's overture is perhaps most valuable for anyone who has made things a little too easy for herself by neglecting to see God's work among her clearest enemies. Leithart reminds us that things are never that clear. If every baptism is (metaphorically) an infant baptism, then it should not surprise anyone that the first Christian emperor only partially abolished sacrifice when he thought he was more thoroughgoing. If, in later generations, some sectors of the church look back and say, "We owe it to your faithfulness to show you where it has hurt Christianity," then surely both the faithfulness and the hurt are genuine.

---

23. This charge of Marcionism is unfortunately common. John Milbank asks: "[D]oes not sheer anti-Constantinianism actually risk Marcionism? As Augustine argued in Book V of *The City of God*, the gospel transcends and fulfils, yet does not abolish, the political level of the Old Testament. . . ." Milbank, "Power is Necessary for Peace." Yet do not some things *in fact* come to an end when they are fulfilled? Jesus fulfilling the everlasting kingship promised to David is an example.

24. E.g., Ignatius of Antioch's letter to the Romans or the Maccabean martyrs.

25. This latter point, of course, is more complicated since many martyr stories tell of the martyrs' enthusiasm for dying at the hands of their executioners. But the church has not usually called these suicides. Enthusiasm for martyrdom was never original or fundamental to the witness they understood their lives to be making.

11 Constantine and Myths of the Fall of the Church

An Anabaptist View

J. ALEXANDER SIDER

> Remember your leaders,
> those who spoke to you the word of God,
> Consider the outcome of their life
> and imitate their faith.
> Jesus Christ is the same yesterday and today and forever.
> Do not be led astray by diverse and strange teachings....
>
> —Hebrews 13:7–9

The reason for remembrance, according to the author of Hebrews, whose previous chapter had reminded readers of a long chain of suffering witnesses, is that Jesus, who continued that chain and brought it to a first "perfection," is the same now and tomorrow and yesterday. The ministry of remembrance, which is the task of the historian, is thus at heart a Christological task. Its vocation is to trace the sameness of Jesus across the generations.[1]

THIS QUOTATION FROM AN essay by John Howard Yoder, "Historiography as a Ministry to Renewal," appeared in a Festschrift for Donald Durnbaugh, a Church of the Brethren historian. The quotation points to a central concern in Christian theological reflection about the past, a concern

---

1. Yoder, "Historiography as a Ministry to Renewal," 216–28. The quotation is from 216.

that Peter Leithart shares with Yoder. The concern is about history as theology: not just history in the service of theology, but the telling of history as a theological enterprise in its own right. When Yoder spelled out what he meant, he claimed that

> "Incarnation" . . . means that in the concrete historical reality of the life and death and rising of Jesus, the otherwise invisible God has been made known normatively. . . . It follow[s] that it must be in the language of concrete history that from then on truth must be communicated, and validated. . . . The news will have to be articulated again and again, always fallible but always open, by grace, to the miracle of faithful communication.[2]

Fallibility and faithfulness blend in the one task of theological communication as a historical enterprise, and it is in this process of communication that the church takes shape. As David Steinmetz, an eminent Methodist historian, put it, "Memory of the past is essential to the Church's self-identity and thus to its mission."[3] History as theology, then, like most theological endeavors, is a risky enterprise, liable to produce self-deception, parochialism, and a false sense of innocence unless it is engaged carefully. This essay explores one set of risks in that pursuit: namely, the appeal to mythic history as a shaping feature in contemporary ecclesiology.

When Peter Leithart engages John Howard Yoder in *Defending Constantine*, he discerns precisely the self-deception, parochialism, and false innocence that accompanies, so Yoder thought, reckless attempts to do historical theology. "Yoder is correct," Leithart argues, "only if he can prove a high degree of early Christian consensus in favor of pacifism." Leithart understands his own task, however, in a rather different way. He continues:

> I do not have to prove that the early church uniformly acknowledged the legitimacy of war and violence to make my case. I have to prove only diversity or ambiguity. If the church was not united on these issues prior to the "Constantinian shift," then it is possible that the church after Constantine took up one thread of earlier teaching, the thread that seemed most relevant to its changed political circumstances. Again, this would be a shift, but it would have been an internal shift of emphasis as the church applied Christ's teaching with a new set of responsibilities, rather than a fall from grace.[4]

2. Yoder, "Historiography as a Ministry to Renewal," 217.
3. Steinmetz, *Memory and Mission*, 9.
4. Leithart, *Defending Constantine*, 259.

Constantine Revisited

While I disagree with Leithart that Yoder's argument concerning Constantinianism crumbles in its entirety if he cannot demonstrate the existence of a consensus in favor of pacifism within the early church, I do agree that Yoder is not off the historical hook. In my dissertation, *To See History Doxologically: History and Holiness in John Howard Yoder's Ecclesiology*, I argued that Yoder's reading of the early church is much more uniform and monological than it ought to be given his convictions about the nature of doing history.[5] Leithart, at various points in *Defending Constantine*, draws attention to this argument. But his analysis also shows that if the church took up one thread of earlier teaching after Constantine (call it pro-imperial or non-pacifist) this implies that other threads of earlier teaching (less pro-imperial, more pacifist) remained. And that, it seems to me, is sufficient to demonstrate the essential point: namely, that distinct ecclesiological trajectories (my phrasing), or, if you wish, "internal shifts of emphasis" (Leithart's phrasing), or divergent "impulses" (Yoder's phrasing), were being entertained in the late ancient church, often, no doubt, in a confused and disunited way. The fundamental question asked by Yoder's historical theology concerning the so-called "Constantinian shift" was not "did a shift occur?" but how do we judge which "change(s) should be welcomed as revelatory and which should be denounced as betrayal"?[6]

Contrary to Leithart's claims, Yoder did at points give an interestingly nuanced account of the Constantinian shift. Leithart is not to be faulted for ignoring these sources—the bibliography of Yoder's work is enormous, and he wrote for many rather inaccessible journals. In one such source from Yoder, an essay called "War as a Moral Problem in the Early Church: The Historian's Hermeneutical Assumptions," he asserted:

> There has been no new information on the topic of war as a moral problem in the early Church for a long time.... Some new authors came to the same old material with new perspectives, but there was even very little of that. Most new authors brought out the same old perspectives, although the tone changed as Roman Catholic historians joined the discussion. There have been no new patristic texts adduced, and the progress of archaeology has not changed much.

---

5. Sider, *To See History Doxologically*.
6. Yoder, "Historiography as a Ministry to Renewal," 217.

According to some surveyors, Yoder continued, the "literature is marked by an 'emotional' tone reflecting the respective authors' own leanings on the issue of pacifism. That is another thing that has not changed."[7]

Given this situation, which Leithart himself might affirm,[8] Yoder concluded that that one ought not embark upon yet another review of patristic sources. Rather, historians of Christianity need to review the "hermeneutical assumptions" on the basis of which they read the texts. "These assumptions," he argued, "need to be made more conscious and to be subjected to methodological scrutiny on grounds other than whether or not the texts can be called on to support one's own ethical predilections."[9] In a footnote to the essay, Yoder clarified something of what he meant. He wrote:

> Johnson says of Cadoux, and Helgeland says of Cadoux, Bainton, and Hornus that their readings are pre-disposed by their pacifism. . . . That is correct; but the opposite view is not exempt from the same critique. Part of the "hermeneutical" self-awareness to which my title refers has to do with the need for a higher level of sophistication about method, which issues like this call for.[10]

Certainly, Leithart's analysis inclines him to agree with Johnson and Helgeland, and to extend their critique of older texts to Yoder. Leithart says, "Yoder argues in many places that the basic problem of Constantinianism is its ecclesiology and eschatology. Yet pacifism looms very large in his analysis of church history, and hence of Constantinianism. Without pacifist assumptions, much of Yoder's edifice crumbles."[11]

What, according to Yoder, are the hermeneutical principles to which one might point that would raise discussion about a "Constantinian shift"

---

7. In *Pacifist Impulse in Historical Perspective*, 90.

8. "*Defending Constantine*," Leithart writes, "is a rather old–fashioned book. I am asking the traditional 'Constantinian questions' that historians have long since tired of answering." *Defending Constantine*, 9.

9. Yoder, "War as a Moral Problem," 91.

10. Ibid. 104.

11. Leithart, *Defending Constantine*, 256 n. 4. I note here only that Leithart refers to Yoder's posthumously published *The War of the Lamb*, a volume edited by Glen Stassen, Mark Nation and Matt Hamsher. As I found out when I did much of the editorial work on Yoder's *Preface to Theology*, many of Yoder's would-be editors think it permissible to improve on his manuscripts. Sometimes this is necessary, as when the sentences are ungrammatical; other times the paraphrases are quite unreliable.

to this higher level of sophistication? Three such principles seem especially relevant to the discussion raised by *Defending Constantine*.

"Pacifism" in the Early Church

Vocabulary is historically-conditioned and polyvalent. Yoder noted that the use of the term "pacifist" in discussions about the early church is usually question-begging. He wrote, "I used to think that with good manners people on both sides of the ethical debate could agree to define their terms 'objectively' enough that the argument could be about substance rather than about words.... That hope, however, has not been sustained."[12] Yoder continued, in his usual fashion, to list a variety of meanings given to "pacifism" within the debate, ranging from James Johnson's relatively benign, though silly, characterization of pacifism as "withdrawal from the world and all its ills," through "the stance of politicians who considered war as not immoral or illegal but inopportune," to the views of Dennis Praeger, who commented in *First Things* on pacifism as "a doctrine that holds that it is morally preferable to allow Dr. Mengele to continue to perform medical experiments on men, women and children than it is to kill him."[13]

Yoder used the term pacifism under protest. He also claimed that within the context of the essay—and, I might add, in a number of other contexts as well, contexts where (a) pacifism functioned for him as shorthand for an argument and (b) he had not distinguished between various sorts of rejections of violence—pacifism meant "the moral rejection of war as incompatible with fidelity to Jesus Christ as Lord."[14]

A number of points should be made in regard to this fairly narrowly circumscribed conception of pacifism:

a. The moral rejection of war does not entail the actual rejection of war. Sometimes, of course, what people think ought to be done and what they in fact do go hand in hand. Often, this is not the case. In any event, we need a much more thorough investigation than either Yoder or Leithart has provided of the history of moral psychology in the so-called Western world over the last two millennia before we can make cogent arguments

---

12. Yoder, "War as a Moral Problem," 91.
13. Ibid. Cf. my comments in Hauerwas and Sider, "Distinctiveness of Christian Ethics," 230–31.
14. Yoder, "War as a Moral Problem," 92.

that reason to moral justification from people's actions. Given the written evidence, could one do this without begging the question? It is difficult to tell without trying.

b. Yoder speaks of the rejection of war and not of many other levels of pro-imperial sentiment. Yoder, for instance, points to the distinction between *militare* (serving in the military) and *bellare* (fighting in war) as not merely verbal. Certainly, Leithart does not dispute Ramsay MacMullen's thesis that Roman soldiers carried out many functions within Roman society beyond fighting in war. And, neither Yoder nor Leithart dispute that Christians did in some cases serve in the military. Where they differ is over their assessment of how "pacifist" this activity was. I, for my part, agree with Leithart that the military functions of the Roman army were often violent quite apart from whether or not they involved acts of war.

c. Debates about the policing function of the Roman military aside, some levels of pro-imperial sentiment among Christians might even have involved elements of support for wars conducted within and outside of the empire. To imply through prayer and written statements that a war is righteous is, for instance, a very different kind of activity than engaging in killing. There is little evidence in the early church for the kind of stance that Christians from the early twentieth century on have identified as "absolute pacifism." In my view there is also relatively little evidence in the early church for the view that it is inconsistent to say both that the empire may fight wars that are righteous and that Christians may not fight in them.[15]

d. Leithart recognizes something like Yoder's protest in *Defending Constantine*: "My use of pacifist throughout this chapter acknowledges Yoder's proviso. I am using it in a loose sense not to denote a specific rationale for Christian opposition to war and violence but in reference to the simple fact of Christian opposition to war and violence." I am not sure what this acknowledgement amounts to, given that Leithart still wants pacifism in the early church to mean the condemnation of "all Christian participation in war, or violent service to the state."[16] Yoder, for his part, asked:

> Were Christians before Constantine pacifist? Certainly not, if we give the term an ahistorically modern definition. . . . Yet none

---

15. Cf. Field, *Liberty, Dominion and the Two Swords*. See especially the fascinating argument of chapter 3, "Imperial Dominion and the Two Swords: Images and Reflections," 45–62.

16. Leithart, *Defending Constantine*, 257.

of [the] ways in which they were not modern pacifists allows us to say that they were non-pacifist or anti-pacifist. The presence of a pacifist "impulse" is not denied by those who claim that Cadoux and Hornus exaggerate its normativity. There is no record of a militaristic, a Machiavellian, or a crusading "impulse." There is not even an Augustinian statement.[17]

Normativity as a Historical Problem

What counts as normative depends on many variables. Throughout *Defending Constantine*, Leithart adduces many different kinds of evidence for ambiguity in the early church record regarding participation in war. That evidence ranges from noticing the implication that some Christians did probably participate in war because other church leaders spoke out against it (although whether we should speak of Origen and Tertullian as "leaders" is itself an interesting question), to arguments from "pacifist" authors recommending certain kinds of military participation and even endorsing some imperial military actions. Lactantius, whom Leithart calls "a patristic poster boy of pacifism," dedicated *The Divine Institutes* to Constantine, whom he "knew to be a soldier," calling Constantine "'the greatest of emperors' because he had 'cast aside error' and determined 'to acknowledge and honor the majesty of the one true God.'"[18] Leithart's point is that the historical record is ambiguous, and Yoder, as we have already seen would have agreed. What Yoder asked for, however, was reflection on how we interpret this ambiguous history. To that end, he offered a number of contemporary analogies, including the following two:

> Americans who have been baptized and who tell the census-takers that they are "Catholic" seem to commit the canonically prohibited actions of contraception, of entering into a new sexual union after divorce, or even of abortion, in proportions not very different from the rest of the American population.[19]

---

17. Yoder, "War as a Moral Problem," 102. By an "Augustinian statement," Yoder meant the kind of negative apologetic Augustine employed in *City of God*. He summarized: "War cannot be forbidden, he argues, because John the Baptist did not forbid it, Jesus did not scold the centurion, Peter did not tell Cornelius to resign, God may have providentially subjected you to an ungodly king, Christian emperors have conquered pagan nations, and the world is miserable anyway." Ibid., 103–4.

18. Leithart, *Defending Constantine*, 272.

19. Yoder, "War as a Moral Problem," 92.

Few would challenge the label of "pacifist" for the Society of Friends, even though only a minority of draft-age men from that constituency took conscientious objector status during the Second World War. Even those young Friends who accepted military service made no attempt to change either the documents or the public image of Quakerism that their individual actions undermined.[20]

In both of these examples, a statistically significant sample of the population in question engages in activities that do not represent a strong and widespread consensus about the moral position of the church in question. This throws any sense of what "counts" as normative in these instances into question. In these cases it makes little sense to insist on a sense of normative practice apart from actual performance. In other words, normativity is not a state; it is a function. So, historians' questions should not stop with "what are the moral positions under consideration?" but rather continue on to "how do those positions function within the society that they describe?" Normativity does not just happen, but is ascribed. These ascriptions are made in politically, socially, and morally charged contexts where diverse understandings of hierarchy and authority, the role of historical and sacred texts, relations with "secular" society, and a handful of other factors are in play. Diversity in one or many of these factors will shape, and in some cases dictate, how normativity works.

Recognition of the historical conditions under which ascriptions of normativity arise will lead historians to a modest set of conclusions. "What to make of this?" is, of course, not an entirely different discussion than "what happened?," but it is a question that highlights certain uncongenial aspects of the historian's task. As David Steinmetz put it:

> Historians, unlike systematic theologians, are left with historical materials that will not conform to their finer theological instincts and with results that force them to conclusions that they find personally disagreeable. There is one commandment and only one that Church historians must scrupulously observe: honor thy father and thy mother. They must accept the past as it offers itself to them. They have no god-like prerogative to bowdlerize and "improve" history. . . . The historical event is beyond the reach of the historian at the level of its sheer givenness.[21]

---

20. Ibid., 93.
21. Steinmetz, *Memory and Mission*, 32.

Constantine Revisited

What kind of problem is this? Historians always make sense out of data. They do this via a variety of processes, including analogies and disanalogies with the present, and they do it in such a way that forges a functional sense of normativity. The problem that presents itself is not about needing to revise interpretations later, or being wrong about one's interpretation in the first place. Nor is the problem about imposing a set of constructed views on "reality." Rather, the danger that looms large when we consider ascriptions of normativity as a historical problem is that of imposing a false (because prematurely final) unity on history that fails to correspond to the complexity of the data. We have decided on grounds other than historical ones what "really" counts as normative. There are, in much simpler terms, always further questions to be asked. It seems to me that this is the main force of Leithart's criticism of Yoder's historiography, but I have just put this criticism in terms that Yoder himself appreciated.[22] To wit:

> Those who say "the early Christians were pacifist" base the generalization mostly on a few writings from literate laymen. Those who most strongly deny the thesis base their claim in circumstantially attested actions of men under arms from who we have no literary communication. The statements on both "sides" may both be true, since they are not talking about the same people. . . . Some of the writers (notably Origen and Tertullian) were later accused of heresy, by other literate men, on grounds unrelated to the issue of military service. Does any of that make any difference?[23]

The Past as Promise and Problem

One conclusion to draw from this, which is my third hermeneutical principle, is that everyone in the debate appeals to some "myth of Christian origins" for a particular polemical purpose. One of the payoffs of the recognition that moral normativity is a functional concept is the discovery that "history as identity is indispensable."[24] And this is no more the case for "radicals" than for anyone else. To quote David Steinmetz again, ". . . a Church that has lost its memory of the past can only wander about

---

22. For a fuller discussion, see chapter 2 of my *To See History Doxologically*.
23. Yoder, "War as a Moral Problem," 93.
24. Yoder, "The Ambivalence of the Appeal to the Fathers," 248.

aimlessly in the present and despair of its future. The Church needs the past, if only for the sake of the present and the future."[25]

To need the past for the sake of the present and the future is both a promise and a problem. Returning to Yoder's statement with which I began, the past's presence can be viewed under Christological warrants; "the retrieval of history is," Yoder said, "christologically mandated."[26] The presence of the past is, in this sense, a cause for hope and a providential occasion for enriching self-knowledge. However, historians and others are often inclined to "sift the story to fit the present need for a usable history."[27] In other words, history writing as an evangelical mandate requires attention not only to "what happened back then" but also to our stakes in characterizing "what happened" in the particular ways we characterize it. Often, our attentiveness to the past, which is driven by intellectual honesty, blinds us to how our uses of the past are less than honest.

a. One effect of this tendency we have already seen. It is that "the historian as historian will be accused of bias and inaccuracy, in that his/her account of origins was predisposed by the intention to find oneself back there."[28] If the past is simply what Rowan Williams has called "the present in fancy dress," then the occasion for enriching self-knowledge will not only be lost, but in fact badly misconstrued. For we will not learn from the difference of the past, but will simply tend to be more securely confirmed in positions that we already hold. Yoder noted that this very dynamic occurred in the academic Mennonite generation immediately preceding his:

> The "school of John Horsch and Harold S. Bender" ignored or declared out of bounds some of the sixteenth-century phenomena which were less sober and less biblical than Horsch's and Bender's own vision for North American Mennonitism. Not all of the first "anabaptists" were nonviolent, not all were soberly Biblicist; but the ones we agreed with made the best fathers.[29]

b. In terms of using the past for the sake of the present and the future, the historian will likely "underestimate those dimensions of his/her

---

25. Steinmetz, *Memory and Mission*, 34.
26. Yoder, "Ambivalence of the Appeal to the Fathers," 248.
27. Ibid., 249. I'm reminded here of Judith Shklar's comment about revising the past so as to outfit the present with a more fitting denouement.
28. Ibid., 249.
29. Ibid., 250.

contemporary loyalty which do not fit the ideal."[30] Steinmetz put the point this way: "In freeing us from theological parochialism, . . . [Church history] also results in the loss of innocence. We see how the tradition that we learned in our parish evolved over the course of the centuries and discover, sometimes to our chagrin, that our tradition, whatever else it may be, is not simply a repristination in the twentieth century of the primitive apostolic faith."[31] When we are not clear about how we use the past, we become less clear about aspects of our present that a more honest assessment of the past might cause us to question. It is not simply that "Anabaptists" in the sixteenth century were not all nonviolent; it is not simply that early Christians were not uniformly pacifist. As a contemporary ecclesiological factor, not all Mennonites espouse nonviolence, and those of us who do are heirs of a historical project with polemical roots in the need for American denominations to provide warrant for conscientious objection to the U.S. government. This is not to say that espousing Christian nonviolence is a bad thing; it is only to suggest that we can be clearer than we characteristically are about the breadth of our reasons for doing so.

Conclusion

While there has been no shortage of ink spilled on the issue of theological abuses of history (I think particularly of Ernst Troeltsch and Van Harvey in this regard, though the stream of inquiry they represent is far wider and deeper than their contributions), it is in practice quite easy to invoke the concept of sober historiography for frankly ideological purposes. Many will find some of those purposes more congenial than others, which is to be expected. Thus, I have not claimed that a conversation, say, about whether Yoder's views of the early sources are more historically adequate than Leithart's is out of place—indeed, from what I have said above it will not be difficult to decide the direction in which I tend. But I do have concerns about the ways in which such a conversation is conducted. If the animating concerns of historical inquiry and debate are ecclesiological or political, as they are in both Yoder's and Leithart's cases, then those concerns demand to be foregrounded, lest they silently shape the inquirer's mindset and thus cover over lessons (congenial or uncongenial) that audiences might learn.

---

30. Ibid.
31. Steinmetz, *Memory and Mission*, 28.

One theologically vital criterion of such conversation is to allow the messy and inconclusive nature of historical inquiry to stand on its own and (maybe more importantly) to take methodological and self-critical steps to do so. How else except via "remembering your leaders" from the past might one be expected to arrive at a durable and unembarrassed sense that the messy and inconclusive nature of many moral and theological concerns today is, dare I say, normal?

12 Afterword

Peter J. Leithart

If a book's success can be judged by the quality of the criticism it receives, I am satisfied that *Defending Constantine* is a successful book. The responses in *Constantine Revisited* are consistently of the highest quality; they challenge, illumine, and inform, and, as importantly, exude the measured and charitable spirit of genuine Christian scholarship. I doubt I would respond with the same grace if one of my heroes were criticized in the way I criticized Yoder. I am impressed and grateful that *Defending Constantine* started a vigorous conversation rather than a Fox News shouting match. You are all truly heirs of Yoder's peaceable zeal.

I have engaged some of these critiques at length elsewhere. I was privileged to defend *Defending Constantine* in response to Craig Hovey and Alex Sider at a Midwest AAR meeting in Rock Island, Illinois, in 2011, and I responded to a version of Mark Nation's essay at the San Francisco AAR meeting in 2011, where I found myself in a room filled with more Mennonites than I have ever seen in one place. I have engaged the criticisms of Nugent, Kreider, and others in a symposium published in the *Mennonite Quarterly Review* (October 2011). One of the blessings of the reception of *Defending Constantine* has been the opportunity to become acquainted with my critics and their work.

A number of these essays expose significant gaps and flaws in *Defending Constantine*. I was not aware of the extent of Yoder's Old Testament work until John Nugent called my attention to it, and we now are fortunate to have his superb *The Politics of Yahweh* (Cascade, 2011). Alan Kreider brought me up short by noting that I gave virtually no attention to the oddity of Constantine's late baptism and by detailing the liturgical evidence for a Constantinian shift, which I had inexcusably ignored.

I will not repeat my responses here, but only develop two points. First, like Yoder, I believe history and theology are two dimensions of the same inquiry. Christian theology concerns the history of God, His people, and His world, and any Christian historian probes God's continuing action. Protestant though I am, I agree wholly with Bill Cavanaugh's "Catholic" insight that "scripture and church history [tell] one continuous story of God's people." Scripture is the narrative of the ragged but recognizable realization of God's promises, and if church history continues that story we should be able to discern similar fulfillments since the first century. To be sure, we walk by faith not by sight, and fulfillments are often paradoxically cruciform. Yet, fulfillments they are, and if we are going to discern the pattern of Christ's rule of His church, we must attend to the particulars of His promises.

From Babel onward, Yahweh promises political salvation—to bless the nations through Abraham's seed and to produce kings from the family of Abraham:

> I will make you exceedingly fruitful, and I will make nations of you, and kings will come forth from you. . . . I will bless [Sarah] and she shall be a mother of nations; kings of peoples will come from her. (Genesis 17:6, 16)

> God also said, "I am God Almighty; be fruitful and multiple; a nation and company of nations shall come from you, and kings shall come forth from you." (Genesis 35:11)

With the Davidic dynasty, the Abrahamic promise reaches an initial fulfillment (2 Samuel 7), and the Davidic monarchy also awkens the hope that Gentile kings will one day acknowledge Yahweh as their High King and David as His deputy. The Queen of Sheba is a figure of the rulers who will offer homage to David's son (1 Kings 10), and the broader promise that the rulers of nations would learn to serve the God of Israel persists through the monarchy and beyond:

> Because of Your temple at Jerusalem, kings will bring gifts to You. (Psalm 68:29)

> The kings of Tarshish and of the islands bring presents; the kings of Sheba and Seba offer gifts. And let all kings bow before him, all nations serve him. (Psalm 72:10–11)

> The nations will fear the name of Yahweh and all kings of the earth Your glory. (Psalm 102:15)

Constantine Revisited

> Praise Yahweh from the earth, sea monsters and all deeps. . . . kings of the earth and all peoples; princes and judges of the earth. (Psalm 148:7, 11)

> In the last days, the mountain of the house of Yahweh will be established as the chief of the mountains, and will be raised above the hills; and all nations will stream to it. . . . He will judge between nations, and will render decisions for many peoples; and they will hammer their swords into plowshares, and their spears into pruning hooks. (Isaiah 2:1–4)

> Kings will be your guardians, and their princesses your rulers. They will bow down to you with their faces to the earth and lick the dust of your feet; and you will know that I am Yahweh. (Isaiah 49:23)

> Nations will come to your light, and kings to the brightness of your rising. . . . Foreigners will build up your walls, and their kings will minister to you. . . . Your gates will be open continually; they will not be closed day or night, so that men may bring to you the wealth of the nations, with their kings in procession. (Isaiah 60:3, 10–11)

This expectation does not end with Malachi. It persists to the very end of the Bible. Kings are destroyed and consumed by beasts in Revelation (19:18–19), but when new Jerusalem descends from heaven, the surviving kings pay homage to Jesus the King of kings (19:16) by bringing treasures into His bridal city. Like the procession of tribal princes offering tribute at Yahweh's tabernacle in the early chapters of Numbers, "the nations will walk by her light, and the kings of the earth will bring their glory into it" (21:24). Kings, while remaining kings, become subjects of the kingdom of Jesus.

Jesus is Yes and Amen to *these* promises. When King Constantine devotes the treasures of the Roman Empire to build the church and gather ecumenical councils and provide justice for the marginal, we should recognize a fulfillment of ancient promise. If Constantine's conversion does not count as fulfillment, it is difficult to imagine what would.

That first point needs to be immediately qualified by a second, which Bill Cavanaugh makes eloquently in his contribution to this volume. In *Defending Constantine*, I describe biblical history as a story of maturation from childhood to adulthood in Christ, but Cavanaugh is right to emphasize that the pedagogy continues through the history of the church. "Is it possible," he asks, "to read the 'Constantinian shift' as something that 'had to' happen . . . in order for the church to learn something it otherwise would not?" My answer is an emphatic "Yes," and I agree with Cavanaugh's further claim that "the learning would not simply be the way one learns from a mistake; there is something more positive to be learned as well." As his essay goes on, it becomes clear that Cavanaugh and I have quite different assessments of what the church should learn from Constantine, but we share the pedagogical reading of the church's history. The biblical theologian James Jordan likes to call the patristic writers the "church babies" rather than "church fathers," because for all their profundity they are only beginning to grasp the full dimensions of the gospel. The Christian political order and political theology that come with Constantine likewise exhibits countless immaturities. We should not expect him or the infant church to get everything right immediately, and we should hope and demand that any future "Constantines" reflect deeply on the failures of the past ones. At the same time, we should not dismiss the real and positive contributions of Constantine and Christendom because, immature as Constantinian order is, it *does* fulfill biblical hope.

The very existence of the present volume is evidence of that maturation, another fulfillment of biblical hope. As John D. Roth notes in his introduction, "in sharp contrast to the disputations with the Anabaptists organized by state churches in the sixteenth century, *Constantine Revisited* models the manner in which deep disagreements among Christians can be debated today in a spirit of charity, without fear of torture, imprisonment, or death by fire, drowning, or the executioner's sword." That, clearly, signals the Spirit's work, an ongoing work of which both my critics and I are the glad beneficiaries.

Bibliography

Agamben, Giorgio. *The Kingdom and the Glory: For a Theological Genealogy of Economy and Government*. Translated by Lorenzo Chiesa. Stanford: Stanford University Press, 2011.

Alexis–Baker, Andy. "*Ad Quirinum* Book Three and Cyprian's Catechumenate." *Journal of Early Christian Studies* 17:3 (2009) 357–80.

Alexis–Baker, Andy. "What about the Centurion's Great Faith?: The Roman Military and Christian Pacifism." In *A Faith Not Worth Fighting For: Addressing Commonly Asked Question about Christian Nonviolence*, edited by Tripp York and Justin Bronson Barringer. Eugene, OR: Cascade, 2012.

Ando, Clifford. "Pagan Apologetics and Christian Intolerance in the Ages of Themistius and Augustine." *Journal of Early Christian Studies* 4 (1996) 171–207.

Ankersmit, Frank. *Historical Representation*. Stanford: Stanford University Press, 2001.

Arner, Rob. *Consistently Pro-Life: The Ethics of Bloodshed in Ancient Christianity*. Eugene, OR: Pickwick, 2010.

Arnobius. *Adversus Nationes*. Online: http://www.thelatinlibrary.com/arnobius/arnobius5.shtml.

Athenagoras. *Legatio Pro Christianis*. Patristische Texte und Studien. Vol 31., edited by Miroslav Marcovich. Berlin: Walter de Gruyter, 1990.

Augustine. *Epistles. The Letters of St. Augustine*. Edited by W. J. Sparrow-Simpson. London: SPCK; New York: Macmillan, 1919.

Augustine, *Sermons*. Online: http://www.theworkofgod.org/Library/Sermons/Agustine.htm

Ayers, Lewis. *Nicea and Its Legacy: An Approach to Fourth-Century Trinitarian Theology*. New York: Oxford, 2004.

Barnes, T. D. *Constantine and Eusebius*. Cambridge: Harvard University Press, 1981.

———. "The Constantinian Reformation." In *The Crake Lectures, 1984: A Classical Symposium held September 27-28 in conjunction with the opening of the Crake Reading Room, Mount Allison University*. Sackville, NB: Crake Institute, 1986.

———. "The Conversion of Constantine." *Classical Views* n.s., 4 (1985) 371–91.

Basil, *Epistles*. In *Nicene and Post-Nicene Fathers*, Second Series, vol. 8. Translated by Blomfield Jackson. Edited by Philip Schaff and Henry Wace. Buffalo, NY: Christian Literature, 1895. Online: http://www.newadvent.org/fathers.

Batiffol, Pierre. "Les Etapes de la conversion de Constantin." *Bulletin d'ancienne littérature et d'archéologie chrétienne* 3 (1913) 178–88, 241–464.

Baucum, Tory K. *Evangelical Hospitality: Catechetical Evangelism in the Early Church and Its Recovery for Today*. Lanham, MD: Scarecrow, 2008.

The Canons of Hippolytus. 2nd ed. Translated by Carol Bebawi. Edited by Paul F. Bradshaw. Bramcote: Grove, 1987.

Bibliography

Bernardin, Joseph Cardinal. *Consistent Ethic of Life*. Kansas City, MO: Sheed & Ward, 1988.

Biggar, Nigel. "The New Testament and Violence: Round Two." *Studies in Christian Ethics* 23.1 (2010) 73–80

———. "Specify and Distinguish: Interpreting the New Testament on 'Nonviolence.'" *Studies in Christian Ethics* 22.2 (2009) 164–84.

Biller, Peter. "Words and the Medieval Notion of 'Religion.'" *Journal of Ecclesiastical History* 36 (July 1985) 351–69.

Bradshaw, Paul F. "The Effects of the Coming of Christendom on Early Christian Worship." In *Origins of Christendom in the West*, edited by Alan Kreider. Edinburgh: T. & T. Clark, 2001.

———. *Early Christian Worship*. Collegeville, MN: Liturgical, 1996.

———. *The Search for the Origins of Christian Worship: Sources and Methods for the Study of Early Liturgy*. 2nd ed. London and New York: SPCK and Oxford University Press, 2002.

Brown, Peter. *Power and Persuasion in Late Antiquity: Towards a Christian Empire*. Madison: University of Wisconsin Press, 1992.

Cameron, Alan. *The Last Pagans of Rome*. New York: Oxford University Press, 2011.

Cameron, Averil. "Education and Literary Culture." In *The Cambridge Ancient History*, edited by Averil Cameron and Peter Garnsey. Cambridge: Cambridge University Press, 1998.

Carey, Philip. "Book Seven: Inner Vision as the Goal of Augustine's Life." In *A Reader's Companion to Augustine's Confessions*, edited by Kim Paffenroth and Robert P. Kennedy, 107–26. Louisville: Westminster John Knox, 2003.

Cartwright, Michael G. "Afterword." In *The Jewish-Christian Schism Revisited*, edited by Michael G. Cartwright and Peter Ochs. Grand Rapids: Eerdmans, 2003.

Cary, Phillip. *Augustine's Invention of the Inner Self: The Legacy of a Christian Platonist*. Oxford: Oxford University Press, 2000.

Cavanaugh, William T. *Migrations of the Holy: God, State, and the Political Meaning of the Church*. Grand Rapids: Eerdmans, 2011.

Cavaugh, William T. *The Myth of Religious Violence*. Oxford: Oxford University Press, 2009.

Cavell, Stanley. *The Claim of Reason: Wittgenstein, Skepticism, Morality, and Tragedy*. Oxford: Oxford University Press, 1979

———. *Conditions Handsome and Unhandsome: The Constitution of Emersonian Perfectionism*. Chicago: The University of Chicago Press, 1990.

Chavalas, Mark W. "Review of *Defending Constantine*." *American Theological Inquiry: A Biannual Journal of Theology, Culture & History* 5:1 (2012) 117–18.

Chomsky, Noam. *Failed States: The Abuse of Power and the Assault on Democracy*. New York: Metropolitan, 2006.

Chronicle of the Hutterian Brethren. Translated and edited by Hutterian Brethren. Vol. 1. Rifton, NY: Plough, 1987.

Clement of Alexandria. *The Pedagogue*. From *Ante-Nicene Fathers* 2. Translated by William Wilson. Edited by Alexander Roberts, James Donaldson, and A. Cleveland Coxe. Buffalo, NY: Christian Literature, 1885. Online: http://www.newadvent.org/fathers/02093.htm.

Codex Theodosianus. Online: http://www.fordham.edu/halsall/source/codex-theod1.asp.

Bibliography

Constantine, *Oration*. In *Nicene and Post-Nicene Fathers*, Second Series, 1. Tranlsated by Cushing Richardson. Edited by Philip Schaff and Henry Wace. Buffalo, NY: Christian Literature, 1890. Online: http://www.newadvent.org/fathers/2503.htm>

Constitutions of the Holy Apostles. Tranlsated by and edited by James Donaldson. Edinburgh: T. & T. Clark, 1996.

Cramer, Peter. *Baptism and Change in the Early Middle Ages, c.200–c.1150* Cambridge: Cambridge University Press, 1993.

Cristiani, Léon. "Essai sur les origines du costume ecclésiastique." In *Miscellanea Guillaume de Jerphanion*. Rome: Pont. Institutum Orientalium Studiorum, 1947.

Curran, John. *Pagan City and Christian Capital: Rome in the Fourth Century*. Oxford: Clarendon, 2000.

Cyprian. *Ad Donatum. Sancti Cypriani Episcopi Opera*. Edited by G. F. Diercks and G. W. Clarke. Turnhout, Belgium: Brepols, 1972.

Cyprian, *Ad Quirinu. Sancti Cypriani Episcopi Opera*. Edited by G. F. Diercks and G. W. Clarke. Turnhout, Belgium: Brepols, 1972.

Cyprian, *De Patientia. Sancti Cypriani Episcopi Opera*. Edited by G F. Diercks and G. W. Clarke. Turnhout, Belgium: Brepols, 1972.

Cyprian. *The Lord's Prayer*. S.l.: Printed for the Scottish Church Tract Society, 1851.

Cyril of Jerusalem. *The Works of Saint Cyril of Jerusalem*. Washington, DC: Catholic University of America Press, 2000. Online: http://site.ebrary.com/id/10382819.

Dawson, John David. *Figural Reading and the Fashioning of Identity*. Berkeley: University of California Press, 2002.

de Lubac, Henri. *Medieval Exegesis: The Four Senses of Scripture, Vol. 1*. Tranlsated by M. Sebanc. Grand Rapids: Eerdmans, 1998.

Deléani, Simone. *Christum sequi: Etude d'un theme dans l'oeuvre de saint Cyprien*. Paris: Etudes Augustiniennes, 1979.

Didascalia Apostolorum. Edited by R. H. Connolly. Oxford: Clarendon, 1929.

Dogmatic Constitution on Divine Revelation (Dei Verbum). Online: http://www.vatican.va/archive/hist_councils/ii_vatican_council/documents/vat-ii_const_19651118_dei-verbum_en.html.

Dörries, Hermann. *Constantine the Great*. New York: Harper, 1972.

Drake, H. A. *Constantine and the Bishops: The Politics of Intolerance*. Baltimore: The Johns Hopkins University Press, 2000.

Edwards, Mark. *Catholicity and Heresy in the Early Church*. Farnham: Ashgate, 2009.

Elton, Hugh. "Warfare and the Military." In *The Cambridge Companion to the Age of Constantine*, edited by Noel Lenski. Cambridge: Cambridge University Press, 2006.

Eoin de Bhaldraithe. "Early Christian Features Preserved in Western Monasticism." In *Origins of Christendom in the West*, edited by Alan Kreider. Edinburgh: T. & T. Clark, 2001.

Eusebius. *Eusebius: Life of Constantine*. Edited by Averil Cameron and Stuart G. Hall. Oxford: Oxford University Press, 1999.

Ferguson, Everett. *Baptism in the Early Church: History, Theology, and Liturgy in the First Five Centuries*. Grand Rapids: Eerdmans, 2009.

———. "Catechesis and Initiation." In *Origins of Christendom in the West*, edited by Alan Kreider. Edinburgh: T. & T. Clark, 2001.

———. "Exhortations to Baptism in the Cappadocians." *Studia Patristica* 33 (1997) 121–29.

Bibliography

———. "Love of Enemies and Nonretaliation in the Second Century." In *The Contentious Triangle: Church, State and University*, edited by Rodney L. Petersen and Calvin Augustine Pater. Kirksville, MO: Thomas Jefferson University Press, 1999.

Field, Jr., Lester L. *Liberty, Dominion and the Two Swords: On the Origin of Western Political Theology (180–398)*. Notre Dame: University of Notre Dame Press, 1998.

Finger, Thomas N. "Christus Victor and the Creeds: Some Historical Considerations." *MQR* 72 (Jan 1998) 31–51.

Finn, Thomas M. *From Death to Rebirth: Ritual and Conversion in Antiquity*. Mahwah, NJ: Paulist, 1997.

———. "It Happened One Saturday Night: Ritual and Conversion in Augustine's North Africa." *Journal of the American Academy of Religion* 58:4 (1990) 589–616.

Finney, Paul Corby. "Images on Finger Rings and Early Christian Art." In *Studies on Art and Archaeology in Honor of Ernst Kitzinger on his Seventy-Fifth Birthday*, edited by William Tronzo and Irving Lavin. Washington, DC: Dumbarton Oaks Research Library and Collection, 1987.

Foucault, Michel. *The Order of Things: An Archaeology of the Human Sciences*. New York: Vintage, 1994.

Frei, Hans. "The 'Literal' Reading of Biblical Narrative in the Christian Tradition." In *The Bible and the Narrative Tradition*, edited by Frank McConnell, 36–77. New York: Oxford, 1986.

Fritz, Georges. "Service Militaire." In *Dictionnaire de Théologie Catholique* 14. Paris: Letouzey et Ané, 1941.

Furry, Timothy J. "From Past to Present and Beyond: The Venerable Bede, Figural Exegesis, and Historical Theory." PhD diss., University of Dayton, 2011.

Fürst, Alfons. *Die Liturgie der alten Kirche: Geschichte und Theologie*. Münster: Aschendorff, 2008.

Girard, René. *I See Satan Fall Like Lightning*. Tranlsated by James G. Williams. Maryknoll, NY: Orbis, 2001.

Goldingay, John. *Israel's Gospel. Old Testament Theology*. Vol. 1. Downers Grove, IL: InterVarsity, 2003.

González, Justo. *The Changing Shape of Church History*. St. Louis: Chalice, 2002.

Gorman, Michael. *Inhabiting the Cruciform God*. Grand Rapids: Eerdmans, 2009.

Grant, Michael. *Constantine the Great: The Man and His Times*. New York: History Book Club, 1993; 2000.

Gross, Leonard, translator. "H. Schnell: Second Generation Anabaptist." *Mennonite Quarterly Review* 68 (July 1994) 351–77.

Hall, Stuart G. "The Sects Under Constantine." In *Voluntary Religion*, edited by W. J. Sheils and Diana Wood. Oxford: Basil Blackwell, 1986.

Halperin, David M. *Saint Foucault: Toward a Gay Hagiography*. New York: Oxford University Press, 1997.

Hanson, R. P. C. "The Achievement of Orthodoxy in the Fourth Century A.D." In *The Making of Orthodoxy: Essays in Honour of Henry Chadwick*, edited by Rowan Williams. Cambridge: Cambridge University Press, 1989.

Hauerwas, Stanley, and J. Alexander Sider. "The Distinctiveness of Christian Ethics." *International Journal of Systematic Theology* 5:2 (2003) 225–33.

Hays, Richard. "Narrate and Embody: A Response to Nigel Biggar, 'Specify and Distinguish.'" *Studies in Christian Ethics* 22.2 (2009) 185–98.

Bibliography

———. "The Thorny Task of Reconciliation: Another Response to Nigel Biggar." *Studies in Christian Ethics* 23.1 (2010) 81–86.

———. "Victory Over Violence: The Significance of N. T. Wright's Jesus for New Testament Ethics." In *Jesus & the Restoration of Israel: A Critical Assessment of N. T. Wright's Jesus and the Victory of God*. Downers Grove, IL: InterVarsity, 1999.

———. *The Moral Vision of the New Testament*. San Francisco: Harper San Francisco, 1996.

Heid, Stefan. "Kreuz." In *Reallexikon für Antike und Christentum*, 21. Stuttgart: Anton Hiersemann, 2004.

Helgeland, John, et al. *Christians and the Military: The Early Experience*. London and Philadelphia: SCM Press and Fortress, 1985.

Helgeland, John. "Christians and the Roman Army from Marcus Aurelius to Constantine." In *Aufstieg und Niedergang der Römischen Welt, II (Prinzipat)* 23.1, edited by Hildegard Temporini and Wolfgang Haase. Berlin/New York: Walter de Gruyter, 1979.

Helgeland, John. "Roman Army Religion." *Aufstieg Und Niedergang Der Romischen Welt II* 16:2 (1978) 1470–1505.

Hill, Edmund. "Translator's Note." In Augustine, *Sermons 1, The Works of Saint Augustine*, 3.1 New York: New City, 1990.

Hornus, Jean-Michel. *It is Not Lawful for Me to Fight: Early Christian Attitudes Toward War, Violence, and the State*. Tranlsated by Alan Kreider and Oliver Coburn. Scottdale, PA: Herald, 1980.

House, H. Wayne and John Howard Yoder. "Against the Death Penalty." In *The Death Penalty Debate: Two Opposing Views of Capital Punishment*. Dallas: Word, 1991.

Hunter, David G. "A Decade of Research on Early Christians and Military Service." *Religious Studies Review* 18:2 (1992) 87–123.

Husbands, Mark. "Introduction." In *Ancient Faith for the Church's Future*, edited by Mark Husbands and Jeffrey P. Greenman. Downers Grove, IL: InterVarsity, 2008.

Irenaeus. *Against Heresies*. Tranlsated by online at http://www.newadvent.org/fathers/0103438.htm.

Janes, Dominic. *God and Gold in Late Antiquity*. Cambridge: Cambridge University Press, 1998.

Johnson, Mark. "Another Look at the Plurality of the Literal Sense." *Medieval Philosophy and Theology* 2 (1992) 117–41.

Johnson, Maxwell E. *The Rites of Christian Initiation: Their Evolution and Interpretation*. Revised ed. Collegeville, MN: Liturgical, 2007.

Justin, 1, *Apol*. In *Ante-Nicene Fathers* 1. Tranlsated by Marcus Dods and George Reith; edited by Alexander Roberts, James Donaldson, and A. Cleveland Coxe. Buffalo, NY: Christian Literature, 1885. Online: http://www.newadvent.org/fathers/0126.htm.

Justin, *Dialogue with Trypho*. Online: http://www.earlychristianwritings.com/text/justinmartyr-dialoguetrypho.html.

Kalantzis, George. *Caesar and the Lamb: Early Christian Attitudes on War and Military Service*. Eugene, OR: Cascade, 2012.

Kissling, Paul J. "John Howard Yoder's Reading of the Old Testament and the Stone-Campbell Movement." In *Radical Ecumenicity: Pursuing Unity and Continuity after John Howard Yoder*, edited by John C. Nugent. Abilene, TX: Abilene Christian University Press, 2010.

Bibliography

Krautheimer, Richard. "The Ecclesiastical Building Policy of Constantine." In *Constantino il Grande dall'antichità all 'umanesimo: Colloquio sul Christianesimo nel mondo antico*. Macerata: Università degli studi di Macerata, 1993.

———. *Rome, Profile of a City, 312–1308*. Princeton, N.J.: Princeton University Press, 1980.

Kreider, Alan. *The Change of Conversion and the Origin of Christendom*. 1999. Reprint, Eugene, OR: Wipf & Stock, 2006.

———. "'Converted' but Not Baptized: Peter Leithart's Constantine Project." *The Mennonite Quarterly Review* 85 (2011) 575–617.

———. "Military Service in the Church Orders." *Journal of Religious Ethics* 31: 3 (2003) 415–42.

———. "Mission and Violence: Inculturation in the Fourth Century—Basil and Ambrose." In *Mission in Context: Festschrift for Andrew Kirk*. Edited by John Corrie and Cathy Ross. Farnham, Surrey, UK: Ashgate, forthcoming.

———. "Peacemaking in Worship in the Syrian Church Orders." *Studia Liturgica* 34:2 (2004) 183–87.

———. "'They Alone Know the Right Way to Live': The Early Church and Evangelism." In *Ancient Faith for the Church's Future*, edited by Mark Husbands and Jeffrey P. Greenman. Downers Grove, IL: InterVarsity, 2008.

———. *Worship and Evangelism in Pre-Christendom*. Cambridge: Grove, 1995.

Lactantius, *Divine Institutes*. In *Ante-Nicene Fathers* 7. Translated by William Fletcher. Edited by Alexander Roberts, James Donaldson, and A. Cleveland Coxe. Buffalo, NY: Christian Literature, 1886. Online: http://www.newadvent.org/fathers/07011.htm.

Leithart, Peter J. *1 & 2 Kings*. Grand Rapids: Brazos, 2006.

———. *Against Christianity*. Moscow, ID: Canon, 2003.

———. *Defending Constantine: The Twilight of an Empire and the Dawn of Christendom*. Downers Grove, IL: InterVarsity, 2010.

———. "Defending *Defending Constantine*: Or, The Trajectory of the Gospel," *Mennonite Quarterly Review* 85 (2011) 643–55.

———. "Infant Baptism in History: An Unfinished Tragicomedy." In *The Case for Covenantal Infant Baptism*, edited by Gregg Strawbridge. Philippsburg, N.J.: P&R Publishing, 2003.

———. "Response to Timothy J. Furry." *Journal of Lutheran Ethics* 11 (2011). Online: https://www.elca.org/What-We-Believe/Social-Issues/Journal-of-Lutheran-Ethics/Issues/September-2011/Response-to-Timothy-J-Furry.aspx.

Lind, Millard. *Yahweh Is a Warrior: The Theology of Warfare in Ancient Israel*. Scottdale, PA: Herald, 1980.

Lizzi Testa, Rita. "The Late Antique Bishop: Image and Reality." In *A Companion to Late Antiquity*, edited by Philip Rousseau and Jutta Raithel. Malden, MA.: Blackwell, 2009.

Lohfink, Gerhard. *Jesus and Community*. Philadelphia: Fortress, 1984.

———. "'Schwerter zu Pflugscharen': Die Rezeption von Jes 2, 1–5 par Mi 4, 1–5 in der Alten Kirche und im Neuen Testament." *Theologische Quartalschrift* 166 (1986) 184–209.

Long, D. Stephen. *John Wesley's Moral Theology*. Abingdon: Kingswood, 2005.

Longman, Timothy. *Christianity and Genocide in Rwanda*. Cambridge: Cambridge University Press, 2011.

Bibliography

MacMullen, Ramsay. *Christianity and Paganism in the Fourth to Eighth Centuries.* New Haven, CT: Yale University Press, 1997.

———. *Christianizing the Roman Empire (A.D. 100–400).* New Haven, CT: Yale University Press, 1984.

———. *Constantine.* London: Croom Helm, 1969.

———. *The Second Church: Popular Christianity A.D. 200–400.* Atlanta: Society of Biblical Literature, 2009.

———. *Soldier and Civilian in the Later Roman Empire.* Cambridge: Harvard University Press, 1963.

Martens, Paul. *The Heterodox Yoder.* Eugene, OR: Cascade, 2012.

Mattox, John Mark. *Saint Augustine and the Theory of Just War.* NY: Continuum, 2006.

McClure, Judith. "Handbooks Against Heresy in the West, from the Late Fourth to the Late Sixth Centuries." *Journal of Theological Studies* 30.1 (1979) 186–89.

Meeks, Wayne A. *The Origins of Christian Morality: The First Two Centuries.* New Haven, CT: Yale University Press, 1993.

Milbank, John. "Power is Necessary for Peace: In Defence of Constantine." Online: http://www.abc.net.au/religion/articles/2010-/10/29/3051980.htm.

Minucius Felix, *Octavius.* Online: http://www.earlychristianwritings.com/octavius.html.

Mühlenkamp, Christine. *'Nicht Wie Die Heiden.' Studien zur Grenze Zwischen Christlicher Gemeinde und Paganer Gesellschaft in Vorkonstantinischer Zeit,* Ergänzungsband, Kleine Reihe 3. *Jahrbuch für Antike und Christentum.* Münster: Aschendorff, 2008.

Nugent, John C. "Biblical Warfare Revisited: Extending the Insights of John Howard Yoder." In *Power and Practices: Engaging the Work of John Howard Yoder,* edited by Jeremy M. Bergen and Anthony G. Siegrist. Scottdale, PA: Herald, 2009.

———. *The End of Sacrifice: The Capital Punishment Writings of John Howard Yoder.* Scottdale, PA: Herald, 2011.

———. "Kingdom Work: John Howard Yoder's Free Church Contributions to an Ecumenical Theology of Vocation." In *Radical Ecumenicity: Pursuing Unity and Continuity after John Howard Yoder,* edited by John C. Nugent. Abilene, TX: Abilene Christian University Press, 2010.

———. "Politics of YHWH: John Howard Yoder's Old Testament Narration and Its Implications for Social Ethics." *Journal of Religious Ethics* 39 (2011) 71–99.

———. *The Politics of Yahweh.* Eugene, OR: Cascade, 2011.

O'Donovan, Oliver. *Resurrection and Moral Order: An Outline for Evangelical Ethics.* Grand Rapids: Eerdmans, 1986.

O'Malley, John W. *What Happened at Vatican II.* Cambridge: Harvard University Press, 2008.

Ochs, Peter. "Commentary on Chap. 10." In *The Jewish-Christian Schism Revisited,* edited by Michael G. Cartwright and Peter Ochs, 166–67. Grand Rapids: Eerdmans, 2003.

Origen, *Contra Celsum.* In *Ante-Nicene Fathers* 4. Tranlsated by Frederick Crombie. Edited by Alexander Roberts, James Donaldson, and A. Cleveland Coxe. Buffalo, NY: Christian Literature, 1885. Online: http://www.newadvent.org/fathers/0416.htm.

———. *Homilies on Exodus.* Online: http://www.john-uebersax.com/plato/origen2.htm.

Bibliography

———. *Homilies on Joshua*. Tranlsated by Barbara Bruce. Washington DC: Catholic University of America Press, 2002.

———. *Letter to Julius Africanus*. Online: http://www.john-uebersax.com/plato/origen2.htm.

———. *On First Principles*. Tranlsated by G. W. Butterworth. Gloucester, MA: Peter Smith, 1973.

Parler, Branson. *Things Hold Together: John Howard Yoder's Trinitarian Theology of Culture*. Harrisonburg, VA: Herald, 2012.

Radner, Ephraim. *A Brutal Unity: The Spiritual Politics of the Church*. Waco, TX: Baylor University Press, 2012.

Rahner, Hugo. *Church and State in Early Christianity*. Tranlsated by Leo Donald Davis. San Francisco: Ignatius, 1992.

Ramsey, Boniface. "Almsgiving in the Latin Church: The Late Fourth and Early Fifth Centuries." *Theological Studies* 43 (1982) 226–59.

Rapp, Claudia. "Bishops in Late Antiquity: A New Social and Urban Elite?" In *Elites Old and New in the Byzantine and Early Islamic Near East: Papers of the Sixth Workshop on Late Antiquity and Early Islam*, edited by John Haldon and Conrad Lawrence. Princeton, NJ: Darwin, 2004.

———. *Holy Bishops in Late Antiquity: The Nature of Christian Leadership in an Age of Transition*. Berkeley: University of California Press, 2005.

Readings in Christian Ethics. Vol. 2, *Issues and Applications*, edited by David K. Clark and Robert V. Rakestraw. Grand Rapids: Eerdmans, 1996.

Rogers, Eugene. "How the Virtues of an Interpreter Presuppose and Perfect Hermeneutics: The Case of Thomas Aquinas." *Journal of Religion* 76 (1996) 64–81.

Rordorf, Willi. "Tertullians Beurteilung des Soldatenstandes." *Vigiliae Christianae* 23 (1969) 105–41.

Russell, Frederick H. *The Just War in the Middle Ages*. Cambridge: Cambridge University Press, 1975.

Russell, James C. *The Germanization of Early Medieval Christianity: A Sociohistorical Approach to Religious Transformation*. New York: Oxford University Press, 1994.

Salzman, Michele Renee. *The Making of a Christian Aristocracy*. Cambridge, Mass: Harvard University Press, 2002.

Sarefield, Daniel. "Bookburning in the Christian Roman Empire: Transforming a Pagan Rite of Purification." In *Violence in Late Antiquity: Perceptions and Practices*, 287–96. edited by H. A. Drake. Burlington, VT: Ashgate, 2006.

Schlabach, Gerald W. *For the Joy Set Before Us: Augustine and Self-Denying Love*. Notre Dame, IN: The University of Notre Dame Press, 2001.

Scobie, Charles. *The Ways of Our God: An Approach to Biblical Theology*. Grand Rapids: Eerdmans, 2003.

Secrétan, Henri. "Le Christianisme des premiers siècles et le service militaire." *Revue de Théologie et de Philosophie* 2 (1914) 345–65.

Shaw, Brent D. "Bad Boys: Circumcellions and Fictive Violence." In *Violence in Late Antiquity: Perceptions and Practices*, edited by H. A. Drake. Burlington, VT: Ashgate, 2006.

Sider, J. Alexander. *To See History Doxologically: History and Holiness in John Howard Yoder's Ecclesiology*. Grand Rapids: Eerdmans, 2011.

Sider, Ronald J. *The Early Church on Killing: A Comprehensive Sourcebook on War, Abortion, and Capital Punishment*. Grand Rapids, MI: Baker Academic, 2012.

Bibliography

Sperry-White, Grant. *The Testamentum Domini: A Text for Students, with Introduction, Translation, and Notes.* Bramcote: Grove, 1991.

Stark, Rodney. *The Rise of Christianity: A Sociologist Reconsiders History.* Princeton, NJ: Princeton University Press, 1996.

Steinmetz, David C. *Memory and Mission: Theological Reflections on the Christian Past.* Nashville: Abingdon, 1988.

Stendahl, Krister. "The Apostle Paul and the Introspective Conscience of the West." In *Paul Among Jews and Gentile*, 78–96. Philadelphia: Fortress, 1976.

Stewart-Sykes, Alistair. *Hippolytus, On the Apostolic Tradition.* Crestwood, NY: St Vladimir's Seminary Press, 2001.

Stroumsa, Guy G. "Religious Dynamics Between Christians and Jews in Late Antiquity (312–640)." In *The Cambridge History of Christianity, II: Constantine to c. 600*, edited by Augustine Casiday and Frederick W. Norris, 151–72. Cambridge: Cambridge University Press, 2007.

Swartley, Willard. *Covenant of Peace: The Missing Peace in New Testament Theology and Ethics.* Grand Rapids: Eerdmans, 2006.

Tanner, Kathryn. "Theology and the Plain Sense." In *Scriptural Authority and Narrative Interpretation*, edited by Garrett Green, 59–78. Philadelphia: Fortress, 1987.

Testamentum Domini. Tranlsated and edited by James Cooper and A. J. MacLean. Edinburgh: T. & T. Clark, 1902.

The Apostolic Tradition: A Commentary. Edited by Paul F. Bradshaw, Maxwell E. Johnson, and L. Edward Phillips. Minneapolis: Fortress, 2002.

The Martyrdom of St Marinus. In *The Acts of the Christian Martyrs*, edited by Herbert Musurillo. Oxford: Clarendon, 1972.

Tomlin, Roger. "Christianity and the Late Roman Army." In *Constantine: History, Historiography and Legend*, edited by Samuel N. C. Lieu and Dominic Montserrat. London: Routledge, 1998.

Tran, Jonathan. *Foucault and Theology.* London: T. & T. Clark, 2011

———. *The Vietnam War and Theologies of Memory: Time and Eternity in the Far Country.* Oxford: Wiley–Blackwell, 2010.

von Balthasar, Hans Urs. *Tragedy Under Grace: Reinhold Schneider and the Experience of the West*, Tranlsated by Brian McNeil. San Francisco: Ignatius, 1997.

Walker, Andrew and Luke Bretherton. *Remembering Our Future: Explorations in Deep Church.* London: Paternoster Press, 2007.

Weaver, Alain Epp. "John Howard Yoder's 'Alternative Perspective' on Christian-Jewish Relations." *The Mennonite Quarterly Review* 79 (July 2005) 295–328.

———. "Missionary Christology: John Howard Yoder and the Creeds." *Mennonite Quarterly Review* 74 (July 1998) 411–40.

Weigel, George. "Moral Clarity in a Time of War." *First Things* 128 (2003) 20–27.

Wesley, John. *The Works of John Wesley.* Edited by Albert C. Outler. Nashville: Abingdon, 1988.

White, Hayden. *Metahistory: The Historical Imagination in Nineteenth–Century Europe.* Baltimore: The Johns Hopkins University Press, 1975.

———. *Tropics of Discourse: Essays in Cultural Criticism.* Baltimore: The Johns Hopkins University Press, 1978.

Wilken, Robert L. *The Christians as the Romans Saw Them.* New Haven, CT: Yale University Press, 1984.

Wright, David F. "Augustine and the Transformation of Baptism." In *Origins of Christendom in the West*, edited by Alan Kreider. Edinburgh: T. & T. Clark, 2001.

Bibliography

———. *What Has Infant Baptism Done to Baptism?* Carlisle, UK: Paternoster, 2005.

Yarnold, Edward J. "The Baptism of Constantine." *Studia Patristica* 26 (1993) 95–102.

———. "Baptism and the Pagan Mysteries in the Fourth Century." *Heythrop Journal* 13 (1972) 247–267.

Yoder, John Howard. "The Ambivalence of the Appeal to the Fathers." In *Practiced in the Presence: Essays in Honor of T. Canby Jones*, edited by D. Neil Snarr and Daniel Smith-Christopher. Richmond, IN: Friends United, 1994.

———. "Behold My Servant Shall Prosper." In *Karl Barth and the Problem of War and Other Essays on Barth*, edited by Mark Thiessen Nation. Eugene, OR: Cascade, 2003.

———. "Biblical Roots of Liberation Theology." *Grail* (1985) 55–74.

———. *Body Politics: Five Practices of the Christian Community Before the Watching World*. Nashville: Discipleship Resources, 1992.

———. *Christian Attitudes to War, Peace, and Revolution*, edited by Theodore J. Koontz and Andy Alexis-Baker. Grand Rapids: Brazos, 2009.

———. *The Christian and Capital Punishment*. Newton, KS: Faith & Life, 1961.

———. *The Christian Witness to the State*. Newton, KS: Faith & Life, 1964. New footnotes added 1977. Reprint, Scottdale, PA: Herald, 2002

———. "Creation and Gospel." *Perspectives—A Journal of Reformed Thought* 3 (1988) 8–10.

———. *Discipleship as Political Responsibility*. Scottdale, PA: Herald, 2003.

———. *The End of Sacrifice: The Capital Punishment Writings of John Howard Yoder*. edited by John C. Nugent. Harrisonburg, VA: Herald, 2012.

———. "Ethics and Eschatology." *Ex Auditu* 6 (1990) 119–28.

———. "Exodus and Exile: The Two Faces of Liberation." *Cross Currents* 23.3 (1973) 297–309.

———. "Exodus: Probing the Meaning of Liberation." *Sojourners* 5 (1976) 26–29.

———. *For the Nations: Essays Public and Evangelical*. Grand Rapids: Eerdmans, 1997.

———. "From the Wars of Joshua to Jewish Pacifism." In *War of the Lamb: The Ethics of Nonviolence and Peacemaking*, edited by Glen Stassen, et al. Grand Rapids: Brazos, 2009.

———. *The Fullness of Christ: Paul's Vision of Universal Ministry*. Elgin, Ill.: Brethren Press, 1987.

———. "Generating Alternative Paradigms." In *Human Values and the Environment: Conference Proceedings*, Report 140, 56–62. Madison, WI: Wisconsin Academy of Sciences, Arts and Letters, 1992.

———. *He Came Preaching Peace*. Scottdale, PA: Herald, 1985.

———. "Historiography as a Ministry to Renewal." In *From Age to Age: Historians and the Modern Church*, edited by David B. Eller. *Brethren Life and Thought* 42:3/4 (1997) 216–28

———. "I Choose Vocation." *Mennonite Community* 2 (1948) 6–7.

———. "Is There Historical Development of Theological Thought." In *Radical Ecumenicity: Pursuing Unity and Continuity after John Howard Yoder*, edited by John C. Nugent. Abilene, TX: Abilene Christian University Press, 2010.

———. "Is There Such a Thing as Being Ready for Another Millennium?" In *The Future of Theology: Essays in Honor of Jürgen Moltmann*, edited by Miroslav Volf, et al. Grand Rapids: Eerdmans, 1996.

———. *The Jewish–Christian Schism Revisited*, edited by Michael G. Cartwright and Peter Ochs. Grand Rapids: Eerdmans, 2003.

Bibliography

———. "Meaning after Babel: With Jeffrey Stout beyond Relativism." *Journal of Religious Ethics* 24 (1996) 125–39.

———. *The Original Revolution: Essays on Christian Pacifism.* Eugene: Wipf and Stock, 1998.

———. *The Pacifist Impulse in Historical Perspective,* edited by Harvey L. Dyck. Toronto: University of Toronto Press, 1996

———. "'Patience' as Method in Moral Reasoning: Is an Ethic of Discipleship 'Absolute'?" In *The Wisdom of the Cross: Essays in Honor of John Howard Yoder,* edited by Stanley Hauerwas, et al. Grand Rapids: Eerdmans, 1999.

———. *The Politics of Jesus: Vicit Agnus Noster.* Grand Rapids: Eerdmans, 1972; 2nd ed. Grand Rapids: Eerdmans, 1994.

———. *Preface to Theology: Christology and Theological Method.* Grand Rapids: Brazos, 2002

———. *The Priestly Kingdom.* Notre Dame, IN: The University of Notre Dame Press, 1985.

———. "Primitivism in the Radical Reformation: Strengths and Weaknesses." In *The Primitive Church in the Modern World,* edited by Richard T. Hughes. Urbana and Chicago: University of Illinois Press, 1995.

———. *Radical Ecumenicity: Pursuing Unity and Continuity after John Howard Yoder,* edited by John C. Nugent. Abilene, Texas: Abilene Christian University Press, 2010.

———. *The Roots of Concern: Writings on Anabaptist Renewal 1952-1957,* edited by Virgil Vogt. Eugene, OR: Cascade, 2009.

———. *The Royal Priesthood: Essays Ecclesiological and Ecumenical,* edited by Michael G. Cartwright. Scottdale, PA: Herald, 1994.

———. "Texts that Serve or Texts that Summon: A Response to Michael Walzer." *Journal of Religious Ethics* 20 (1992) 229–34.

———. "Thinking Theologically from a Free Church Perspective." In *Doing Theology in Today's World: Essays in Honor of Kenneth S. Kantzer,* edited by John D. Woodbridge and Thomas Edward Comiskey. Grand Rapids: Zondervan, 1991, 251–65.

———. *To Hear the Word,* 2nd ed. Eugene, OR: Cascade, 2010.

———. "'To Your Tents, O Israel': The Legacy of Israel's Experience with Holy War." *Studies in Religion* 18.3 (1989) 545–62.

———. "War as a Moral Problem in the Early Church: The Historian's Hermeneutical Assumptions." In *The Pacifist Impulse in Historical Perspective,* edited by Harvey L. Dyck. Toronto: University of Toronto Press, 1996.

———. *The War of the Lamb: The Ethics of Nonviolence and Peacemaking.* Grand Rapids: Brazos, 2009.

———. and David A. Shank. "Biblicism and the Church." In *The Roots of Concern: Writings on Anabaptist Renewal 1952–1957,* edited by Virgil Vogt. Eugene, OR: Cascade, 2009.

Young, Frances. "Paideia—What Can We Learn from the First Four Centuries?" In *Essentials of Christian Community: Essays for Daniel W. Hardy,* edited by David F. Ford and Dennis L. Stamps. Edinburgh: T. & T. Clark, 1996.